The Roman Salute

The Roman Salute
Cinema, History, Ideology

Martin M. Winkler

THE OHIO STATE UNIVERSITY PRESS
COLUMBUS

Copyright © 2009 by The Ohio State University.
All rights reserved.

Library of Congress Cataloging-in-Publication Data
Winkler, Martin M.
  The Roman salute : cinema, history, ideology / Martin M. Winkler.
      p. cm.
  Includes bibliographical references and index.
  ISBN-13: 978-0-8142-0864-9 (cloth : alk. paper)
  ISBN-10: 0-8142-0864-9 (cloth : alk. paper)
  1. Rome—In motion pictures. 2. Rome—In art. 3. Rome—In literature.
  4. Salutations. I. Title.
  PN1995.9.R68W56 2009
  700'.45837
  [22]
                                                    2008041124

This book is available in the following editions:
Cloth (ISBN 978-0-8142-0864-9)
CD-ROM (ISBN 978-0-8142-9194-8)
Paper (ISBN 978-0-8142-5830-9)

Cover design by Dan O'Dair
Text design by Juliet Williams
Type set in Adobe Bembo

contents

Illustrations	vii
Acknowledgments	xi
INTRODUCTION	1
1. History and Ideology: Half-Truths and Untruths	1
2. Ideology and Spectacle: The Importance of Cinema	6
3. About This Book	11
ONE Saluting Gestures in Roman Art and Literature	17
TWO Jacques-Louis David's *Oath of the Horatii*	42
THREE Raised-Arm Salutes in the United States before Fascism: From the Pledge of Allegiance to *Ben-Hur* on Stage	57
FOUR Early Cinema: American and European Epics	77
FIVE *Cabiria:* The Intersection of Cinema and Politics	94
1. *Gabriele D'Annunzio and Cabiria*	95
2. *Fiume: The Roman Salute Becomes a Political Symbol*	101
3. *From D'Annunzio to Mussolini*	109
SIX Nazi Cinema and Its Impact on Hollywood's Roman Epics: From Leni Riefenstahl to *Quo Vadis*	122

SEVEN	Visual Legacies: Antiquity on the Screen from *Quo Vadis* to *Rome*	151
	1. *Cinema: From* Salome *to* Alexander	151
	2. *Television: From* Star Trek *to* Rome	169

CONCLUSION 178

Appendices 185
   1. *Livy's Account of the Horatii and Curiatii* 185
   2. *The Roman Salute According to* Il Capo-Squadra Balilla 190
   3. *Modern Scholarship on Fascism, Nazism, and Classical Antiquity* 192

Works Cited 195
Index of Film Titles 213
General Index 217

illustrations

1. Trajan's Column, Scenes LXXXIV–LXXXV. Trajan conducting sacrifice. From Conrad Cichorius, *Die Reliefs der Trajanssäule,* vol. 4 (Berlin: Riemer, 1900).   19

2. Trajan's Column, Scenes CI–CII. Trajan being saluted. From Conrad Cichorius, *Die Reliefs der Trajanssäule,* vol. 4 (Berlin: Riemer, 1900).   20

3. Trajan's Column, Scene CXLI. Trajan receiving Dacian chiefs. From Conrad Cichorius, *Die Reliefs der Trajanssäule,* vol. 4 (Berlin: Riemer, 1900).   21

4. Detail from Dionysus and Ariadne sarcophagus. Author's photograph.   32

5. Equestrian statue of Marcus Aurelius from "Fascist" angle. Author's photograph.   35

6. Marble statue of Marcus Aurelius. Author's photograph.   38

7. *The Robe/Demetrius and the Gladiators.* Gladiators saluting Caligula. Twentieth Century-Fox.   41

8–10. *The Vanishing American.* The pledge and flag salute. Famous Players-Lasky/Paramount.   63

11. *The Indian Fighter.* Indian chief greeting white officer. Bryna Productions/United Artists.   64

12.	*Jeremiah Johnson*. Crow warrior saluting. Warner Bros.	65
13.	Souvenir program of stage production of *Ben-Hur*; Act III, Tableau 3. Author's collection.	72
14.	Souvenir program of stage production of *Ben-Hur*; second image of Act IV, Tableau 1. Author's collection.	74
15.	*La vie et la passion de Jésus-Christ, n. s.* Jesus, age twelve, greeting Mary and Joseph in the Temple. Pathé Frères.	83
16.	*Nerone*. The opening tableau: Nero, far r., being saluted. Ambrosio.	86
17.	*Gli ultimi giorni di Pompeii* (1913). The opening shot. Ambrosio.	90
18.	*Cabiria*. Furius Axilla taking his leave from his hosts. Itala Film.	100
19.	*Cabiria*. Sophonisba and Syphax formally saluting each other. Itala Film.	100
20.	*Cabiria*. Maciste foreshadowing Mussolini. Itala Film.	116
21.	*Scipione l'Africano*. Scipio (center background, behind row of lictors) and the crowd. Ente Nazionale Industrie Cinematografiche.	118
22.	*Scipione l'Africano*. Hannibal saluted by messenger. Ente Nazionale Industrie Cinematografiche.	120
23.	Statue of athlete in front of the Amsterdam Olympic stadium, 1928. Author's collection.	130
24.	*Cleopatra* (1934). Cleopatra saluting Caesar. Paramount/Universal.	137
25.	*Quo Vadis* (1951). Marcus Vinicius, holding his triumph, saluting Nero. Metro-Goldwyn-Mayer.	144
26.	*Quo Vadis* (1951). Nero returning salute. Metro-Goldwyn-Mayer.	144
27.	*Helen of Troy* (1956). Priam (back to camera) saluting Trojan officer. Warner Bros.	153
28.	Rex Warner, *The Young Caesar*. Cover illustration of paperback edition. Author's collection.	154

29.	*Ben-Hur* (1959). Messala arriving in Jerusalem. Metro-Goldwyn-Mayer.	155
30.	*The Greatest Story Ever Told.* King Herod receiving Roman officer. United Artists/Metro-Goldwyn-Mayer.	156
31.	*Solomon and Sheba.* Pharaoh, his court, and Adonijah's henchman hailing the false king of Israel. United Artists/Metro-Goldwyn-Mayer.	157
32.	*Spartacus* (1960). "Hail Crassus!" Julius Caesar and senators except Gracchus acknowledging the new powers of Crassus. Bryna Productions/Universal.	158
33.	*Cleopatra* (1963). Julius Caesar, unimpressed by Egyptian pomp, salutes King Ptolemy while looking for Cleopatra. Twentieth Century-Fox.	159
34.	*The Fall of the Roman Empire.* Commodus saluting the crowd during his triumphal entry into Rome. Samuel Bronston Productions.	163
35.	*Titus.* An inebriated Emperor Saturninus giving the Roman salute in front of the Fascist *Colosseo quadrato.* Twentieth Century-Fox.	164
36.	*Gladiator.* Tigris of Gaul entering the Colosseum on his chariot. Dreamworks/Universal.	165
37.	*Alexander.* Alexander on his triumphant entry into Babylon. Warner Bros.	168
38–39.	*Star Trek:* "Mirror, Mirror." Varieties of the Roman salute in outer space. Paramount.	170
40–41.	*Rome.* Caesar receiving combination pectoral and straight-arm salute. HBO.	175
42.	*Apache Gold.* The salute in the American West as imagined in Western Germany. Rialto Film.	177
43.	*Fahrenheit 451.* A variant of the salute in a futuristic totalitarian society. Enterprise Vineyard/Universal.	177
44.	*The Bible: In the Beginning. . . .* Adam's first gesture at the culmination of the world's creation. Twentieth-Century Fox.	180

acknowledgments

FOR VALUABLE INFORMATION about references and sources, for a variety of important points, and for other kinds of support I am greatly indebted to several friends and colleagues, primarily Frederick Ahl, the late Max Baeumer, Richard Bosworth, Ward Briggs, Paul-Georg Brisken, William Calder III, Anthony Corbeill, James Dee, Julia Gaisser, Irvin Matus, Hartmut Rahm, Jon Solomon, and the late Egon Verheyen. I have incorporated a number of their suggestions but not all; the reason is my *pertinacia,* as ancient Romans might have called it. In Washington, D.C., I owe thanks to Rosemary Hanes and Thomas Mann at the Library of Congress and to Betsy Walsh and Erin Blake at the Folger Shakespeare Library. None of those here named is responsible for any errors of fact or judgment.

introduction

THIS BOOK is the first systematic study of the *saluto romano,* the Roman or Fascist salute, in the various cultural contexts that were decisive for the origin of this gesture, its appropriation by totalitarian ideologies, and its dissemination. It also traces the survival of the raised-arm salute in the popular media until today, adducing and interpreting extensive textual and visual evidence since well before the birth of Fascism. Popular theater and even more so the cinema are of particular importance in this. Since European and American visual culture from the 1890s to the 1920s had made forms of the raised-arm salute widely familiar, these were readily available to be adopted for political purposes. The book demonstrates that what came to be known as the Roman salute was invented on the nineteenth-century stage in long-running productions of "toga plays," melodramas set in the Roman Empire, and that the gesture then reached the cinema screen. Film, the most powerful new mass medium, became the chief means for the dissemination of various supposedly authentic aspects of the visual reconstructions of antiquity. European and American silent films about ancient cultures were most influential for the popularity and eager acceptance of the Roman salute in political contexts.

1. History and Ideology: Half-Truths and Untruths

In the twentieth century the Roman salute was the most familiar symbol of Fascism in Italy, Nazism in Germany, Falangism in Spain, and several other right-wing or nationalist movements. Those executing this gesture extended their stiff right arm frontally and raised it to roughly 135 degrees from the body's vertical axis, with the palm of the hand facing down and the fingers touching. According to the Fascist ideology of the 1920s and in common perceptions still current, this salute was based on an ancient Roman custom, just as the term Fascism itself is associated with the Roman *fasces,* the bundles of rods with an axe in their middle that were a symbol of the power of office held by higher Roman magistracies and some priests. As will be seen, however, the term "Roman salute" is a misnomer. Not a single Roman work of art—sculpture, coinage, or painting—displays a salute of the kind that is found in Fascism, Nazism, and related ideologies. It is also unknown to Roman literature and is never mentioned by ancient historians of either republican or imperial Rome. The gesture of the raised right arm or hand in Roman and other ancient cultures that *is* attested in surviving art and literature had a significantly different function and is never identical with the modern straight-arm salute. Until comparatively recently, historians have tended to neglect modern popular culture in general and the cinema in particular; as a result, misconceptions about the origin of the Roman salute have remained unexamined and uncorrected. This book refutes the distortions of the past. It does so from a perspective that is critical of errors in modern portrayals of antiquity but at the same time remains sympathetic to popular art and media culture.

Although the ideologies which popularized it in the 1920s and 1930s have been thoroughly discredited, the raised-arm salute can still be observed today, sometimes in mainstream politics but more often on far-right or extreme fringes of society and in more esoteric circles.[1] American and European Skinheads, especially prominent in Germany in the 1980s and 1990s, are a familiar example.[2] One of the more bizarre American

---

1. An example of these is The Hermetic Order of the Golden Dawn (*Stella Matutina*), founded in 1888 and a self-described "system of magic." Its "Neophyte Ritual" includes a raised-right arm gesture as the sign of the "zelator"; an illustration appears at Regardie 1997, 133.

2. On these see, among numerous other works, Cadalanu 1994; Ridgeway 1995; Hasselbach and Reiss 1996, turned into a 2002 feature film by Winfried Bonengel, co-author of the original German version of Hasselbach's book; Langer 2004; Ryan 2004. Bonengel's 1993 film *Profession: Neo-Nazi* is a German documentary, Tony Kaye's *American History X* (1998) a fiction film dealing with the same topic. The essays in Fenner and Weitz 2004 deal with various aspects of the phenomenon. See further Eatwell 1996, 245–362 and 384–92 (notes), on neofascism in different European countries and especially Laqueur 1996 on Fascism, neofascism, and postfascism.—The modern German variation of the straight-arm salute, the *Kühnengruß*, so named after Michael Kühnen, a former neo-Nazi, and the public display of the *saluto romano* on the part of a popular Italian soccer player indicate the continuing attraction of the Nazi and Fascist past to some. On the latter see, e.g., Duff 2005 and Fenton 2005.

manifestations is The World Church of the Creator, an organization replete with a supreme leader, a Pontifex Maximus, and the Roman salute.[3] Right-wing politics in Italy even returned a measure of acceptability to Fascism on the level of a national government within the European Union.[4] Political organizations of various stripes regularly employ straight-arm salutes.[5] So the continuing presence of certain aspects of Fascism and modern extremism makes an examination desirable, especially when the true origins of such a potent and persistent symbol as the raised-arm salute and its history are barely known. Even professional classicists and historians of ancient Rome and scholars of twentieth-century European history and culture have contented themselves with perpetuating vague opinions based on insufficient evidence, often taken uncritically from earlier writings. The following two examples are representative.

The two-volume *Dizionario del fascismo,* published in 2003 by one of Italy's most reputable publishing houses, ought to be a reliable source of information. Its entry on the Roman salute, however, begins as follows:

Il modello cui il fascismo attinse per il cosidetto saluto romano fu certamente l'antichità classica, ma il primo ad aver utilizzato questa forma di saluto nel Novecento sembra essere stato Gabriele D'Annunzio, durante l'impresa di Fiume.

The model on which Fascism drew for the so-called Roman salute was certainly classical antiquity, but the first to have used this form of salute in the twentieth century seems to have been Gabriele D'Annunzio during the occupation of Fiume.[6]

---

3. Cf. Wilgoren 2003.
4. Cf., for example, Quaranta 1998.
5. For examples see Bulathsinghala 2003 and Daniel Johnson 2006. The Black Tigers interviewed in Bulathsinghala are the suicide force of the Liberation Tigers of Tamil Eelam (Tamil Tigers).
6. Stefano Cavazza, "Saluto romano," in de Grazia and Luzzatto 2003, vol. 2, 578–79; quotation at 578. The next paragraph begins: *Il gesto del saluto, che richiamava alla memoria la tradizione romana* ... ("The gesture of the salute, which recalled the Roman tradition ... "). This statement is correct only if any generally held belief is included in the meaning of "tradition," regardless of historical fact. For an earlier example of such misperception cf. Salvemini 1973, 229: "the so-called Roman salute, made by raising the right hand in the air, [was] ... the salute of the 'arditi' [i.e. the Italian shock troops in World War I] during the war and [was] adopted in Fiume." A footnote to this sentence explains: "In classical antiquity it was the slaves who saluted their masters by raising the right hand. Free men greeted one another by shaking hands." No source references are provided. The *arditi* ("Daring Ones") raised their arms holding their daggers; see, e.g., Rochat 1997, 88: *saluto collettivo con il pugnale snudato e sollevato al cielo* (a "collective

The statement that Fascism took ancient Rome for its model is true enough but does not address the question whether the Fascists were concerned with historical accuracy in their use of antiquity, not least in connection with their ritual use of the raised-arm salute. Expressions like "certainly" and "seems to have been" are too vague to assure readers that the description here provided is factually correct. Classical antiquity was demonstrably *not* the true model of the Roman salute, although in the 1920s such a perspective was foisted on a people willing enough to believe that it was. The one to do so was indeed Gabriele D'Annunzio. But D'Annunzio was not at all "the first" to employ the raised-arm salute in the twentieth century. He *was* the first to give it an explicit ideological and propagandistic turn when he made it part of his rituals at Fiume in 1919, and the salute was soon adopted by Mussolini and the Italian Fascists. However, in 1919 the gesture was anything but new.

Modern scholarship in English is equally unreliable. In it we may find the following assertion: "The PNF [Partito Nazionale Fascista, the National Fascist Party] insisted on the adoption of the virile Roman straight-armed salute in place of the degenerate, effeminate (and germ-ridden) bourgeois handshake."[7] This statement is correct in mentioning the Fascists' contempt for the traditional—and entirely unpolitical—custom of shaking hands, but it merely presupposes the antiquity of the raised-arm salute without any concern for actual Roman culture.

The main reason for such lack of accuracy is that a thorough analysis of the history of the raised-arm salute requires a synthesis of various areas of knowledge that scholars usually keep separate: the history, literature, and art of ancient Rome; the cultural and political history of modern Italy, Germany, and the United States; the history of late-eighteenth-century European painting and late-nineteenth-century popular theater; and film history from its beginnings to today. For this reason no comprehensive scholarship on the raised-arm salute has previously been attempted. My subject is therefore by nature wide-ranging. It incorporates Roman civilization, its influence on modern politics, and its connections to popular culture and its most influential medium, film. At the same time it remains focused on a specific symbolic gesture. My book aims to deepen our understanding of a particular, and particularly effective, way in which the past—imperial Rome—has been appropriated

---

salute with the dagger naked and raised to the sky"); cf. Rochat 1997, 91 note 33. I discuss the *arditi* in context in chapter 5.

7. Koon 1985, 20. The slogan in the title of this book is Mussolini's exhortation to the Fascist Youth; it was introduced in 1930. Heller 2008, 83, provides a photograph of the slogan. Another instance of the incorrect view concerning the antiquity of the raised-arm salute occurs in Ledeen 2002, vii.

for purposes of modern political propaganda and has become an integral, if incorrectly understood, part of our view of this past.

As an especially revealing example of the common misperceptions about Romans and Fascists—or even about Romans as Fascists—I quote, without the slightest editorial interference, from the now defunct Internet site of the American Falangist Party, which had this to say under the heading "The Roman Salute":

> No, it's not a Nazi salute, though most people in the United States think that's what it is when they see it given and it has been called that in this country for so long that you really can't blame the people too much. what it really should be called though, is a Roman Salute because that's where it came from, ancient Rome and is the oldest known form of salute. It was made popular in the early 1920's by Benito Mussolini and his Fascist Party who wanted to revive the Roman Empire and save Western Christian Civilization from the Communist/Socialist forces that were spreading like a cancer throughout Europe and the World. Hitler copied it from the Italians as did many other ant-Communist movements at the time.
>
> Anyone who has seen old movies where the Roman Centurian would come into the room give this salute and say "Hail Cesear!" knows that this salute was around a long time ago. Yes the Nazis and Fascists use it, but so do a lot of other people, especially in the Middle East and Latin America. It was even used in the United States during the Revolutionary war and in the early part of the 1900's when new citizens took their oath of allegiance to the United States. If you go to our photo page you'll see a photograph of president Franklin Roosevelt being saluted in this manner. mostly because of tradition, we've been using it since the early 1930's when the Communist used the closed fist salute, the opposite of that being the Roman Salute.
>
> The American Falangist Party discourages Party members from using this salute too much in public until people become more informed.

This text is telling for several reasons. Blind adherence to ideology replaces any knowledge of ancient and modern history. Carelessness of grammar, style, orthography, and punctuation reveals carelessness of thought. So the simple belief in the accuracy and reliability of films set in the past that the text evinces is to be expected. The words here quoted appeared below a color still from the 1951 Hollywood film *Quo Vadis*, in which the commander of a Roman legion gives the raised-arm salute to Emperor Nero.[8]

---

8. The entire Falangist text and the illustration from *Quo Vadis* used to be accessible at

(The film and the sequence in which this moment occurs will be discussed in chapter 6.) The Falangist party provided no information about the origin of the image it displayed with such prominence, as if it were as good as a historical document that needed no explanation. (Did none of the Falangists recognize actor Robert Taylor in the part of the Roman commander?) The other pages of the Falangist site were instructive, too; evidently, knowing the past or learning from it is not for everybody.

2. Ideology and Spectacle: The Importance of Cinema

Unintentionally the American Falangist Party provides a strong justification for a detailed inquiry into the history of the Roman salute. But the Falangists also make clear, again inadvertently, how pervasive and important the visual media have become in modern culture, not only in terms of apparently innocuous entertainment but also, and more importantly, as purveyors of political ideologies. All manner of spectacle, not least the historical epics on our screens, were and are politically important, nowhere more so than in systems of totalitarian power in the twentieth century: "The spectacle is the self-portrait of power in the age of power's totalitarian rule over the conditions of existence."[9] My book will make and reinforce this point on most of its pages. So it is appropriate for us to be aware that mass entertainments, not least the cinematic ones, are potent social and political factors. French cultural critic Guy Debord has commented on the nature of spectacle:

> It is the sun that never sets on the empire of passivity. It covers the entire globe, basking in the perpetual warmth of its own glory.... The

---

http://www.falange.org/roman.htm. The caption to the photo mentioned in the text here quoted read as follows: "U.S President Roosevelt being given the Roman Salute in Beaumont, Mississippi '1938.'" The Falangists' Internet site ceased to exist in 2004. That of the Christian Falangist Party of America (www.falangist.com) does not contain this text or illustration. However, a related Internet site (www.warbaby.com/dh2k/html/p-falangist.html), which dates to the year 2000, concludes its "Party Overview" with the following text: "The Falangist salute, identical to the one made infamous by the Nazis, is described as the Roman salute and is understandably not used in public. The party is waiting hopefully for the day when 'people become more informed' before they flash it too often in the streets." The Christian Falangist Party uses a "pectoral salute," in which the right arm, bent at the elbow, is extended from the heart, palm down. We will encounter this salute in chapter 7. The party takes pains to distance itself from Nazism and Neo-Nazism, but its symbols, not least the stylized spread-eagle graphic that is on display at the top of its home page, tell a different story.

9. Debord 1994, 19.

spectacle, being the reigning social organization of a paralyzed history, of a paralyzed memory, of an abandonment of any history founded in historical time, is in effect a *false consciousness of time*.[10]

The false historical consciousness of Fascists and Nazis concerning the raised-arm salute, their common symbol, is the subject of my book. The spectacles of twentieth-century totalitarian states reveal the need of ruling elites for pomp and circumstance to impress the masses emotionally. They also provide compelling evidence for the political importance of ritualized mass shows. In the words of Debord:

> In all its specific manifestations—news or propaganda, advertising or actual consumption of entertainment—the spectacle epitomizes the prevailing model of social life. . . . In form as in content the spectacle serves as total justification for the conditions and aims of the existing system. It further ensures the *permanent presence* of that justification.[11]

Small wonder that the raised-arm salute should have been Fascism's and Nazism's most powerful common aspect, the only one that survived both politically (among right-wingers and radicals) and in popular culture at large. A particular film contemporary with Fascism and Nazism gives us the best proof that the raised-arm salute was the chief defining visual side of both ideologies. This film is Charles Chaplin's *The Great Dictator* (1940), the first popular exposé of twentieth-century European totalitarianism and its vanity and barbarism. Adolf Hitler's Germany appears as Adenoid Hynkel's Tomainia. The country's name is a pun on *ptomaine* that is as clever as it is revealing. Chaplin's verbal satire of the megalomaniacal dictator centers on Hitler's speeches, delivered as linguistic nonsense of Chaplin's own invention. His visual ridicule of the Nazis is equally sophisticated. The swastika, the German *Hakenkreuz*—literally, "hooked cross"—has become the Tomainian Double Cross. But the straight-arm salute is Chaplin's most effective means of satire. It is frequently given in an exaggerated fashion that makes it look ridiculous, as when Hynkel and his fellow dictator, Benzino Napaloni of Bacteria, hectically exchange salutes when they first meet during Napaloni's state visit to Tomainia. (The sequence satirizes Mussolini's trip to Berlin in 1937.) The most telling instances of the raised-arm salute occur early in the film. Hynkel's motorcade along a broad avenue that is meant to evoke the Siegesallee

---

10. Debord 1994, 15 and 114. Emphasis in original.
11. Debord 1994, 13. Emphasis in original.

("Victory Avenue") in Berlin passes before oversize statues of the Venus de Milo and of Auguste Rodin's *Thinker*. Both statues are giving the raised-arm salute. As in a newsreel, a voice-over explains to us that these are "the new Venus" and "the new Thinker." Their brief appearance on the screen speaks volumes, for here two iconic images of the greatness of Western civilization have been claimed for a new and supposedly superior society. In the process both have been utterly subverted. By implication, so has all of European culture. It is no coincidence that the names of the two totalitarian countries in *The Great Dictator* evoke disease and decay. ("Tomainia," given as "Tomania" in some sources, also carries an overtone of madness.) The raised-arm salute with all its *faux*-classical connotations is Chaplin's most concise visual means to make the point.[12]

Sometimes one specific scene or image from a film can be instructive. An epic-scale sequence in Carmine Gallone's *Scipione l'Africano* (*Scipio Africanus*, 1937) shows us Scipio returning to the people of Rome from the senate house. He is descending an open-air staircase ahead of a group of lictors with *fasces* in their arms while on either side a huge crowd greets them with the raised-arm salute. Scipio returns their greetings.[13] The moment is of emblematic significance in regard to Debord's sense of spectacle. It points to the most powerful aspects of the mass appeal of Fascism: an anonymous crowd of people is united in near-mystical ecstasy with an elevated individual in absolute power. An intermediary group—the stern-faced lictors, heroically looking straight ahead and past the camera—share both anonymity and closeness to that power. On prominent display are the symbols of this power, the *fasces* and the straight-arm salute. As my examination of Gallone's film in chapter 5 will show, the analogies between the two leaders, Scipio then and Mussolini at the time of the film's making, are intentional. In historical retrospect and from our vantage point of the fall of Fascism and Nazism and our knowledge of the reasons for that fall, this scene in the film is almost uncanny. It is as if, lemming-like, the idolized leader, his entourage, and the people were all marching straight to their doom.

Films have been our greatest means of mass communication for more than a century. The cinema has shown itself capable of reaching the most remote corners of our global village. More importantly, it is also a kind of cultural seismograph. Films have the ability to detect and reveal currents

---

12. Extensive up-to-date information on Chaplin's film may be found in *The Dictator and the Tramp* (2002), a documentary directed by Kevin Brownlow, in Scheide and Mehran 2004, and on the DVD edition of *The Great Dictator*.

13. Aristarco 1996, 92 (fig. 21), provides a still image of the same moment, as does figure 21 in the present book.

of social issues or political trends. Often they do so unconsciously, sometimes intentionally in works of political or social criticism.[14] So careful attention to the filmic record is indispensable for any historical account of the raised-arm salute.

This circumstance points to wider ramifications. Beginning with the late nineteenth century, the visual media of photography, film, television, and now the computer have become mass media. Their images have increasingly shaped historical consciousness and what people consider historical knowledge or awareness. The history of the Roman salute as traced here is a case in point because of the cinema's central role in twentieth-century politics and ideologies. Far from merely providing to later generations a factual or documentary record of something the camera had recorded, cinema influenced and even made history in a manner not previously possible for a visual art or craft. The historical film, chiefly as costume drama or epic spectacle, became a significant historical force and generated its own tradition of how people raised on mass-media images saw the past, particularly those past times in which such mass media had not yet been invented and for which therefore no competing sets of images existed as correctives to errors, misperceptions, or even deliberate distortions. What American historian, historical novelist, and screenwriter Gore Vidal observed in the early 1990s is highly apposite:

> Today, where literature was movies are . . . there can be no other reality for us [besides film and television] since reality does not begin to *mean* until it has been made art of . . .
> Movies changed our world forever. Henceforth, history would be screened; first, in meeting houses known as movie houses; then at home through television. As the whole world is more and more linked by satellites, the world's view of the world can be whatever a producer chooses to make it . . . through ear and eye, we are both defined and manipulated by fictions of such potency that they are able to replace our own experience, often becoming our *sole* experience of a reality become . . . irreal.

Vidal's conclusion from all this may be alarming, but it is unavoidable and entirely correct: "In the end, he who screens the history makes the

---

14. I deal with this aspect of the nature of cinema in the "Introduction" to Winkler 2001, 3–22, at 8, with examples adduced in note 7. Kracauer 1947 made the case for German cinema between World War I and 1933. As he observes: "Inner life manifests itself in various elements and conglomerations of external life, especially in those almost imperceptible surface data which form an essential part of screen treatment. In recording the visible world—whether current reality or an imaginary universe—films therefore provide clues to hidden processes" (7).

history."¹⁵ Many of the pages in my book will bear him out. So does the text of the American Falangists quoted above.

The screening of what purports to be history is of special importance in today's largely visual culture. Surrounded by images, we live in a world of appearance almost more than in one of reality; the images, as this book demonstrates, supersede reality. Classical scholars may be reminded of Plato's Cave Allegory, whose subject is the distinction between reality (objects) and images (their shadows projected against a wall). The shadows in Plato's cave moved but were comparatively small; for us, images of moving objects have taken on a kind of pseudo- or even hyperreality: they can be huge, are usually in vivid color, and are accompanied by varieties of sounds (words, music, effects) to enhance their apparent reality. Deceptively realistic-looking images that move across our screens easily reconstruct the present or the past, in the latter case often without direct reference to any real historical world. Once we have seen the irreal past recreated for us often enough, familiarity breeds—no, not contempt but rather a sense of intimacy which, in turn, leads to what we take or mistake for knowledge.¹⁶ As a result, whatever *is* right—historically accurate, correct, authentic—may *look* wrong and is readily regarded to *be* wrong; what is wrong replaces what is right.

Many epic films exemplify the truth of this effect of our false consciousness of history. The appeal of pseudohistory is at its most powerful when the past can be viewed through the lens of hindsight. Filmmakers assume a cultural, spiritual, or political superiority over this past and inspire the same in their viewers. At the same time the cinema works its spectacular magic by pitting a heroic good side against abject evil. *Quo Vadis*, the first Hollywood epic after World War II, is a case in point for this approach to history. My discussion of this film in chapter 6 will demonstrate that Nero's Rome, presented as an evil empire par excellence, is intentionally patterned on recent history. The film's emphasis on the "bad guys," primarily Nero himself, only serves to intensify the edifying appeal that historical cinema usually claims for itself: to be a thrilling and inspiring history lesson. The souvenir program of *Quo Vadis* that was sold in theaters makes the point as explicitly as we may wish. On the first page of text ("The Story Behind *Quo Vadis*") we read that "the studio has felt the urge and the ambition to create a film which, with all the technical improvements and resources of modern cinema-making, would carry a message of beauty and inspiration to the people of the earth." A longer

---

15. Vidal 1992, 5, 32, and 81.
16. On this subject see the work of Jean Baudrillard, in particular Baudrillard 1994 and 2002.

section later on ("The Making of *Quo Vadis*") sounds the same note with a crescendo:

> The story has in it the stuff of immortality.... M-G-M feels that it has been privileged to add something permanent to the cultural treasurehouse of civilization.[17]

The immortality that *Quo Vadis* imparts to history is synonymous with the false consciousness of time described by Debord. The film also imparts to the present and to the future a particular image of the ancient Romans that is still going strong. What greater story than that of an evil empire overthrown, as *Quo Vadis* makes clear, spiritually and, if not quite yet at film's end, militarily and politically as well? We can thrill equally to the excesses and debauches of a megalomaniacal despot and his society and to the edification of being able to side with the noble and humbly triumphant with whom we identify.

The message is clear: History is good for you, but what is presented as history is also good for you. What is shown as history on the screen is particularly good for you. The filmmakers are your best educators, more effective than your favorite teachers, even if the cinema is largely a commercial undertaking. The money that you pay at the box office for historical epics does not only buy you excitement but also an educational and spiritually uplifting experience. The false history on the giant screen looks real enough, sometimes even to experts, but it is a modern creation and so remains irreal. This irreality is good for you. The potent fiction of cinema edges out real history and replaces it in people's awareness. As we will see, when irreal history is combined with ideology, the result can be irresistible.

3. About This Book

The specific example of a potent fiction that has made reality irreal and the subject of this book is the Roman salute. In view of the ramifications, outlined above, of its history and because of the cinema's power to create apparent facts and ideological manipulation with equal facility, I present an extensive amount of ancient and modern evidence concerning this gesture: its absence in antiquity, its invention in the late nineteenth

---

17. *M-G-M Presents* Quo Vadis (1951; unpaginated souvenir book; no publishing data provided), 2 and 9.

century, and its uses in the twentieth and early twenty-first centuries. I discuss numerous and varied instances of its occurrence.[18] As we will see, however, the gesture is not Roman. Why not? Chapter 1 answers this question by showing that it is neither Roman nor even ancient. Where, then, does it come from, and when and why? Chapters 2–4 provide answers to these questions. Chapter 5 then shows how the salute acquired its misnomer, and chapters 6–7 examine what effect it has had until today. I begin by reviewing, in chapter 1, the ancient record of Roman art, literature, and historiography. Since Roman culture was closely connected to Greek culture, I include, in this chapter and wherever appropriate later on, briefer considerations of Greek and some other ancient contexts. In chapter 2 I discuss Jacques-Louis David's painting *The Oath of the Horatii* in its historical and cultural contexts and examine its political influence. Appendix 1 provides readers with my translation of the Roman historian Livy's account of the Horatii and Curiatii that is the basis of David's painting and the material dealt with in this chapter. Chapter 3 turns to two aspects of late-nineteenth-century American culture: the Pledge of Allegiance to the Flag, a quintessential American custom that originally included a straight-arm salute, and popular stage plays dealing with imperial Rome. After this the cinema, the most influential medium of the twentieth century, will provide me with my main body of evidence. I examine its cultural and political importance for Fascism and Nazism, the two totalitarian ideologies with the most extensive conscious recourse to ancient Rome, and the iconography of imperial Rome in European and American films. Chapter 4 demonstrates the widespread occurrence of the raised-arm salute in silent epic cinema and makes evident how lasting an influence a particular convention may exert once it has become firmly established—once it has made irreality real and has begun to look right even when it is wrong. Chapter 5 analyzes the intersection of cinema and politics through the importance of D'Annunzio, first in his involvement with a particular epic film and then as a crucial force in the earliest stages of Fascism. Appendix 2 provides an excerpt from the handbook of the Italian Fascists' youth organization concerning the Roman

---

18. I omit, however, a number of curiosities, of which the following may be a representative instance. The international online edition of the German newsweekly *Der Spiegel* reported on November, 30, 2006, that readers of the German daily mass publication *Bild* had made a shocking discovery, which their tabloid duly featured with a picture and an article. I quote from *Spiegel Online* (http://www.spiegel.de/international/0,1518,451645,00.html): "Christmas shoppers in Germany are horrified. Across the country, models of Santa Claus in shop windows appear to be giving the Nazi salute. Some chains have already removed them from the shelves." The headline reads: "Is Santa Claus a Nazi?"

salute. It shows how important the gesture was to the Fascist party and how seriously it took it as a means for the education along party lines of Italy's future generations. Chapter 6 turns to Nazi cinema as political propaganda and in connection with the Olympic salute, a variant on the political straight-arm salute, and to the influence of silent film epics and Nazi propaganda films on Hollywood's Roman epics. Chapter 7 takes the cinematic history of the Roman salute down to our time and in turn leads to a retrospective conclusion. Altogether I hope to show the extent to which popular culture, especially film, has exerted its influence on modern history and politics and has shaped both our understanding of history and our historical imagination. I also hope to demonstrate the importance of cinema for the study of past ages—in this case, classical antiquity—that did not know and could not conceive of the technology that made this powerful medium possible.

In view of the wide range of areas on which my book touches, I support each part of my argument and the conclusions I draw with extensive documentation. I adduce quotations from historical, literary, and scholarly works and from film dialogues, and I describe specific scenes or moments in stage plays and films. The notes provide abbreviated references to the scholarship that is important for my topic, while full information about everything cited there appears in my bibliography. An exhaustive bibliography on all aspects of history, culture, cinema, theater, art, ideology, and theory is evidently impossible (and pointless), but I have attempted to be comprehensive enough in my listings of secondary sources to enable readers easily to follow up on individual topics that may be of further interest to them or on questions about my presentation or conclusions. In addition, a number of standard recent works on the connections between Fascism and Nazism on the one hand and classical antiquity on the other are listed in appendix 3. My chief aim has been to provide as solid a basis of primary and secondary texts (including filmic texts) on which to build my argument as readers could expect from an author who addresses several fields of scholarship simultaneously. For this reason I adduce a considerably larger number of sources and references to specific details than might be considered customary or strictly necessary. But this material has provided me with the foundation and evidence to trace the history of the Roman salute with more than a reasonable degree of certainty.

Given the importance of films for the history of the raised-arm salute, readers should keep in mind that complete documentation is impossible. In popular culture, record-keeping and preservation have long been incomplete and haphazard. This is especially true for early cinema but also for the nineteenth-century stage, both of which are crucial for our understanding of the origins of the raised-arm salute. Moreover, a high percentage of silent films do not survive at all, survive only in a fragmentary state, or are difficult to reach. Nevertheless it has been my aim to develop as coherent an argument as possible about early cinema and its cultural and historical importance.

Since no examination of the different aspects of the raised-arm salute in history, politics, cinema, and popular culture has existed so far, I hope that my book will close a considerable gap in our historical and cultural awareness of ancient Rome and of the classical tradition. The book is therefore intended for scholars, teachers, and advanced students in classical studies, Roman history, art history, twentieth-century European and American history, and film, media, and cultural studies. It also addresses readers outside the academy who are interested in ancient and modern history, in cinema, and in the connections between antiquity and contemporary culture. The book is free of academic jargon and specialized terminology to make it easy for all readers to reach their own conclusions about the evidence I adduce without first having to come to terms with a narrow and frequently obfuscating linguistic code. All passages quoted in languages other than English also appear in translation. Unless otherwise indicated, these translations are my own.

Finally, a word about illustrations. Images of Nazis or Fascists from the 1920s to the 1940s or, more recently, of members of comparable political or ideological organizations (neofascists, Skinheads, etc.) will be familiar to most readers; if they are not, they are easily accessible in printed and electronic sources. For these reasons they have been excluded from this book as not being essential to its argument. In addition, the cost of reproducing a significant number of illustrations in academic publications borders on the prohibitive, and authors of specialized monographs such as this have to make difficult choices about excluding or including certain images. Evidently I would have preferred a far larger number of illustrations to support individual points than appear on these pages. The images included have been selected for their intrinsic value and usefulness, especially those coming from films of the silent era, the most important period in the history of the raised-arm salute of the twentieth century. References to other images—paintings, drawings, posters, or others—that could not be reproduced are provided in my notes, so readers can easily find on their own what I describe. I am aware that this is a compromise, but scholarly publishing is, like politics, the art of the possible. In my discussions of films for which stills were not available or could not be included I describe the relevant scenes or moments in sufficient detail for readers to be able to form a good idea about what is important. I also discuss, without being complete or exhaustive, a large number of often obscure films. Not each of them is crucial for my argument, but, taken together, all of them support my theses about the origin and spread of the straight-arm salute better than a more selective approach could have done. Specialists may well be able to point to yet additional examples, but I am confident that these will support rather than question my conclusions. With these words I do not maintain or imply that this book contains the last word on all cultural, artistic, historical, political, cinematic, and theatrical aspects of the Roman salute and its variants, but I hope to give readers a solid introduction to a fascinating side of modern life from a new perspective. If they find the book useful for pursuing certain parts of my argument further, whether as the basis of future research or in scholarly disagreement, I will have reached my goal.

one

Saluting Gestures in Roman Art and Literature

SALUTES TOOK A variety of forms in the different cultures of antiquity.[1] Among the gestures important for our subject are those involving one or both hands. In the ancient Near East, for example, raising one's right hand to one's forehead seems to have been the standard form of greeting.[2] In classical Greece, raising one's hand when greeting someone in the street existed alongside linking hands.[3] Ancient Roman hand gestures were similar to those of the Greeks and encompassed hands grasped—*dextrarum iunctio:* the joining of right hands—and, in military contexts, a salute comparable to the modern military salute: the right hand raised to one's head.[4]

Sculptures commemorating military campaigns and victories such as those on the arches of Titus and Constantine or on the columns of Trajan and Marcus Aurelius, to mention only the best-known examples, are the most obvious candidates for visual evidence of scenes incorporating the raised-arm or "Roman" salute if such a form of greeting had existed at the time, but these monuments do not display a single clear instance.

---

1. Zilliacus 1983 provides a convenient summary and further references.
2. Zilliacus 1983, col. 1207.
3. Zilliacus 1983, cols. 1210–11.
4. Zilliacus 1983, cols. 1216–17. Knippschild 2002 presents a detailed update on hand gestures in various ancient contexts of what we would today call international relations. Cf. especially Knippschild, 16–54 and 55–63 (chapters entitled "Die rechte Hand und der Handschlag" and "Die Handerhebung"; in these 29–48 and 59–61, respectively, on Greece and Rome); see also below on *fides*/*Fides*.

18 / *Chapter One*

Three scenes on Trajan's Column, here identified according to the standard numbering system first employed by Conrad Cichorius, deserve mention; I quote relevant excerpts from the description accompanying photographs of them in the recent work of Filippo Coarelli.[5] These are (Figures 1–3):

> Plate LXII, Scenes LXXXIV–LXXXV (Cichorius) = Plate 99 (Coarelli): Before Trajan conducts a sacrifice, "crowds of onlookers . . . raise their arms to salute the emperor." Only half of the six or so raised arms are clearly extended straight, the others are bent at the elbow. On the straight arms, only one palm is open but held vertically; on the others, thumb and index finger are extended, the other fingers are bent back. The fingers on the hands of three of the bent arms are pointing downwards.
>
> Plates LXXIV–LXXVI, Scenes CI–CII (Cichorius) = Plates 122–123 (Coarelli): "The emperor on horseback . . . is welcomed outside the walls of a city by a unit of legionaries, preceded by a high-ranking officer, trumpeters (*cornicines*) and standard-bearers." Of the fifteen or so legionaries depicted, none is raising his entire arm. The officer, facing Trajan, is holding his upper right arm close to his body; the lower arm is raised, with the index finger pointing up and the other fingers closed. Above (i.e., behind) him, two raised right arms display hands with fingers spread wide. Trajan himself is holding his upper right arm close to his body, extending only the lower part. The marble forming his hand is damaged, so the exact position of the fingers is unrecognizable. No straight-arm salute occurs in this scene.
>
> Plate CIII, Scene CXLI (Cichorius) = Plate 167 (Coarelli): In his last appearance on the column, Trajan "is about to receive an embassy of Dacian *pileati* [men wearing felt caps] who are escorted by auxiliary troops." Three of the Dacians are extending their right arms toward Trajan, their open hands held vertically and their fingers spread. None of the Romans is returning their gesture.[6]

The later Column of Marcus Aurelius is comparable to Trajan's Column in this regard. It shows raised-right-arm gestures but with fingers apart.[7]

---

5. Cichorius 1896–1900; Coarelli 2000. Cichorius was the first to provide a complete photographic record of the sculptures on Trajan's Column, taken from casts; the photographs in Coarelli's book are of the column itself, taken 1989–91 for the German Archaeological Institute in Rome.

6. The quotations in these descriptions are from Coarelli 2000, 143, 166, and 211.

7. Cf. Scheid and Huet 2000, 361–62 (figs. 71–72). Those authors who examine gestures in this collection of essays do not mention the raised-arm salute. Hölscher 1967, 56, observes

Figure 1. Trajan's Column, Scenes LXXXIV–LXXXV. Trajan conducting sacrifice. From Conrad Cichorius, *Die Reliefs der Trajanssäule*, vol. 4 (Berlin: Riemer, 1900).

Figure 2. Trajan's Column, Scenes CI–CII. Trajan being saluted. From Conrad Cichorius, *Die Reliefs der Trajanssäule,* vol. 4 (Berlin: Riemer, 1900).

Closest to the raised-arm salute, although by no means identical to it, are scenes in Roman sculpture and on coins and medallions which show an *adlocutio* ("address") or *acclamatio* ("acclamation") or an *adventus* ("arrival") or *profectio* ("departure"). These are occasions on which a high-ranking official, most often a general or the emperor, addresses or greets individuals or a group, the latter usually soldiers. The *History* of Ammianus Marcellinus, a late Roman historian, provides a detailed description of an *adventus,* that of Emperor Constantius II in the city of Rome in A.D. 357.[8] Unlike the modern custom, in which both the

---

that representations of Roman emperors since Hadrian show them with their right hand raised "in repräsentativem Gruß" (i.e., in a representative greeting) but admits that the meaning of the gesture seems unclear and that further research is desirable (56–57 note 30; he adduces references to different interpretations). Bergemann 1990, 6–8, discusses raised-right hand gestures in equestrian statuary—cf. Plates 8d (from an early Augustan group of statues from Cartoceto di Pergola now in the National Museum, Ancona), 14 (equestrian statue of Augustus now in the National Museum, Athens, with only the lower right arm and hand raised), and 68–69 (early Augustan Pompeian statue now in the National Museum, Naples)—and summarizes different scholarly views of their potential meanings, giving extensive references. He emphasizes that none of these interpretations can be documented conclusively and that the gesture is chiefly a visual demonstration of, e.g., an emperor's active or decisive participation in a particular action, such as a battle. Cf. Bergemann, 42–43.

8. Ammianus Marcellinus, *Res Gestae* 16.10.1–13. The most detailed modern analyses of *adventus* are Koeppel 1969 and MacCormack 1981, 17–89 and 280–313 (notes, with quotations

Figure 3. Trajan's Column, Scene CXLI. Trajan receiving Dacian chiefs. From Conrad Cichorius, *Die Reliefs der Trajanssäule,* vol. 4 (Berlin: Riemer, 1900).

leader and the mass of people he addresses raise their arms, most of these Roman scenes—but not all; the iconography varies—show only the man of rank with his right arm extended as a sign of greeting and benevolence but chiefly as an indication of his power.

This latter aspect is worth our attention at some length. A marble relief with the departure of Emperor Domitian on a military campaign as depicted on a frieze now in the Palazzo della Cancellaria in Rome contains two figures as idealized representations of the Senate and the Roman People, the *genius populi* and the *genius senatus*.[9] Both raise their right arms in a farewell greeting. The gesture of neither resembles the modern raised-arm salute even slightly. Before them, Domitian's right arm is raised as well, not as high as that of the Senate figure but only horizontally. From parallel scenes on imperial Roman coins depicting

from ancient texts). The emperor's *adventus* is, or at least can be, a kind of triumphal procession (*triumphus*), as Ammianus' description makes evident. Its iconography, based on ancient textual and visual sources, was made popular by Andrea Mantegna's late-fifteenth-century series of nine paintings, *The Triumphs of Caesar,* on which cf. Martindale 1979, especially 55–74 (chapter entitled "*The Triumphs of Caesar* and Classical Antiquity"). Cf. also Alföldi 1970, 79–118, on public ceremonies of saluting the emperor, with 93–100 on his parades and triumphs, and Hölscher 1967, 48–67 (*adventus* and *profectio*) and 68–97 (*triumphus*).

9. The scene is discussed in detail by Koeppel 1969, 138–44, whom I follow here; his Ill. 3 provides a photograph of Frieze A.

an *adventus*, on which the emperor raises only his lower arm from the elbow held close to and low beside his body, scholars have concluded that such gestures are not primarily gestures of salute but rather gestures of power.[10] For this view there exists extensive visual evidence which, in turn, is borne out by Roman imperial literature. The emperor's raised right hand (*dextra elata*) becomes an eloquent symbol of imperial power in poems by Statius and Martial. In a consolation on the death of his wife composed for Abascantus, Domitian's "secretary of state" (*ab epistulis*), Statius has the dying wife recall her husband's closeness to the emperor: "I saw you approach ever more closely the right hand on high" (*vidi altae propius propiusque accedere dextrae*). In another poem the same emperor's favorite boy, Earinus, is said to have been "chosen to touch so many times the mighty [lit., huge] right hand" of Domitian (*ingentem totiens contingere dextram / electus*).[11] The immediately following mention of foreign nations—Getae, Persians, Armenians, Indians—reveals that an emphasis on imperial power underlies these references to the ruler's hand. This view is corroborated by some epigrams of Martial in which the emperor's right hand is described as the greatest—i.e., most powerful—on earth (*manumque . . . / illam qua nihil est in orbe maius*, in a phrase following immediately on the word *dominum*, "lord") or carries the same or a synonymous attribute that Statius gives it: *ingenti manu* ("in his mighty hand") or *magnas Caesaris in manus* ("into Caesar's mighty hands").[12]

So it is no surprise that the author of the standard modern work on the subject should frequently speak of "the uplifted hand of gesture" in Roman art. He comments: "Behind all these usages lies the element of force, given or received, which is fundamental to the symbolic character of the hand."[13] He never refers to a Roman salute or mentions the modern straight-arm salute but simply and appropriately describes saluting figures as "gesticulate."

---

10. On this see especially the detailed study by L'Orange 1982, 139–70 (chapter entitled "The Gesture of Power. Cosmocrator's Sign"), with section "The Emperor's 'Huge Hand'" at 139–53. Koeppel 1969, 142–43, follows L'Orange.

11. Statius, *Silvae* 5.1.183 and 3.4.61–62.

12. Martial, *Epigrams* 4.30.4–5, 4.8.10, and 6.1.5. Cf. Groß 1985, 403–12, on the divine emperor's hand.

13. Brilliant 1963, 215. He provides an appendix on *manus* and its implications at 215–216. Cf. also Vincenzo Saladino, "Dal saluto alla salvezza: valori simbolici della mano destra nell'arte greca e romana," in Bertelli and Centanni 1995, 31–52 and figs. 1–14; see especially 35–36 (on the raised right hand) and 43–46 (on *adventus*).—In a different but influential ancient context, the Old Testament contains numerous textual examples of the raised arm or hand of power, e.g. at 2 Mos. 6.6 and 17.11; 5 Mos. 4.34, 5.15, 7.19, 9.29, 11.2, 26.8; 1 Kings 8.42, 2 Kings 17.36; 2 Chron. 6.32; Jes. 5.25, 9.11, and 40.10. New Testament examples are significantly fewer (Luke 1.51, 1 Peter 5.6).

Here it is worth our while to consider what Quintilian, the first-century-A.D. teacher of rhetoric and author of the most detailed Roman handbook on oratory, had to say about hand and arm gestures in Book 11, chapter 3, of *The Instruction of the Orator*.[14] He states that an orator's arm can be "stretched out to the side" (*expatiatur in latus*), but this is only to accommodate moments in which words are being delivered in grand style; otherwise Quintilian refers to "restrained extension of the arm" (*bracchii moderata proiectio*) during which the fingers are being opened while the hand goes up (11.3.84). The more emphatic gesture appears to be parallel to one described in earlier rhetorical treatises.[15] But to deduce from any of these passages that Roman orators employed any gestures even vaguely resembling the rigid raised-arm gesture toward the front of their bodies or slightly to its side is unwarranted.

Quintilian observes that a hand may be raised above shoulder height as if in warning: *illa cava et rara et super umeri altitudinem elata . . . velut hortatrix manus* (11.3.103). But he condemns the raising of the hand above eye level and any excessive gesticulations with the arms (11.3.112 and 118–19). An emperor's mighty raised hand or arm, then, may well have been intended as clearly signaling to his subjects his awareness of virtually unlimited power. If such a view is indeed correct, it may even throw light on a particular aspect of the modern straight-arm salute in Nazi Germany. There, the man in absolute power very often, and almost casually, bent his raised right arm so far back that his palm could be horizontal while those facing him made their salutes as smart and snappy and as straight as possible—playing by the rules, as it were, and thereby demonstrating their faith, their unquestioning obedience, and their inferiority.

Pertinent passages from Roman literature are comparable to the ancient visual evidence. The historian Livy reports that Pacuvius Calavius, a nobleman from Capua, had been instrumental in handing over his city to Hannibal after the latter's great victory over the Romans at Cannae in 216 B.C. Pacuvius' son, however, had been strongly against his father's action. In violation of the principle of hospitality, one of the most com-

---

14. On Quintilian and Cicero see in particular Fantham 1982; Maier-Eichhorn 1989, with a commentary on all relevant passages and expressions; Hall and Bond 2002; and Hall 2004. The last two contain up-to-date additional references. Maier-Eichhorn, 137–43, provides illustrations of the hand gestures Quintilian describes; none of them fits any raised-arm saluting gesture. Fritz Graf, "Gestures and Conventions: The Gestures of Roman Actors and Orators," in Bremmer and Roodenburg 1992, 36–58, likewise does not mention this kind of gesture.

15. Cicero, *Orator* 18.59: *brachii porrectione* ("the arm extended") at impassioned speaking; *Rhetoric to Herennius* 3.15.27: *porrectione perceleri bracchii* ("with a very quick extension of the arm").

pelling ancient moral codes, the son then planned to assassinate Hannibal at a banquet. When he revealed his intention to his father, Pacuvius succeeded in dissuading him with an impassioned speech. At its beginning the father refers to the right hand of *fides* ("trust, reliability"):

> "Per ego te," inquit, "fili, quaecumque iura liberos iungunt parentibus, precor quaesoque ne ante oculos patris facere et pati omnia infanda velis. Paucae horae sunt intra quas iurantes per quidquid deorum est, dextrae dextras iungentes, fidem obstrinximus—ut sacratas fide manus, digressi a conloquio, extemplo in eum armaremus?"

> "By all the lawful ties, my son," he said, "which join children to their parents, I beg and implore you not to commit any such unspeakable crimes before your father's eyes or allow them to be done. It has been only a few hours since we pledged our trust, swearing by all the gods and joining right hands to right hands—only to arm our hands, hallowed by this trust, against him immediately after we leave our conference with him?"[16]

Fides, allegorized as a goddess, may herself be said to stretch out her right hand to humans. Valerius Maximus characterizes her in the following terms: *venerabile Fidei numen dexteram suam, certissimum salutis humanae pignus, ostentat* ("the venerable divine power of Trust, the most reliable pledge of human security, stretches out her right hand").[17] Virgil says of Anchises: *dextram Anchises . . . / dat iuveni atque animum praesenti pignore firmat* ("Anchises . . . gives the young man his hand and encourages him with this pledge").[18] Ovid refers to the joining of right hands as a token of trust in the context of Odysseus' confrontation with the sorceress Circe: *fides dextraeque datae* ("right hands given in trust").[19] Tacitus summarizes the mission of the king of Parthia's ambassadors to Germanicus in comparable terms: *Miserat amicitiam ac foedus memoraturos, et cupere novari dextras* ("He had sent them in commemoration of their friendly alliance and because he wished to renew their treaty [lit., their right hands]").[20] It is evident that throughout Roman culture the goddess Fides and the right hand were closely associated.[21]

---

16. Livy, *From the Foundation of the City* 23.9.3. Cf. Karl-Joachim Hölkeskamp, "*Fides*—deditio in fidem—dextra data et accepta*: Recht, Religion und Ritual in Rom," in Bruun 2000, 223–50.
17. Valerius Maximus, *Memorabilia* 6.6 praef.
18. Virgil, *Aeneid* 3.610–11.
19. Ovid, *Metamorphoses* 14.297.
20. Tacitus, *Annals* 2.58.1.
21. Cf. Groß 1985, 389–93.

To Romans, *fides* and *foedus* ("treaty") were related as words and concepts. Both are closely related to hand gestures or handshakes.[22] But more important for our topic are what Romans called *supinae manus,* hands stretched toward heaven. For these Horace and Virgil provide literary evidence to supplement the surviving visual examples, which occur mainly on Roman coins. Horace begins one of his *Odes* with the description of a poor countrywoman's simple prayer and sacrifice: *Caelo supinas si tuleris manus . . .* ("If you stretch your hands to the sky . . .").[23] In Book Three of the *Aeneid* Aeneas receives in his sleep a vision of the Penates, the household gods, rescued from the burning city of Troy; he reports:

corripio e stratis corpus tendoque supinas
ad caelum cum voce manus et munera libo
intemerata focis.

I jump up from my bed and stretch my hands up to the sky, praying, and pour an offering of undiluted wine on the hearth.[24]

In his biography of Marius Plutarch describes a similar moment when Marius, solemnly pledging a sacrifice to the gods, stretches both his hands toward heaven.[25]

The raised hands with which Aeneas, Marius, and the ancients in general prayed to the gods signify both a salute to the gods and an acknowledgment of their superior powers. But these hand gestures do not express the routine kind of greeting on social occasions among humans. Such gestures are not identical to the modern Roman salute in either purpose or appearance, for hands were held vertically or with palms facing up, not down. Parallel to this is the ancient custom of raising one's hands in acknowledgment of earthly power.

Related to the religious aspects of the raised right hand is that of swearing an oath. This side will become important in chapter 2, which deals with a famous painting of a supposedly archaic Roman oath scene. Therefore the ancient literature referring to this gesture deserves our

---

22. Cf. Galinsky 1996, 60–61 and 63 ill. 31.
23. Horace, *Odes* 3.23.1.
24. Virgil, *Aeneid* 3.175–77. Cf. Sullivan 1967.
25. Plutarch, *Marius* 26.2. John Bulwer (fl. 1654) adduces this text in his *Chirologia,* one of his detailed and highly influential treatises on hand gestures—its title page identifies him as "J. B. Gent. Philochirosophus"—under *Gestus XVII: Juro* ("I swear"). The accompanying illustration (R) shows a hand held up vertically. Bulwer's *Chirologia: Or, The Natural Language of the Hand* and his *Chironomia: Or, The Art of Manual Rhetoric* (both 1644) are easily accessible in a modern edition (Bulwer 1974), where see pages 47–48 and 115 (ill.).

attention.[26] Clear evidence of Roman oaths involving raised arms or hands is scant.[27] Early in the last book of the *Aeneid,* Aeneas, in a religious context—he invokes the gods, and a priest and animals are present for a sacrifice—delivers a promise about the Trojans' future treatment of the Latins according to the outcome of his impending duel with Turnus. Latinus, king of the Latins, then replies with a comparable oath, and the sacrifice confirms their solemn agreement *(foedera,* 212).[28] While he swears, Latinus looks up at the sky "and stretches his right hand to the stars" *(tenditque ad sidera dextram,* 196). If this were all Virgil says about his gesture, we could assume that Latinus' palm is facing upward while he invokes the gods above and that, when he mentions the underworld (199), he turns his palm downward and lowers his arm as well; further that, when he touches the altar *(tango aras,* 201), his right hand is on the altar palm down and remains in that position. This, then, would be a clear case of an oath ceremony resembling a salute—after all, an invocation of gods implies a greeting. But Virgil tells us that Latinus' right hand was not empty: he was holding his scepter *(dextra sceptrum nam forte gerebat,* 206). It is possible that Latinus began his oath with an empty right hand and during its delivery picked up his staff. But it is more realistic to assume that he was holding it all along. The passage does not provide any clear evidence for a salute-plus-oath gesture that involves a raised right arm and an open palm.

Less ambiguous is Ovid's description of Clymene's reaction to her son Phaethon's question concerning the identity of his father. This, Phaethon is about to learn, is none other than Sol, the god of the sun:

---

26. Cf. in this context Bleicken 1963 and for its background Groß 1985, 219–21. Herrmann 1968 deals with the oaths sworn to Roman emperors and with the Hellenistic Greek background of this custom only on a textual, not a gestural, basis. Cf. further L'Orange 1982, 153–59 (section entitled "The Oriental Origin of the Gesture of the Raised Right Hand").

27. Given its context and the general spirit of irreverent wit and satire in Petronius' *Satyricon,* the moment in which Trimalchio's dinner guests raise their hands and swear to their host's ingenuity (40.1) is not necessarily conclusive but reveals ironic exaggeration, although it is doubtless based on custom. It expresses, at least in part, utter astonishment, as does the same gesture at, e.g., Cicero, *Letters to His Friends* 7.5.2 *(sustulimus manus:* "we threw up our hands").

28. Cf. *Aeneid* 7.234–35 in a speech by Ilioneus, who swears by Aeneas' fate "and his mighty right hand" *(dextramque potentem),* with *fides* mentioned in the following line. Different is *Aeneid* 3.610–11, where Anchises gives Achaemenides his right hand as a pledge *(pignus)* of his good faith. Achaemenides may well have accompanied his earlier invocation of heavenly gods (599–600) by raising his arm or arms, but Virgil does not say so. The plea of Volteius Mena at Horace, *Epistles* 1.7.94–95, does involve his right hand, but there is no description of the gesture he may be employing while speaking. A miniature Pompeian wall painting depicts a priestess, her right arm raised and held straight, her palm (probably) facing down, before Apollo and Diana; illustration at Berry 2007, 186–87.

>   utraque caelo
> bracchia porrexit spectansque ad lumina solis
> "per iubar hoc" inquit "radiis insigne coruscis,
> nate, tibi iuro, quod nos auditque videtque,
> hoc te, quem spectas, hoc te, qui temperat orbem,
> Sole satum . . . ."

> she stretched both arms to the sky and, looking at the light of the sun, said: "By this bright light clearly visible in its flashing radiance, my son, I swear to you: this which hears and sees us, this one at whom you are looking, this one who masters the world and the sun's course, from him, the Sun, you are born. . . ."[29]

It is self-evident that both mother and son are looking up at the sky while this scene is going on. Equally clearly Clymene keeps her arms raised during her entire speech, which continues for several lines. But it is reasonable to assume that she keeps her palms turned upward, pointing them, as it were, at the sun. Her gesture is intended to reinforce what her words reveal to be a highly emotional moment to her, for Ovid gives her speech an excited, almost breathless rhythm and a sentence structure that is anything but smooth.

Another comparable epic passage occurs in Lucan's *Pharsalia,* a poem on the subject of the civil war between Julius Caesar and Pompey the Great, a war that will culminate in the bloody battle of Pharsalus of 48 B.C. and leave Caesar sole ruler of Rome and its dominions. In Book 1 Caesar's soldiers, swayed by inflammatory speeches, promise him unconditional allegiance in the upcoming campaign:

>   His cunctae simul adsensere cohortes
> elatasque alte, quaecumque ad bella vocaret,
> promisere manus.

> All army cohorts unanimously agreed to these words; they stretched out their hands, raised high, and promised their support for whatever campaigns he would call them to.[30]

My translation is no more than an attempt to render the complexity of Lucan's words intelligible. The poet emphasizes the decisive importance

---

29. Ovid, *Metamorphoses* 1.766–71.
30. Lucan, *Pharsalia* 1.386–88.

of the moment that set an irrevocable course of history ruinous for Rome by compressing—cross-wise, as it were—two meanings into the phrase *promisere manus*. The verb *promittere* literally means "to send forth," here in the sense of stretching out (i.e., one's hands), and "to promise," the word's most common meaning. As a result, *manus* both keeps its literal meaning ("hands") and acquires the figurative meaning of "support" (cf. an English expression like "giving someone a hand" in an emergency). But exactly how the cohorts sent forth their hands at this moment, characterized by such great noise and general commotion that Lucan can only describe it with an epic simile (389–391) that is actually more detailed than what it describes, remains unclear to us. It is possible, if unlikely, that the soldiers all employed the same kind of hand or arm movement and for the moment would have appeared far too orderly. Large-scale disorder of a kind that leads to even larger discord is Lucan's very point here.

In his epic *Punica* Silius Italicus has Regulus, a famous Roman hero, invoke the goddesses Fides and Juno, by whom he had sworn to return to Carthage. Regulus informs the Roman senate about the weakness of the Carthaginians and urges the Romans not to accede to an ignominious peace with Carthage. By way of emphasis Regulus lifts his open palms and eyes to the sky before he begins his speech: *palmas simul attollens ac lumina caelo*.[31] His hands will have been held in the palms-up position common for such prayers, oaths, or invocations. The gesture, of course, has nothing to do with the modern raised-arm salute.

Although they mention and describe acts of salutation, Greek texts are equally inconclusive about raised arms. Greek art works also do not provide substantial evidence for the straight-arm salute. I adduce only a few pertinent instances from Greek literature and art here since Roman, not Greek, saluting customs are my chief concern. In his *Anabasis of Alexander* the historian Arrian reports an episode from the life of Alexander the Great in which his serious wound disconcerted his soldiers to such an extent that they readily believed rumors which pronounced him dead. They were reassured only when they saw him alive with their own eyes. Alexander, Arrian says, "stretched out his hand upward to the crowd" to convince them; they in turn "shouted out, stretching their hands to the sky and some to Alexander himself."[32] Arrian provides no further description of their mutual greetings, and it seems unlikely that either a weakened Alexander or his soldiers employed anything as rigid or formal as the straight-arm salute or indeed any other gesture resembling it. The

---

31. Silius Italicus, *Punica* 6.466. The references to Fides and Regulus' oath are at lines 468–69.

32. Arrian, *Anabasis of Alexander* 6.13.1–3; quotation at 13.2.

soldiers in their joyous relief at seeing Alexander alive may well have waved their arms and hands about excitedly.

My first example from Greek art is especially striking in view of a modern work that takes recourse to its ancient precursor. The gigantic statue of the sun god Helios that Chares, the disciple of the famous Hellenistic sculptor Lycippus, built for the Rhodians in the third century B.C. was a marvel to the ancients and deservedly counts among the Seven Wonders of the ancient world. The bronze colossus, said to be about 30–35 meters high, was destroyed in an earthquake.[33] Although it could be seen in its ruined state for centuries, no trace of it has survived, and ancient Greek and Roman descriptions of it are inconclusive as to the god's posture.[34] The Renaissance view that Helios' legs were straddling the entrance to the harbor has now been abandoned. It is likely, though, that the statue carried a torch and so served as a kind of lighthouse.[35] The American Statue of Liberty is loosely modeled on this traditional view of the Colossus of Rhodes.[36] Modern archaeologists and art historians have proposed a variety of reconstructions of what the statue may have looked like. Possible evidence derives from small-scale representations of Helios that show the god with his right arm raised and extended, palm down but fingers slightly spread.[37] His arm is bent at the elbow, sometimes more, sometimes less. The posture clearly indicates a saluting gesture, but it is in no instance identical to the modern form.[38]

A marble relief by Archelaus of Priene shows the hill of the Muses with Zeus, Apollo, and the Muses on its two top panels. Below, on the third panel, a seated Homer is being crowned by the personifications of

---

33. Cf. Pliny the Elder, *Natural History* 34.41; Polybius, *The Histories* 5.88–89.

34. Pindar, *Olympian Ode* 7.54–76, recounts the myth that explains why Helios was associated with the island of Rhodes. Scholarly literature on the colossus is extensive; see especially Vedder 1999–2000. See further Reynold Higgins, "The Colossus of Rhodes," in Clayton and Price 1988, 124–37 and 171–72 (notes); Vedder 2003; and Brodersen 2004. Brodersen provides the texts of the ancient sources.

35. Belief in the ancient Colossus' torch is based on the literal understanding of a phrase in its dedicatory inscription that refers to the torch of freedom; cf. *Greek Anthology* 6.171. Langglotz 1975–76 corroborates that the Colossus of Rhodes had held a torch in his right hand.

36. The Statue of Liberty was referred to as "The New Colossus" in Emma Lazarus' well-known poem by that name (1883); see Lazarus 2005, 58.

37. Cf. especially the illustrations in Hoepfner 2003, 65–73, ills. 91–97, 99–101, and 103 (bronze statuettes, gems, and coins). Hoepfner, 66 ill. 96, shows a bronze statuette with Helios' upper arm stretched out horizontally but his lower arm raised at a ninety-degree angle; his right hand is held vertically.

38. Cf. especially Hoepfner 2003, 80–82 (section entitled "Die Skenographia des grüßenden Helios"), with color drawings of a reconstruction of the Colossus greeting sailors approaching Rhodes and discussion of the suitability of this gesture. See also note 24 in chapter 6 below on a modern painting of the Colossus.

World and Time; facing him across an altar are several male and female figures. Two of these have raised their right arms in salute, but their fingers and thumbs are kept well apart. In front of them another figure has raised both arms at the same angle; significantly, both hands hold flaming torches. Behind them there appears yet another saluting figure, partly covered, whose right arm is raised but held considerably lower than the others'. Presumably this third figure is greeting Homer by raising only the lower arm, a common way of saluting. The relief, found at Bovillae near Rome, dates to around 150–125 B.C.

Back to Rome. If, as we have seen, Roman literature is at best inconclusive, although tantalizing, about raised-arm gestures, what can the visual evidence tell us beyond the information considered above? Raising one's arms in prayer—commonly both, but sometimes only one and then usually the right arm—is a universal religious gesture that can be traced back to prehistoric art. Frequently the upper arm or arms are held close to the body, the lower arm is raised from the elbow, with the open palm held vertically and facing out.[39] A well-known example appears on Relief B of the Cancellaria scenes, in which we witness an *adventus*. Emperor Vespasian, facing the viewer but looking to his right at his son Domitian, has raised his right hand in this manner.[40] An instructive scene of what an elaborate religious ceremony will have looked like occurs in a wall painting from Herculaneum, now in the National Museum of Naples. Although it depicts an Egyptian cult, it is representative of the syncretism prevalent in the Roman world since the late republic. (By the time of the early empire, Eastern and especially Egyptian cults had spread to Rome and Italy.) The Herculaneum painting shows the central figure of a priest extending his right arm horizontally toward a group of musicians and worshippers on the viewer's left, while some members of another group of worshippers on the right raise their right arms, either stretched out or lifted from the elbow.[41] This is one of the earliest mass scenes in Roman

---

39. As the title indicates, the study by Demisch 1984 deals primarily with the prayer gesture in which both arms are raised, but see pages 131–34 and 232 (notes), ills. 168–76, and ill. 14 (page 331) for examples of the raised right arm. Cf. further Neumann 1965, 41–48, on saluting gestures in Greek art (with ills. 19–22 of right-arm salutes with elbows bent, open palms, and fingers spread) and 78–82 (with ills. 37–39) on comparable postures as gestures of prayer, and Groß 1985, 25–28 and, for an overview of the importance of the gods' hands in Roman cults, 383–417.

40. Koeppel 1969, 172–74, discusses this image and provides a photograph. Cf also Koeppel, 184, on a comparable coin type.

41. Mielsch 2001, 175 with ill. 206, provides a description and a color photograph of this painting. So does Berry 2007, 208.

painting.⁴² In retrospect it may remind us of similar (but not identical) modern gestures and contexts.

Other Roman examples are more pertinent to our topic. The so-called Altar of Domitius Ahenobarbus, dating to before 107 B.C., shows the standing figure of a soldier who is attending a *census* ceremony. He is holding a shield in his left hand and appears to be saluting with his right arm. His hand touches his helmet at the temple in a gesture familiar to us from modern military salutes, so his arm is bent, not straight. This gesture may be a salute or not; if it is one, it is not analogous to the raised-arm salute.⁴³ A closely similar gesture appears considerably later on a sarcophagus from the early third century A.D. that depicts Dionysus and Ariadne and is now in the National Museum in Rome. (Figure 4) Earlier, the posture of Nero on the Augustan cameo showing Augustus' apotheosis—the *Grand Camée de France,* now in Paris—is somewhat comparable to that of the soldier on the Altar of Ahenobarbus as well. The cameo further shows Drusus Caesar saluting Augustus with his outstretched right arm, fingers slightly bent and apart.⁴⁴ The apotheosis of Emperor Antoninus Pius and his wife Faustina, originally on the base of the column of Antoninus dating from the second century A.D., shows the goddess Roma as an observer; she is seated in a relaxed position and raising her right arm and open palm toward the imperial couple above. In keeping with her relaxed posture, her arm is bent at the elbow, and the fingers of her right hand are slightly bent forward while her thumb points straight up.⁴⁵ A Pompeian wall painting in the house of the Vettii showing the victory of Apollo over the dragon Python includes a standing female figure saluting Apollo with her raised right arm. The gesture appears to be formal, as is appropriate in the god's presence.⁴⁶ Such examples, isolated as they are, cannot sufficiently account for the supposedly Roman nature of the raised-arm salute in the political ideology of the twentieth century. More common variants of the ancient gesture occur with statues of orators addressing their audiences, although even these conform to the modern

---

42. So Mielsch 2001, 175.
43. Andreae 1999, 52–55, gives a description and interpretation of the monument. (It is a pedestal rather than an altar.) Cf. also Ann Kuttner, "Some New Grounds for Narrative: Marcus Antonius's Base (The *Ara Domitti* [sic] *Ahenobarbi*) and Republican Biographies," in Holliday 1993, 198–229, with illustration of the *census* at 200–201 ill. 69. Further illustrations appear in Andreae, 360–61 ill. 220; Brilliant 1963, ill. 2.74; Henig 1983, 72 ill. 53; and, in greatest detail, in Stilp 2001, figs. 22–23, 40–41, 48, and 51. Stilp, 67–68, discusses the figure of the soldier and follows earlier scholarship in his conclusion that the soldier's gesture is inexplicable to us.
44. Cf. the color plate at Andreae 1999, 141 ill. 54.
45. Color illustration at Andreae 1999, 232 ill. 111.
46. Color plate at Andreae 1999, 155 ill. 69.

Figure 4. Detail from Dionysus and Ariadne sarcophagus. Author's photograph.

salute only loosely if at all. Some Etruscan statues and statuettes, including the *Arringatore* or *Orator* (Aule Metele, i.e., Aulus Metellus) now in Florence, are familiar examples.[47] As we have seen, however, ancient Roman rhetorical treatises refer chiefly the orator's *hand* gestures, not to his raised arm or arms.

The Prima Porta (or Primaporta) marble statue of Emperor Augustus, discovered in 1862 and now in the Vatican Museums, may be the most famous statue of a Roman addressing someone with his right arm raised.[48] Later ones are the equestrian bronze statues of an emperor, possibly Caligula, in Naples, of Nero in Ancona, and of Marcus Aurelius on the Campidoglio in Rome.[49] But the statue of Augustus did not represent him as saluting or in an act of *adlocutio* at all, as has been and still is popularly assumed.[50] The statue's right arm is not original but seems to have been restored in antiquity, perhaps more than once.[51] Originally the

---

47. Illustrations in Brilliant 1963, figs. 1.24–31 (all with palms outward but vertical, elbows bent), and 1.43 (the *Orator*). Andreae 1999, 64 ill. 20, provides a large color plate of the *Arringatore*. Cf. also Aldrete 1999, figs. 1 (schematic drawing of an orator exhorting his audience with raised and open right hand, arm bent at elbow), 18 (coin of Emperor Hadrian addressing and being greeted by a group of people, right arms raised; cf. Aldrete, 93 and 185 note 15, and see below). Cf. further Aldrete, 94 (on a coin of Trajan) and 104–14 (section entitled "Greeting and Praise"). Corbeill 2004, 20–24 (section entitled "Hands"), does not specifically refer to hand gestures as salutes. Neither Aldrete nor Corbeill refers to any modern analogies, connections, or connotations that the Roman gestures they examine might have acquired. Flaig 2003 presents a different theoretical perspective but does not include the raised-arm salute. Neither do Boegehold 1999, Morstein-Marx 2004 (with a photograph of the *Arringatore* on the dust jacket), or the essays collected in Cairns 2005.

48. Simon 1986, Plate 1, and Andreae 1999, 104 ill. 36, furnish large color photographs.

49. Illustrations in Brilliant 1963, figs. 2.23, 2.25, and 2.105. Cf. also Brilliant, figs. 1.84, 2.42, 2.92–93, 3.13, 3.60, 3.62, 3.88, 3.90, and 4.127–33. Comparable scenes of *adlocutio* at Brilliant, figs. 3.5, 3.9, 3.58, 3.64–65, 3.74, 3.111, 4.1–7, 4.10, 4.12–13; of *adventus* at 3.91, 4.24, and 4.26–34. Andreae 1999, 247 ill. 113, has an exceptional color plate of Marcus Aurelius' statue. Types of *adlocutio* scenes recur in the later history of Western art; cf., e.g., Panofsky 1969, 74–77, with additional references, and figs. 83–88 (including paintings by Titian, Giulio Romano, and Tiepolo).

50. For recent statements of this view see Kleiner 1992, 63–66, and Galinsky 1996, 24–28, both with illustrations. Several other examples could be mentioned. Galinsky, 24 and 27 ill. 7, adduces as a parallel a *denarius* of Octavian from ca. 31–28 B.C. whose reverse shows "Octavian addressing the troops." Elsner 1995, 161–62, is less decided: Augustus "appears to be proclaiming victory to the army or the people, or at any rate addressing the spectator." The epic-size painting by Thomas Couture, *The Romans of the Decadence* (1847), one of the most famous and iconic works about the moral and implicitly political decline of Rome, shows on its far right a statue modeled on that of the Augustus of Prima Porta, right arm raised but fingers spread.

51. So already Köhler 1863, at 433. Köhler's essay is more accessible in a German translation (slightly abridged): "Eine Statue des Caesar Augustus," in Binder 1991, 187–203; here 188–89. Köhler, 435–36 (original) or 190–91 (translation), discusses the traditional position of the restored right arm as a representation of an *adlocutio* on the part of the world's most powerful

hand of his raised arm was holding a spear, its tip on the ground. The ring finger of this hand has survived separately; it is pointing downward.[52] In the case of Marcus Aurelius' statue, the emperor's extended right arm is not raised to even a horizontal level, and his hand and fingers are not stretched out.[53] Nevertheless the statue was made to serve as model for an equestrian statue of Benito Mussolini by Giuseppe Graziosi and provided the backdrop to Fascist rallies.[54] It is, of course, possible to view the statue from a low angle which makes the emperor appear to be giving a kind of pre-Fascist salute. (Figure 5) But this would be no more than a calculated perspective on the part of a photographer, far removed from the impression the statue makes on a neutral observer. Rather, it expresses a combination of both majestic power and dignified benignity. A modern literary author perhaps shows best the impression that the statue of Marcus Aurelius makes on its viewer. In chapter XVIII of his 1860 novel *The Marble Faun* Nathaniel Hawthorne gives the following description:

> The moonlight glistened upon traces of the gilding, which had once covered both rider and steed; these were almost gone; but the aspect of dignity was still perfect, clothing the figure as it were with an imperial robe of light. It is the most majestic representation of the kingly character that ever the world has seen. A sight of this old heathen Emperour is enough to create an evanescent sentiment of loyalty even in a democratic bosom; so august does he look, so fit to rule, so worthy of man's profoundest homage and obedience, so inevitably attractive of his love! He stretches forth his hand, with an air of grand beneficence and unlimited authority, as if uttering a decree from which no appeal was permissible, but in which the obedient subject would find his highest interests consulted; a command, that was in itself a benediction.[55]

---

ruler. Brilliant 1963, 65–68, also discusses the statue in detail. Cf. further Boschung 1993, 96–103, especially 97.

52. Simon 1986, 56–57, gives a reconstruction of the Prima Porta statue, with illustration (ill. 59) and supporting iconographic evidence. (Galinsky 1996, 396 note 54, cites this among other studies.) Cf. also Simon's essay "Altes und Neues zur Statue des Augustus von Primaporta," written in 1983 but not published until 1991 in Binder 1991, 204–33 and Plates 30–35; see especially Plate 34. Bergemann 1990, 6 note 58, follows her. Andreae 1999, 89–90, adheres to the traditional reconstruction of the right arm.

53. Cf. the gold coin (*aureus*) of ca. 29 B.C. and the *denarius* of ca. 41 B.C. depicting the equestrian statue of Octavian, the later Emperor Augustus, in Galinsky 1996, 46 ill. 21 and 167 ill. 78. On both coins the emperor's raised arm is slightly bent at the elbow.

54. Cf. the illustration in Malvano 1988, ill. 30.

55. The text of *The Marble Faun; or, The Romance of Monte Beni* is here quoted from Hawthorne 1983, 990–91. The description of Emperor Justinian's equestrian statue in the Augustaeum in Constantinople by the historian Procopius (*On Buildings* 1.2.10–12) indicates how closely Melville captured the spirit of such statuary. Procopius' text is translated and quoted in

Figure 5. Equestrian statue of Marcus Aurelius from "Fascist" angle. Author's photograph.

Hawthorne's words are admirably sensitive to the aura of unlimited and, in this case, benign imperial power that is embodied in an emperor's mighty hand, the *ingens dextra* of imperial Roman literature.[56] A modern

---

MacCormack 1981, 77 and 308 note 305. L'Orange 1982, 147 ill. 104, reproduces an image of Justinian's statue. (His right arm, raised from the elbow up, and its open hand are positioned significantly differently from Marcus Aurelius'.) L'Orange, 143, further remarks: "After Constantine [the Great] the raised right hand is repeated as a typical gesture of majesty right down to the middle ages."

56. Koeppel 1969, 182 and 192, emphasizes that this posture of the emperor's arm is not only a greeting and that it is a standard aspect of equestrian statues of Roman emperors.

art historian, discussing this statue's fate in the Middle Ages, similarly speaks of the emperor's "commanding gesture of benediction" and continues:

> The sense of the gesture of Marcus Aurelius' right hand and, in consequence, the effect of the entire work would, indeed, be quite different were that gesture deprived of the universal meaning with which it greets and blesses its viewers.[57]

Art historian Hans Peter L'Orange called this imperial posture the "gesture of power and benediction" and observed:

> The supernatural redeeming power in the emperor's outstretched right hand presupposes higher powers and abilities dwelling in him. Through the emperor, manifesting his power in this gesture, divine interference in human affairs takes place.[58]

So it is difficult to agree with the assessment by a modern military historian that Marcus Aurelius here "is returning the equestrian military salute with his right arm raised and extended."[59] That the gesture is military is open to doubt. Nevertheless even recent scholars somewhat fancifully and, as seems likely, under the influence of the gesture's modern history retroactively apply it to the military culture of the Roman Empire.[60]

---

57. Fehl 1974; quotations at 365 and 366. Presicce 1990, 89–108, gives an illustrated overview of the statue's history.

58. L'Orange 1982, 145 and 147. Comparable points may be made about the tradition of Christian iconography, especially images of Christ enthroned as cosmic ruler (*pantokrator*) and of scenes with angels. One random but important example of late-ancient to early-Christian art illustrating the latter kind of image is the *Reiderische Tafel*, an ivory tablet from Northern Italy (about 400 A.D.) now in the Nationalmuseum, Munich. It shows Christ's empty tomb and his ascension, with a seated figure in the left foreground, presumably the angel at the tomb, greeting the three Marys with his raised right arm, index and middle fingers extended. Descriptions and illustrations in Gutberlet 1935, 63–83 (description and interpretation, but without mention of the salute) and Plate II, and Schiller 1971, 21–22 and ill. 12. This angel's saluting gesture frequently recurs; representative examples from later centuries may be seen in Schiller, figs. 8 and 17–21. The topic of Christian iconography is too large to be incorporated into the present argument, nor is it crucial for our purpose.

59. Rankov 1994, 15 (part of a caption accompanying a low-angle photograph of the statue that hints at its military purpose).

60. Here is an example taken from Rankov 1994. This slim volume has color plates by Richard Hook. Plate G on page 39 shows a scene Rankov describes on page 51 in part as follows: "A trooper of the Emperor's Horse Guards (*Equites Singulares Augusti*) reports to his decurion during Trajan's First Dacian War [A.D. 101–102]... The trooper greets his officer with the cavalry salute of the extended right arm." The color picture shows the trooper giving what

Other equestrian statues of Roman emperors also show them raising their right hand or arm in salute, so an over-lifesize statue of Augustus in the National Museum, Athens, and a reconstructed gilded statue of Nero Caesar, son of Germanicus, now in the Palazzo della Gherardesca in Florence. The latter horseman raises his right hand above his head. Both riders exemplify the *adlocutio* type of Roman statuary.[61] The life-size marble statue of Marcus Aurelius standing, his right arm raised and elbow bent, now in the National Museum in Rome, is a comparable type. (Figure 6)

We may now conclude that the open raised hand sends the viewer an obvious message of power and authority but that its Roman examples do so in ways not consistent with the modern political iconography of a "Roman" salute.[62] Concerning such a salute the record of Roman art is inconclusive. Nor does any Roman text refer to or describe it. It is revealing that in his exhaustive 1890 study of Greek and Roman gestures Carl Sittl neither discussed nor illustrated raised-arm salutes, as he would doubtless have done if he had found any evidence for them.[63] (At his time German *Altertumswissenschaft* was famously, or notoriously, thorough and exhaustive.) Nevertheless their ubiquity in the modern popular imagination has led even classical scholars to assign them to the ancient Romans. A representative example is the following statement by Jérôme Carcopino in his widely read book *Daily Life in Ancient Rome* about the arrival of gladiators in the Colosseum:

> The gladiators . . . marched round the arena in military array. . . . They walked nonchalantly, their hands swinging freely, followed by valets

---

is virtually indistinguishable from the Fascist or Nazi salute. Plate I on page 41 then has another salute scene set at the same time, described by Rankov on page 53: "A Praetorian tribune receives a battlefield report from a centurion. . . . The centurion gives his commander the infantry salute, raising the right hand to the helmet, palm inwards: this is shown on a number of reliefs." Perhaps more to the point, this salute is identical with the modern military, i.e., nonpolitical and nonideological, salute. Cf. Koeppel 1969, 179, for a brief discussion of Praetorians greeting the emperor in a scene on Trajan's Column.

61. For illustrations see Junkelmann 1998, 182 ill. 183 (Nero) and 202 ill. 210 (Augustus). Cf. in general Junkelmann, 196–207, a chapter on equestrian monuments.

62. Cf. Brilliant 1963, 208–11 ("Hand Up") and, e.g., 68 ("the frontal hand of . . . world dominion" in later imperial art). Cf. Brilliant, 107, on the raised arms of the mass of anonymous citizens.

63. Sittl 1890, a classic work. Likewise Andrea de Jorio, *La mimica degli antichi investigata nel gestire Napolitano* (Naples, 1832), another standard work, neither mentions nor depicts the salute. The latter is now easily accessible in English (de Jorio 2000). Gilbert Austin, *Chironomia, or A Treatise on Rhetorical Delivery* (1806; now Austin 1966), refers to ancient gestures on several occasions but does not know the raised-arm salute.

Figure 6. Marble statue of Marcus Aurelius. Author's photograph.

carrying their arms; and when they arrived opposite the imperial *pulvinar* [boxed seat] they turned toward the emperor, their right hands extended in sign of homage, and addressed to him the justifiably melancholy salutation: "Hail, Emperor, those who are about to die salute thee. *Ave, Imperator, morituri te salutant!*" [64]

---

64. Carcopino 1940, 239–40.

A note now refers the reader to the author's source, a passage in Suetonius' biography of the Emperor Claudius. Suetonius, however, describes an entirely different situation, which did not even take place in Rome. It occurred well before the building of the Colosseum, the most famous site of Roman gladiatorial games, and did not involve gladiators. A closer look at Suetonius' text is therefore in order. He reports:

> Quin et emissurus Fucinum lacum naumachiam ante commisit. Sed cum proclamantibus naumachiariis: "Have imperator, morituri te salutant!" respondisset: "aut non," neque post hanc vocem quasi venia data quisquam dimicare vellet, diu cunctatus an omnes igni ferroque absumeret, tandem e sede sua prosiluit ac per ambitum lacus non sine foeda vacillatione discurrens partim minando partim adhortando ad pugnam compulit.

> Even when he [Claudius] was about to drain Lake Fucinus, he commissioned a sea battle first. But when the combatants in the sea battle exclaimed "Hail, Emperor, those about to die salute you!" he answered "Or not," and when after these words no one wanted to fight, as if they had been pardoned, and he hesitated for quite a while whether he should have them all killed by fire or sword, he finally jumped up from his seat and, running along the edge of the lake with his repulsive reeling walk, he finally got them to fight, partly with threats, partly with promises.[65]

Suetonius only reports the combatants' words and does not mention any gesture accompanying their greeting. And he avoids using the term gladiators, which would have been inappropriate anyway. The kind of sea battle (*naumachia*) here described occurred only at irregular intervals in Roman history, unlike the regularly offered gladiatorial games, and the words reported by Suetonius are not a customary or standard greeting.[66] Moreover, the whole scene is replete with absurdity: Claudius' joke in reply to the fighters' words, their reaction to it, his weird behavior, and the futility, not recorded here, of the entire undertaking because

---

65. Suetonius, *Claudius* 21.6. The event is also reported by Cassius Dio, *Roman History* 60.33, who quotes the greeting slightly differently and in Greek, and by Tacitus, *Annals* 12.56.

66. This was recognized several decades ago by Leon 1939; he surveys occasions of *naumachia* and describes the differences between gladiators and *naumachiarii*, men condemned to death as criminals or captives. He also cites (46 note 1) Carcopino and older scholarship that attributes the fighters' phrase to gladiators. He concludes that the words of the *naumachiarii* were not a regular salute at all but were uttered on this one occasion only.

Claudius' attempt to drain the lake failed.⁶⁷ So this passage in Suetonius does not bear out Carcopino's conclusion about gladiatorial customs, nor does Carcopino's description warrant a reference to Suetonius except as a source for his Latin quotation of the fighters' words. On these a modern expert on gladiatorial Roman combat concludes: "there are no records proving that this famous remark was ever uttered by gladiators in the amphitheatre."⁶⁸ But Carcopino's error has drawn wide circles and appears to be ineradicable, both in popular culture and in works of scholarship.⁶⁹ Its verbal part is still indispensable in Ridley Scott's *Gladiator* (2000).

The standard iconography of the moment when gladiators salute the emperor in the arena owes much to cinematic recreations, which show them either extending their right arms and holding their swords in their hands—unlike Carcopino's, these gladiators do not have valets—or, like Carcopino's, extending their right arms and empty hands. Both ways occur frequently. An early example of the former occurs in Carmine Gallone and Amleto Palermi's *Gli ultimi giorni di Pompei* (1926; *The Last Days of Pompeii*).⁷⁰ A prominent example of the latter is the opening shot of Henry Koster's *The Robe* (1953), the first widescreen film Hollywood released after World War II. The identical shot recurs in the sequel, Delmer Daves's *Demetrius and the Gladiators* (1954), since both films were made almost at the same time. (Figure 7) It is possible that Carcopino's book was consulted by historical advisors or researchers for a number of films with scenes of gladiatorial combat. Another possible inspiration is painting: the gladiators in Jean-Léon Gérôme's popular *Ave Caesar! Morituri te salutant* (1859) are all raising their right or left arms, holding tridents and other weapons. Even so, there is no uniformity in the gladiators' greeting in *Demetrius and the Gladiators*. Some arms are held out straight, others are bent. The opening scene of Nick Nostro's *Spartacus e i dieci gladiatori* (*Spartacus and the Ten Gladiators* or *Day of Vengeance*, 1964) shows gladiators in the arena saluting first the presiding official and then, after a 180-degree turn, even the crowd of spectators; they hold up their sword arms and say "Hail!" but nothing else. Conversely, a scene in Douglas Sirk's *Sign of the Pagan* (1954) shows a contingent of Roman

---

67. The biographer of Emperor Hadrian in the *Augustan History* reports that Hadrian drained the lake in the following century (*HA Hadrian* 22.10). Complete drainage was not achieved until 1875.
68. Marcus Junkelmann, "*Familia Gladiatoria*: The Heroes of the Amphitheatre," in Köhne and Ewigleben 2000, 31–74; quotation at 74.
69. It appears in, e.g., Quennell 1971, 45; Hopkins 1983, 26; and Aldrete 2004, 124.
70. Redi 1994, 164, provides a still image of this moment.

Figure 7. *The Robe/Demetrius and the Gladiators.* Gladiators saluting Caligula. Twentieth Century-Fox.

soldiers greeting Attila's daughter by carrying their right arms straight up while holding swords in their hands. The gesture, which combines the regular raised-arm salute and the gladiatorial salute, goes back at least to 1917, when it occurred in an Egyptian context. In J. Gordon Edwards's *Cleopatra,* a film that survives only in a number of stills mainly featuring its star Theda Bara, Cleopatra is walking past two lines of an Egyptian honor guard whose sword arms are raised in salute. As will become clear in my later discussions, to film directors it is not historical accuracy that counts but only spectacle. The answer to the question "How will a scene or a particular moment look on the screen?" decides about salutes and other gestures, just as it does about practically everything else.

If, then, the straight-raised-arm salute is not actually Roman, what is its origin, how did it come to be appropriated for Fascist ideology, and why did it become popular so easily? To answer these questions we must turn to the visual culture of the modern era. The early appearances of the salute in fact predate Fascism and do not carry any Fascist connotations, just as the salute was originally not as fixed a gesture as it was to become in twentieth-century political contexts. A thorough answer to our questions must begin with late eighteenth-century painting.

two

Jacques-Louis David's *Oath of the Horatii*

ONE OF THE MOST influential works in the history of painting is Jacques-Louis David's *Le serment des Horaces entre les mains de leur père* (*The Oath of the Horatii*, 1784–1785). It was painted and first shown in Rome, then caused a sensation when it was exhibited in Paris at the Salon of 1785. David's studies of Roman art during his time in Italy exerted a major influence on his work.[1] Scholars are agreed that *The Oath of the Horatii* represents a decisive turning point in the history of painting.[2] It has rightly been called "the quintessential, neo-classic picture. . . .

---

1. Cf., e.g., the essays in *David et Rome / David e Roma* 1981 (exhibition catalogue), with pages 133–43 on *The Oath of the Horatii*. See also Howard 1975 on David's 1778 drawing, done in Rome, *Funeral of a Warrior* (or *Funeral of Patroclus*), especially 83–90 (section entitled "Oaths") on its connections to David's later work. Hautecoeur 1912 is a detailed survey of its topic; cf. pages 151–62 on the "triumph" of David's *Horatii*. Cf. now also Bordes 2005, 183–95 and 349–51 (notes; chapter entitled "Antiquity Revisited").

2. On the painting see especially Boime 1987, 392–405 and 506–7 (notes), and Schnapper and Sérullaz 1989 (exhibition catalogue), 162–75 (nos. 67–74); also 138–41 (nos. 52–53). Crow 1995, 31, observes: "To the world this was to be David's break-through work, the painting that established his leadership in historical painting." See also Rosenblum 1969, 67–74, with references to previous scholarship on the painting, its origin, and the tradition of oath paintings. Cf. Maria Grazia Messina, "Dalla retorica dei gesti al silenzio delle passioni: il quadro di storia intorno a Jacques-Louis David," in Bertelli and Centanni 1995, 272–97 and figs. 56–64. Boime 1990, 20, reproduces an amusing—better: amazing—decorative piece that reverses the original intention of the painting: an Empire clock from 1810–1815, now in the Royal Pavilion at Brighton, with gilded bronze figures of the Horatii (ill. 1.12). Boime, 21, comments: "It is the decorative complement to authority without the energy and conviction that informed the original."

It united the generations and the nations."³ One scholar even considers David's picture to be a metaphorical equivalent of the American constitution of 1789 and of the French constitutions of the 1790s.⁴ This well accords with the iconographic model provided by Johann Heinrich Füssli (Fuseli) and his painting *Die drei Schweizer* (*The Three Swiss*, 1779–1781), whose subject is the oath on the Rütli which was the foundation of the Swiss Confederation in the late thirteenth century, and it accords with the example for republican self-government set by Switzerland.⁵

The subject of David's painting is part of an episode from early Roman history, a period that had been shrouded in mythic-heroic and, in numerous cases, fictional stories since antiquity. The chief ancient sources of the story are Livy and Dionysius of Halicarnassus.⁶ Livy's became the more influential and better known version of the two in postclassical times because the Roman historian exerted far greater influence than the Greek one, because Latin was taught more commonly in schools than Greek, and because Roman historical, architectural, linguistic, and other cultural influences were farther-reaching and more directly comprehensible than Greek ones in France, the former Roman province of Gaul that Julius Caesar had Romanized.⁷ David had recourse to the story via Pierre Corneille's tragedy *Horace* (1639), which David had seen

---

3. Levey 1966, 190. The painting appears on the cover of the present volume.

4. Ratcliff 1990.

5. For descriptions of Füssli's painting, also called *The Oath on the Rütli*, his earlier studies for it (originally without a sword and different positions of arms and hands), and its background and influence see, e.g., Franz Zelger, "Der Schwur," in Gamboni and Germann 1991 (exhibition catalogue), 128–31 (on cat. no. 1–4), and Boime 1987, 272–77 and 398–99 (comparison with David). Earlier and later variants are, e.g., Joseph Werner, *Der Schwur auf dem Rütli* (1677; Gamboni and Germann, 190–91 [no. 58]), and at least three versions by Jean Léonard Lugardon; cf. Gamboni and Germann, 635–36 (no. 423). In the tradition of David, Joseph Anton Koch's etching *Schwur der 1500 Republikaner bei Montenesimo* (1797; Gamboni and Germann, 527–28 [no. 338]), shows numerous raised-arm gestures, palms down and up. Honoré Daumier parodied David with his *Renewal of the Oath of the Horatii* and *Les Horaces des Elysées* (both 1851); cf. Gamboni and Germann, 722–24 (no. 490). *The Oath of the Calico Sellers*, an anonymous lithograph of around 1817, satirizes David's scene; illustration and comment in Porterfield and Siegfried 2006, 168–69. A recently discovered drawing by Louis Curtat, *L'Helvétie*, dating to ca. 1900, shows a standing female figure in flowing archaizing dress raising her right arm and extending her fingers, palm out, as an allegory of Swiss liberty; cf. Gamboni and Germann, 325–26 (no. 148).

6. Livy, *From the Foundation of the City* 1.24–26; Dionysius of Halicarnassus, *Roman Antiquities* 3.13–22. Ogilvie 1965, 109–17, is the standard modern study of Livy's account and provides additional references to ancient literature and modern scholarship. A translation of Livy's complete text appears below in appendix 1.

7. Wind 1941–1942, 125 note 2, reports that the *Histoire romaine* (1738) of Charles Rollin was "the most popular text book of Roman history in David's youth." Rollin followed Livy, not Dionysius, in his account of the Horatii and Curiatii but without mention of their oath.

on the stage in a revival.⁸ The moment depicted in the painting, however, is David's own invention.⁹ The three Horatius brothers swear an oath to their father to defend their country as champions of Rome in combat against three opposing brothers, the Curiatii, champions of the city of Alba but their cousins by blood. One of the Horatii is married to a sister of the Curiatii—a detail not in the ancient sources—and one of the Curiatii brothers is engaged to a sister of the Horatii. Together with three other figures, these women appear on the right-hand side of David's painting. A family tragedy inevitably ensues. David heightens the emotional power of the story by depicting its most dramatic moment, the point from which there is no return for the brothers. Dominating the center of the picture is the brothers' father, facing left. He has raised both arms. His left hand is holding up three swords; behind it, his right hand is empty, its fingers stretched out but not touching. Facing him on the left are his sons, ready to go to battle. Each is extending one arm toward his father and the swords; they are in the act of swearing their oath. The position of their arms and hands is important. The brother closest to the viewer is holding his arm almost horizontally. The arm of the brother on his left is raised slightly higher, while the third brother, furthest back, holds his arm a little higher yet. In addition the first brother, the one closest to the viewer, is extending his *right* arm; the others are extending their *left* arms. The painter's reason for giving his figures these arm positions is to keep all three arms and hands clearly in view, just as the brothers' legs and helmeted heads are all visible. But the succession of arms raised progressively higher eventually leads to a gesture closely approximating the Fascist salute, if with the "wrong" arm on the part of the brothers further away from the viewer. As in the modern salute, the brothers' palms are facing downward, although the first two brothers' fingers do not touch. The position of the third brother's hand is such that

---

8. On Livy as Corneille's inspiration see especially lines 1101–40 of *Horace* and, e.g., Corneille [n. d.], 795–96 note 178. In his letter on the play to Cardinal Richelieu, Corneille quotes Livy in translation (Corneille [n. d.], 658–59, at 658). His "Examen" of 1660 ends with the characterization of his Horace as *un Romain à la française* ("a Roman in the French manner"; Corneille [n. d.], 659–63, at 663).

9. Brookner 1987, 70–77, traces the process of David's invention of the brothers' oath and provides a skeptical analysis and partial refutation of earlier scholarship, of which the following is still noteworthy: Wind 1941–1942 (an influential demonstration that Corneille's play could not have provided David with direct inspiration for the scene he chose to paint; cf. Howard 1975, 120 notes 190–92, especially the last of these); Hazlehurst 1960; Ettlinger 1967; and Rosenblum 1970. These works discuss several textual analogies to David's work and related scenes in paintings of people with raised or outstretched arms as at moments of swearing an oath. See also Calvet 1968 on David's preparatory drawings of the Horatii.

the viewer does not see his fingers except for his thumb and cannot tell if they touch or not. Both ways are possible.

Classical scholarship has long recognized that the story of the Horatii and Curiatii is more mythical than historical—even in Livy's telling, which strives to give it an air of authenticity.[10] So the fact that ancient or modern variations are imposed on an archaic heroic theme should not surprise us. But neither Livy nor Dionysius mentions any oath sworn by the Horatii to their father. Rather, Dionysius, the more detailed source, reports that the father had left to his sons the decision to fight and then raised his hands to the heavens to thank the gods for their moral excellence because they had not accepted the championship of Rome without consulting his authority.[11] To ancient readers this circumstance expresses what the Romans called *pietas* on the part of the three sons: a sense of filial duty that was the cardinal Roman virtue. Here it confirms the rightness of their cause. But it is ironic that full-color reproductions of David's painting can be found on the covers of academic books on Livy and on Roman history as if the oath of the Horatii were historical.[12]

No more than loose analogies to David's oath scene from Roman history can be observed on a few ancient coins. Images on the reverse of a gold *stater* and half-*stater* minted in Rome ca. 225–212 B.C. show an oath-taking scene in which two warriors, facing each other, with their swords touch a pig held on the ground by a figure kneeling between them. The same scene recurs on a *denarius* coin minted in Rome in 137 B.C.[13] During the Social War of 91–88 B.C., conducted over Rome's denial of citizenship to its allies (*socii,* hence the name of the war) in Picenum, Samnium, and Apulia, gold coins were struck whose reverse images show the same oath scenes as mentioned before, but with soldiers

---

10. Ogilvie 1965, 109, gives parallels from classical Greek and Roman literature and adduces the Irish legend of Cuchulain as a particularly close analogy and observes: "We may recognize here [in Livy] the Roman form of a very ancient legend.... The legend was certainly prized by the family of the Curiatii ... and is likely to have enjoyed a wide currency" in Rome. Ogilvie, 110, calls Livy's versions of the ancient Roman legal texts that appear in his account "an archaizing reconstruction." Cf. also Ogilvie, 105–6.
11. Dionysius of Halicarnassus, *Roman Antiquities* 3.17.3 and 3.17.5.
12. Minkova and Tunberg 2005, a Latin textbook intended for American undergraduates; Mackay 2005, a general history published by a leading university press. A paperback reprint of Lewis Grassic Gibbon's 1933 novel *Spartacus* (Gibbon 2006 shows the center of David's painting, the three sons' and their father's hands.
13. On these coins see Crawford 1974, vol. 1, 144–45 and 266 (nos. 28.1–2, 29.1–2, and 234.1), and vol. 2, plates II.10–12, V. 5–6, and XXXV.23. For a historical explanation of the *denarius* reverse see Crawford, vol. 1, 266. Cf. Sydenham 1952, 6 (nos. 69–70: Roman *stater* and half-*stater*) and 66 (no. 527: non-Roman *denarius* of 110–108 B.C.); illustrations on plates 13 and 18.

arranged on either side in even numbers from two to eight pointing their swords toward the ground. They represent the tribes of the confederacy at war with Rome.[14] But on all these coins the warriors are holding or pointing their swords *down;* they are not raising them upward as in David's painting.[15]

The brothers' oath is not the only invention by David in this picture. The clothing worn by the four men, their helmets, and the background architecture are all anachronistic. This is especially true for the swords: no Roman soldier, least of all in the seventh century B.C., ever had or even knew of a sword of such size and appearance. Nevertheless David intended to be authentic and to recreate the archaic Roman spirit characterized by *pietas, virtus* (bravery, moral uprightness), and *severitas* (sternness).[16] Although no such gesture as the father's or the brothers' is demonstrably part of any ancient Roman ceremony of oath-taking or pledging, viewers of David's picture will hardly have been conscious of this fact.

A brief mention of two other paintings that also purport to represent scenes from Roman history, one painted before, the other after David, is instructive. In the 1660s, Rembrandt van Rijn had commemorated the Batavian rebellion of A.D. 69 led by Julius Civilis, a member of the Batavian royal house, against the Romans that Tacitus describes in detail in Books Four and Five of his *Histories*. The extraordinarily large painting, titled "The Conspiracy of the Batavians Under Claudius [= Julius] Civilis," now in the National Museum in Stockholm, was intended for the Great Hall of the Stadhuis in Amsterdam. It showed a kingly Julius seated behind a kind of banquet table and holding an upright sword before him as co-conspirators touch the blades of their swords to his. A preparatory drawing by Rembrandt dated October 25, 1661, and now in the Staatliche Graphische Sammlung in Munich shows a variant of the scene: Julius is still seated, but those before him extending their swords are standing.

---

14. Sydenham 1952, 91–94 (nos. 619–21, 626, 629, 634, 637, and 640: *denarii*); illustrations on plate 19 (nos. 620 and 637).

15. This posture appears before David's *Oath of the Horatii* in a 1771 painting by, or attributed to, Jacques-Antoine Beaufort that shows another famous scene from early Roman legendary history, the story of Lucretia: *Le serment de Brutus sur le corps de Lucrèce* (*The Oath of Brutus over the Body of Lucretia*). On this see especially Rosenblum 1970, who also gives the painting's rather cumbersome full title, and Brookner 1987, 77–79. Illustrations at, e.g., Rosenblum, figs. 1 and 6; Brookner, ill. 39 (with ill. 38, a closely comparable *Serment de Brutus* attributed to David); and Bordes 1983, plate 26.

16. Rosenblum 1969, 72, quotes (note 77) from a 1785 French review of the picture to that effect. The film version of the story, Ferdinando Baldi's *Orazi e Curiazi* (1961; *Duel of Champions*) is a very loose adaptation, indebted more to cinematic genre conventions than to ancient sources or to David. It contains no oath scene.

Tacitus summarizes Julius' speech that incites the conspirators' alliance and mentions that they took an oath. But he does not mention any swords; instead, he only refers to the barbarians' ancestral customs and oaths.[17] The details and atmosphere in Rembrandt's drawing and painting are invented, just as David was later to invent *his* scene—if to greater historical and art-historical effect.[18]

In 1867, popular French painter Jean-Léon Gérôme, who turned to Roman history in several of his works (cf. above in chapter 1), exhibited *La mort de César* (*The Death of Caesar*), illustrating the moment just after the dictator's assassination on the Ides of March, 44 B.C. The conspirators, crowded together, are all raising their right arms, lifting their swords or daggers into the air. The gesture is intended, first and foremost, to communicate to the painting's spectators the conspirators' triumphant elation at their success, but after David the gesture may also express a kind of reaffirmation of their allegiance, a renewal, as it were, of their sworn brotherhood. The moment shown is, however, once again an invention. In his account of Caesar's assassination Suetonius immediately follows his report of Caesar's dying words to Brutus (in Greek) with the statement that Caesar's body was now lying on the floor—as it is in the foreground of Gérôme's painting—while everybody was running away.[19] There is no reason to assume that Suetonius intended to exclude the conspirators from this sensible reaction. Such unheroic flight is unsuitable for a painting that aims for the greatest dramatic impact.

David's picture reflects the atmosphere of the political and social upheaval that was about to take place in France and that in its radicalism parallels that in the Fascist countries of the early twentieth century. What some art and cultural historians have said about David's picture resounds to future events in Europe. These scholars deal only with the painting's own time. But anyone who keeps a broader perspective in mind may detect an ominous undertone in their analyses. Anita Brookner, for example, calls the painting a "fantasy of strength, calm, power, and indifference to public opinion."[20] About its political aspects she concludes:

> We cannot dismiss out of hand the notion that David's picture is a political picture, more specifically a republican picture, although the evidence is against it. Although Rome was a kingdom when the Horatii

---

17. Tacitus, *Histories* 4.14–15: *barbaro ritu et patriis exsecrationibus* (4.15.1).
18. On Rembrandt's painting cf. Wilfried A. M. Hessing, "Foreign Oppressor *versus* Civiliser: The Batavian Myth as the Source for Contrasting Associations of Rome in Dutch Historiography," in Hingley 2001, 126–43, at 131–34.
19. Suetonius, *Caesar* 82.2–3. The text reads at 82.3: *Exanimis diffugientibus cunctis aliquamdiu iacuit* ("Lifeless he lay there for a while, everybody scattering and running off").
20. Brookner 1987, 74.

fought their battle, although the picture was a royal commission, there is about it the feeling of a call to arms.... One might also reflect on the extraordinary history and reputation of this picture which the painter gleaned from a variety of sources, none of them particularly obscure but all transformed into an image of such force and tension that it was rightly regarded as revelatory by the public of the day, unaccustomed to seeing Antique symbols invested with such violent emotion.[21]

This violence of emotion is expressed primarily through the father's and brothers' hands, which are at the center of the image literally and figuratively. Cultural historian Jean Starobinski observes:

the central point of the painting is the left hand of the old Horatio [sic], lifting up the three swords that symbolically unite three wills. The father looks at the hilts of the swords, and it is toward the same point that the sons stretch out their arms; the eyes of the sons meet those of the father on the three separate yet united hilts, so that the focal point of the brothers' communion is the fasces, the sheaf, of death-dealing weapons sanctified by the paternal hand that proffers them.[22]

To this we may add Dorothy Johnson's more recent description:

One's gaze is directed to the central focus of a transfixing hand, highlighted against a dark neutral ground. The father's authority, his absolute control over the destiny of his sons, which is emblematized in the power of this hand, is also emphasized by David in the original title of the painting: *The Oath of the Horatii in the Hands of Their Father.* The opened right hand, which symbolizes authority as well as the appeal to a higher allegiance to which the sons and the father swear, is contrasted with the eloquently rendered left fist of Horatius, which clenches the sharp blades of the heavy iron swords in a seemingly effortless and painless

---

21. Brookner 1987, 78–79. Proof that David's *Oath* became an influential political picture is to be found in, e.g., Hofmann 1989 (exhibition catalogue), 216–17, 277–78, and 282 (cat. nos. 243a, 244–45, 357, and 361; the last-mentioned shows an oath scene, with arms raised, as illustration of the *Droits de l'Homme et du Citoyen,* frontispiece of *Tableaux Historiques de la Révolution Française,* vol. 3 [1802]). Hofmann, 207 (no. 225), reproduces Armand Charles Caraffe's 1791 drawing *Le serment des Horaces,* in which a seated Horatius is holding up one sword toward which his three sons are swearing. They are standing in a quarter circle before and beside him. Their arms, palms down, are stretched out in a slightly downward direction. This and another drawing are the models for Caraffe's painting of the scene.

22. Starobinski 1982, 103. The term *fasces* is not, strictly speaking, applicable here since no *fasces* appear in David's painting.

fashion.... The sons are similarly attempting to transfer their own force of will to the weapons—the objects that will ensure their success or failure in battle.... On an essential level, then, *The Oath* is a painting about will and the use of will to sacrifice the self and extensions of the self—the family—to political ideals ... at the most basic political and cultural level, David's *Oath* was a revolutionary call to a type of physical (and concomitant moral) regeneration and perfectability of the self.[23]

This is in keeping with contemporary thought about man and his body. As the Comte de Buffon had put it in his *General and Particular Natural History* of 1749:

> His [i.e., man's] hand was not meant to dig in the earth.... His arm and hand are made to serve more noble purposes, to execute the orders of his will, to grasp things at a distance, to push away obstacles, to prevent encounters and the shock of harmful things, to embrace and hold onto whatever pleases him and to make it available to his other senses.[24]

The will to power on the part of superhumanly heroic figures and that will's eventual triumph at all cost was to come about both in the French Revolution and in the rise of Fascism. The political appropriation of the raised-arm oath sworn by the Horatii to the artist's contemporary history, and with it the appropriation of antiquity to a radical upheaval in modern history at large, becomes manifest in the painting's companion piece, David's *Le serment du jeu de paume* (*The Tennis Court Oath,* 1791–1792). A drawing for this immense canvas, which David did not complete, shows us what the finished product would have been like.[25] Its subject was the meeting of members of the Third Estate and several clergymen in the hall of the *jeu de paume* at Versailles on June 20, 1789. With one exception, all swore an oath "never to be separated and to meet wherever circumstances so require, until the Constitution of the Kingdom is established firmly on solid foundations." This was the beginning of the French Revolution.[26]

---

23. Dorothy Johnson 1993, 60–62 and 66, in a chapter entitled "The Eloquent Body." Johnson, 60–61, links the postures of the male figures to Mesmerism.

24. Quoted from Dorothy Johnson 1993, 65, in her translation. She prints the original French text at 281 note 108 from Georges-Louis Leclerc, Comte de Buffon, *Histoire naturelle générale et particulière,* vol. 2 (Paris, 1749), 519.

25. Details at Boime 1987, 424–32; Schnapper and Sérullaz, 242–75 (nos. 100–14). Boime, 432–33 and 436–40, connects this image to the American Revolution.

26. On the historical and political background to this projected painting and its artistic significance see Brookner 1987, 95–97; Dorothy Johnson 1993, 77–90; Crow 1995, 197–98; and Roberts 2000, 227–68. Bordes 1983 gives a detailed study of *The Tennis Court Oath,* its artistic sources and historical contexts, and the relevant documents.

In 1794, David and Robespierre were to organize a large ceremony at which young and old men re-enacted the oath of the Horatii.[27]

Not only did David "transpos[e] the male figures of the *Oath of the Horatii* onto the *Tennis Court Oath*," but he also exhibited the sketch of the *Tennis Court Oath* beneath *The Oath of the Horatii* "to emphasize the analogy between the antique and the modern oaths which shared a fervent, patriotic meaning."[28] Albert Boime comments:

> As in the earlier picture, David signifies the unity of minds and bodies in the service of a patriotic ideal; this time, however, the union reaches across family ties to envelop more realistically different class, religious, and philosophical opinions. . . . It is altogether consistent with his artistic and political development that he joined the *Horatii* to his drawing of the *Oath of the Tennis Court* in the Salon exhibition of 1791.[29]

The sketch shows the mass of the assembly given over to revolutionary ardor, but with the exception of one dissenter. To impress this ecstasy on the viewer most powerfully and to express visually the momentous nature of the act of swearing their oath, David renders his figures with outstretched and raised arms at varying angles, from almost horizontal to heavenward. Jean Starobinski has observed about oaths: "The act of taking the oath . . . was based on an antique model. At the same time as it inaugurated the future, it also repeated a very ancient archetype for entering into a contract."[30] But the supposedly antique model that David portrays was, as we know, his own invention. The prominence in the drawing of the solitary dissenter "strengthens the allusion to individual conscience: The great collective impulse is in the first place the decision of each particular will." Besides the ineffectual nature of the dissenting will, we witness the overwhelming triumph of the collective will. David,

---

27. Dowd 1948, 122–24. Dowd, 123, comments:"This great festival marks the apex of the Jacobin regime."

28. Quotations from Roberts 2000, 231, and Dorothy Johnson 1993, 80–81. In view of the great influence of the ancient works of art which David had studied (and sketched) while in Rome, this juxtaposition is not surprising. In particular the sculptures on Trajan's Column, which influenced the postures David gave to some of the figures in both *The Oath of the Horatii* and *The Tennis Court Oath,* had proved decisive to him, as he himself attested. On this see Bordes 1983, 43 (in connection with the raised-arm postures in David and on Trajan's Column). Bordes, 174–75 (Document 19) reprints an autobiographical statement, written in the third person, at whose beginning David mentions the importance of Trajan's Column to his artistic development.

29. Boime 1987, 429.

30. Starobinski 1982, 102–4. Starobinski, 99–124 (chapter entitled "The Oath: David"), examines the cultural and political background and the iconography of oaths.

Starobinski concludes, "was at his best . . . as a painter of the sacred, of dread, able to make the visible most intensely present just when he was subjecting it to the domination of an implacable absolute."[31] The domination of a sacred and dread absolute was to assert itself most forcefully in the first half of the twentieth century.

While the *Tennis Court Oath* extols the virtue and dedication of the people, a third image by David transposes a comparable theme to a mighty imperial subject. This is *Le serment de l'armée fait à l'Empereur après la distribution des aigles au Champs-de-Mars le 5 décembre 1804* (*The Distribution of the Eagle Standards*, 1810) in commemoration of Napoleon's coronation.[32] In a grand military ceremony three days later Napoleon exhorted his military leaders to swear allegiance to him, which they did. (In this, Mussolini and Hitler followed Napoleon's example.) Anita Brookner comments: "Here is the mutation of *The Oath of the Horatii* into yet another guise, this time an Imperial and autocratic one."[33] Appropriately for both the religious and imperial nature of the moment, several of the army leaders raise their arms. What Dorothy Johnson observes about the army's new flags, the eagle standards, is important for our context: "The uniformity of the new flags conveys the power of centralized control, the new bureaucracy that Napoleon established for the military as he did for society as a whole."[34] But the comments by Albert Boime, who connects this third of David's oath pictures to the earlier two, are even more telling:

> The series of oath pictures may be seen as the coding of key developments in the history of the Revolution and its culmination in Napoleonic authoritarianism. The ancient Roman republican model served as a standard for the moderns . . . , but the collapse of the Revolution paved the way for a despotic figure swollen with the blood of military and foreign conquest indispensable for the retention of his hold over the French people. As under the old regime, obedience and loyalty were sworn to the sovereign. It is by no means fortuitous that the last

---

31. The two quotations are from Starobinski 1982, 110 and 124.
32. On this painting and its style, David's earlier design of 1808, and the work's eventual reception cf. Brookner 1987, 158–61, and Dorothy Johnson 1993, 206–16. Details at Boime 1990, 44–46; Schnapper and Sérullaz, 443–72 (nos. 187–204); and Bordes 2005, 103–12 and 122–23. On Roman overtones of Napoleon's imperial self-presentation see, e.g., Valérie Huet, "Napoleon I: A New Augustus?" in Edwards 1999, 53–69.
33. Brookner 1987, 160. Cf. Wind 1941–1942, 135, on connections to Napoleon in David's painting. On David and Napoleon cf. Bordes 2005, 19–74 and 338–47 (notes; chapter entitled "In the Service of Napoleon").
34. Dorothy Johnson 1993, 215.

and final oath was ... almost exclusively military: the *vaincre ou mourir* ["conquer or die"] implied in the *Horatii* was literally written into the Napoleonic ceremony of the eagles and symbolically demonstrated the ascendance of the military over the civil domain and the force of arms over collective expression. The civil pride of French nationalism won during the Revolution had been displaced onto pride in battlefield glory, and the welfare of the French citizenry taken as a whole became subordinated to the prestige of the troops. Symbolically this was further represented by shifting the ancient paradigm from the republic to the empire.[35]

Here we can detect certain modern parallels. Centralized control expressing the general will and new bureaucracies based on an autocratic leader's personal will and fervently embraced by the people who see the dawn of a new age after years of social and political instability will be the order of the day again in the twentieth century. It is therefore important for us to remember that the roots of Fascist ideology go back to eighteenth-century France. A case in point is the thought of Joseph de Maistre, as one of the leading philosophers of the twentieth century, Isaiah Berlin, has shown conclusively.[36] Revolutionary republican and then imperial France, Fascist Italy, and Nazi Germany all took recourse to Roman iconography in various ways of presenting and representing themselves. The radical republicanism of the French Revolution and of early Fascism, marked by violence and a collective will to power in either case, gave way to an all-encompassing ideology of rule and empire, in France with Napoleon, in Italy and Germany with Mussolini and Hitler, and in all three countries with military campaigns of expansion.[37] The comparatively modest titles of twentieth-century dictators such as Mussolini (*Duce*), Hitler (*Führer*), and Francisco Franco (*Caudillo*) all mean simply "leader" and roughly correspond to that of Roman emperor Augustus, who never

---

35. Boime 1990, 46.

36. Berlin 1991, 91–174 (essay entitled "Joseph de Maistre and the Origins of Fascism"). Cf. also Canfora 1980, 9–159 (= part 1 of this book, entitled "Dai giacobini al Terzo Reich"), especially 20–30; Mosse 1989; and Koon 1985, 4–6.

37. On cultural and historical connections between Napoleon on the one hand and Mussolini and Hitler on the other in terms of their common Roman (Caesarian) parallels see, e.g., Mangoni 1976; Giardina and Vauchez 2000, 246–47 (Napoleon and Mussolini). Horne 2004, 195, observes about Napoleon: "Inevitably dictators in the evil twentieth century, like Hitler, Stalin, and Mao, as well [as] tin-pot demagogues in Africa and South America, reach out to his image." Cf. Buruma 2005, 36: "Few dictators after Napoleon escaped from his influence. His court painter, Jacques-Louis David, set the tone for images of grandeur in Communist as well as fascist courts.... Hitler's plans for the transformation of Berlin into a monstrous imperial capital owed much to Napoleon's architectural hubris." See now also Campi 2007.

called himself an emperor but merely a *princeps* (first citizen). Mussolini was also referred to as *Dux,* the Latin for *Duce.* That revolutionary and imperial France and later Fascist countries should have the supposedly Roman raised-arm oath or salute in common is therefore not surprising. Napoleon's power spanned both republic and empire, as his titles of First Consul and Emperor attest. The titles of consul and emperor in themselves tell us that the model to which Napoleon harks back is ancient Rome. Karl Marx was one of the earliest writers to point out, in 1852, the Roman look of the French Revolution and of what followed:

> The tradition of all the dead generations weighs like a nightmare on the brain of the living. And just when they seem engaged in revolutionizing themselves and things, in creating something that has never yet existed ... they anxiously conjure up the spirits of the past to their service and borrow from them names, battle cries and costumes in order to present the new scene of world history in this time-honoured disguise and this borrowed language. Thus ... the Revolution of 1789 to 1814 draped itself alternately as the Roman republic and the Roman empire ... [the revolutionaries and Napoleon] performed the task of their time in Roman costume and with Roman phrases, the task of unchaining and setting up modern *bourgeois* society.... The new social formation once established, the antediluvian Colossi disappeared and with them resurrected Romanity.[38]

David's *Distribution of the Eagle Standards* makes this evident visually as well. Another painting that does so is *Napoléon sur le trône impérial* (*Napoleon I on His Imperial Throne;* English titles vary slightly) by Jean Auguste Dominique Ingres of 1806. Here, too, Roman-style eagles are prominent, one as a decoration of the emperor's throne on the left and a much larger one woven into the carpet on the floor before his throne. Napoleon's scepter is topped by a statuette of the Holy Roman Emperor Charlemagne. No viewer of either painting could be left unaware of Napoleon's claims, expressed by these iconographical details, of founding or intending to found an empire that succeeds the two most famous empires in European history, the Roman Empire and the Holy Roman

---

38. Quoted from Marx 1963, 15–16. An amusing moment occurs on screen in Jean Renoir's *French Cancan* (1955), a fictional history of the opening of the famous Moulin Rouge in 1889. An aspiring cabaret singer informally auditions with a song about Napoleon; then, carried away by his own enthusiasm, he exclaims "Vive l'Empereur!" while giving the straight-arm salute—with his left arm, which is away from the camera and so does not obstruct our view of him.

Empire.[39] The decorative arts furnish additional evidence in abundance. The Empire Style is replete with classical or classicizing images, not least Roman eagles.[40]

To viewers today, the emotional impact of David's painting of the Horatii carries obvious visual associations with the twentieth century, although it would be anachronistic to impute such an ideology to David himself. So it is appropriate to end this discussion of David with two longer quotations from art historians because here we can recognize a clear parallelism to the spirit and the esthetics of a later age. *The Oath of the Horatii,* Michael Levey writes, is

> shot through with frightening, dramatic intensity. The picture shrieks of the sword; nowhere does the light glitter more threateningly than on the cluster of blades—unless on those sword-like arms thrust out so greedily towards them. Though there is poignancy in the group of grieving women, it is subordinated to stern patriotism. Men toe the line at the moment of exultation and self-sacrifice. In this republican world there is no place for anything else . . . the picture perhaps partly owed its tremendous success to the fright it gave the spectators . . . the Horatii, presented with powerful realism, are fighting for Rome, putting the state before all personal considerations; they are men in a world without gods, trusting in their swords. . . . It is an exciting prospect. . . . Soon it would not be in mere painted rhetoric that men swore oaths and seized their swords.
>
> Painting is about to affect people, with a vengeance. . . . Perhaps the deepest conviction behind his picture is that violence will provide a solution.[41]

Some of the terms that Levey employs to express the haunting force of David's image more than hint at modern horrors. Albert Boime provides an even more explicit parallel to Levey's observations:

> The brothers stretch out their arms in a salute that has since become associated with tyranny. The "Hail Caesar" of antiquity [although at the time of the Horatii a Caesar had yet to be born] was transformed into

---

39. On this painting see now Porterfield and Siegfried 2006, 24–61, with instructive illustrations.

40. Cf., e.g., Nouvel-Kammerer 2007 (exhibition catalogue), with extensive illustrations and further references, and in this Daniela Gallo, "On the Antique Models of the Empire Style" (40–51).

41. Levey 1966, 190–91.

the "Heil Hitler" of the modern period. The fraternal intimacy brought about by the Horatii's dedication to absolute principles of victory or death [and the resultant] emphasis on the destruction of all intermediate loyalties between citizen and state, and on the absolute sovereignty of state power, is closely related to the establishment of the fraternal order.... In the total commitment or blind obedience of a single, exclusivistic group lies the potentiality of the authoritarian state.[42]

The raised arm, first stretched out as a symbol of righteous fervor—as the Horatii evince it—and later as a symbol of political allegiance and religious-political unity between a people and its leader, becomes an important part of the iconography of new societies. In addition to its specific contemporary use the gesture comes to express, in a fashion that appears timeless and even mystical, an appeal to a higher being and to a heroic ancient past that had served as a model for most of Western civilization for centuries, although often in ways not supported by historical fact. David's *Oath of the Horatii* provided the starting point for an arresting gesture that progressed from oath-taking to what will become known as the Roman salute.

Two classic French films, one with a contemporary, one with a historical setting, contain telling visual reminiscences of David's oath gesture. In Louis Feuillade's crime melodrama *Judex* (1917), an elaborate serial in twelve parts, the titular hero, aided by his brother, is an aristocratic master of disguise and avenger of injustice. A flashback explains why: ruined by an unscrupulous banker, his father had committed suicide. Before his body lying in state the mother makes the two young boys swear to avenge their father's death. They so swear, raising their right arms horizontally in the direction of their father's dead body. Their mother then makes a similar gesture. There are no direct references to David's painting, but the brief moment in a film well over five hours long is dramatically powerful and impressive for its impeccable visual composition. By contrast, Jean Renoir's *La Marseillaise* (1938), an elaborate homage to the French Revolution, returns us to David's time and the gesture of the raised-arm oath. The film includes a short scene in which volunteers from Marseilles are enlisting in a military unit that is being formed for a march to Paris. To qualify, they have to meet certain requirements. When asked, one of the film's central characters exclaims that he indeed qualifies: "I swear by the nation!" At the same time he raises his straight right arm. At the time of the film's production, however, raised arms had become prominent again

---

42. Boime 1987, 400–401.

through Fascism and Nazism, and Renoir is likely to have remembered the flap that occurred two years earlier over some of the French athletes giving raised-arm salutes at the opening ceremony of the Olympic Games in Berlin. (This episode and its context will be discussed in chapter 6.) Renoir could not have had his actor perform a historic gesture in a manner that contemporary audiences might misunderstand. So he avoids ambiguity by having the man enlisting raise his hand no more than horizontally and away from his body. The gesture is easily overlooked, but the moment is remarkable for the way in which Renoir stages it. In an earlier scene arms had been raised higher and in front of the body but had been de-emphasized by the general excitement of revolutionary fervor depicted on the screen. Evidently Renoir was aware of the historical importance of the gesture as well as of its modern implications. He succeeded in expressing the former and completely avoiding the latter.

Ancient Rome advanced from a small city to a mighty empire spanning the civilized world. Often it had to struggle for its survival against overwhelming odds, as the story of the Horatii and Curiatii illustrates. No wonder that a gesture thought to have been part and parcel of this heroic and powerful society was to achieve a lasting appeal among the easily impressed. But before it acquired a different symbolic character in radical, and radically new, twentieth-century political movements, the raised-arm gesture had already become prominent in another country, one that had modeled itself in several important aspects on ancient Rome and that had also begun its expansion into empire. The United States of America adopted a raised-arm salute in the late nineteenth century as a patriotic symbol. But around that time the same gesture also became prominent in entirely nonpolitical contexts when it appeared in the popular arts of stage and screen. Since that time, popular culture has been most influential in the dissemination of the raised-arm gesture. Now the visual record becomes decisive for our tracing its development further. We have already seen that the modern raised-arm salute is not based on any ancient custom; we shall soon see that its origin and appeal both lie in its visual impact.

three

Raised-Arm Salutes in the United States before Fascism

From the Pledge of Allegiance to *Ben-Hur* on Stage

THE EARLY FORM of the American Pledge of Allegiance to the Flag contained both an oath and a saluting gesture, in this way combining the two decisive verbal and visual aspects inherent in such a ritual.[1] The Pledge was introduced in 1892 at the dedication ceremony of the World's Columbian Exposition in Chicago, which opened the following year. The Exposition, a world's fair and simultaneously a commemoration of the quadricentennial of Columbus' arrival in America, had more than twenty million visitors. Its White City, as it was commonly called, could boast of amazing "palatial plaster-of-paris neoclassical buildings."[2] These included the Palace of Fine Arts and the Agricultural Building as oversize Roman Pantheons, the Peristyle topped by a four-horse chariot, an obelisk, and recreations of Pompeii. Although contemporaries also prominently mentioned other ancient cities such as Jerusalem and Athens as models, it seems likely that imperial Rome was the chief Old-World inspiration for the White City. In the words of Barr Ferree, professor of architecture at the University of Pennsylvania and editor of *Engineering Magazine:* "No

---

1. On the political and social causes for the origin of the Pledge of Allegiance and on its dissemination and changes in wording see Paul 1992 and Rydell 1996. Rydell, 24 note 4, cites additional sources. Baer 1992, a pamphlet published and distributed by the author, contains much of the same information. Cf. also Leepson 2005, 163–76 and 290–91 (notes; chapter entitled "One Nation Indivisible"). Ellis 2005 is the most detailed account and provides up-to-date scholarship and references.

2. Rydell 1996, 16. On the White City's neoclassical architecture and its context see Burg 1976, 297–309. On the exposition's cultural and architectural (neoclassical) influences, which included the foundation of the American Academy in Rome, see Badger 1979, 115–18.

Roman emperor in the plenitude of his power ever conceived so vast a festival as this."³ The design for the Art Building, for example, was criticized as having been plagiarized from a French *Prix de Rome* project.⁴ The railway station, from which most visitors entered the fair, was modeled on the Baths of Caracalla in Rome. The fair even had a Rostral Column, a homage to the famous *columna rostrata* in the Roman Forum. But most imposing to visitors was Daniel Chester French's statue "The Republic," patterned on Roman victory statues and on the Statue of Liberty. This was a gilded plaster statue sixty-five feet high—over a hundred feet if we include the height of its base—and placed prominently in the exposition's Court of Honor. The "Golden Lady," French's copy at one-third of the original's size, now stands in Chicago's Jackson Park.

Despite its eclectic mixture of architectural styles from different times and places, the Exposition—"that city of the ideal" with its "white, classic loveliness"—must have struck many visitors as being quite in the Roman spirit.⁵ To judge by contemporary photographs, it appears to have been irresistible in its imperial-Roman gaudiness.⁶ An encomium to the White City by American poet Richard Watson Gilder is instructive:

> Say not, "Greece is no more!"
> Through the clear morn
> On light winds borne
> Her white-winged soul sinks on the New World's breast [.]
> Ah, happy West—
> Greece flowers anew, and all her temples soar!

Given the combination of neoclassical art and unabashed Kitsch on display in the White City, these lines make much better sense if we substi-

---

3. Barr Ferree, "Architecture," *Engineering Magazine* 5 (June 1893), quoted from Burg 1976, 299. Cf. Gilbert 1991, 75–130 and 243–51 (notes), a chapter on the White City.

4. On this see Badger 1979, 104. On fairs and expositions in the larger context of spectacle cf. Rydell 1984 and Glassberg 1990.

5. The quotation is from Rainsford 1922, 329. The Rev. Rainsford was a major figure of social reform during the Gilded Age.

6. An extensive collection of photographs appears in *The Columbian Exposition Album* 1893. This commemorative volume bears a suitably epic title for what American showman P. T. Barnum had urged during the fair's planning stage: "Make it the Greatest Show on Earth"; quoted from Badger 1979, 54. A collection of photos also appears in Appelbaum 1980. For only the most obvious examples of neoclassical and in particular "Roman" buildings and architectural details see the following illustrations in the book last mentioned: frontispiece, figs. 3–6, 15, 18–21 (basin and Court of Honor), 22–23, 27 (with rostral column), 29–32, 37–39, 52 (again with rostral column), 93–94, 96, and 109 (vault of banqueting hall with classicizing decoration and painting).

tute "Rome" for "Greece." Some views of the White City evoke Thomas Cole's "The Consummation of Empire," the central and largest painting in his famous series *The Course of Empire* (1834–1836).[7]

None of this is surprising, because ancient Rome had already been lavishly and bombastically recreated in other quintessentially American environments. "Nero; or, The Destruction of Rome," written and produced by Imre Kiralfy, had first been shown in New York City in 1888 and was then taken over by P. T. Barnum for his circus, "The Greatest Show on Earth." In 1889 Barnum took Kiralfy's spectacle to London and in the following year on a tour through the United States. In both venues Barnum's success was huge. Audiences could admire an immense set of the imperial city, populated by about a thousand actors and dancers.[8]

U.S. President Benjamin Harrison proclaimed October 21, 1892, the National School Celebration of Columbus Day. The earliest publication of the wording of the Pledge of Allegiance and a description of the saluting gestures that were to accompany it appeared on September 8, 1892, in *The Youth's Companion,* "a popular children's magazine filled with stories of moral virtue, adventure, and patriotism."[9] The third item about the sequence of ceremonies was as follows:

3. SALUTE TO THE FLAG, *by the Pupils.*

At a signal from the Principal the pupils, in ordered ranks, hands to the side, face the Flag. Another signal is given: every pupil gives the

---

7. Gilder's lines are quoted from Gilbert 1991, 90. For analogies to Cole's painting cf. the illustrations at Gilbert, 85, 90, 106, and 219.—In view of the imminent emergence of cinema I note in passing that Eadweard Muybridge showed his motion studies in the Zoöpraxographic Hall of the Chicago fair and that Thomas Alva Edison's new kinetoscope may have been on exhibit in its Electricity Building.

8. Verdone 1970, 140–47 (chapter entitled "P. T. Barnum e la 'distruzione di Roma'"), describes this spectacle and furnishes several illustrations. Most impressive is the two-page color spread of Rome with the Colosseum in the background (142–43). Cf. also Saxon 1989, 319–20, for a description and an eyewitness account. On Kiralfy, Barnum, and comparable Roman spectacles shown in a variety of New York places, including Coney Island, see Malamud 2001a or 2001b. Verdone, 146–47, links Barnum's show to early cinema epics, and indeed Barnum's production was redone as a film by the Edison Company. Verdone's book has the merit of delineating the tradition of spectacle from ancient Rome to the age of silent cinema, with stops on the way concerning medieval and Renaissance pageants, circuses, and even Buffalo Bill's Wild West show.

9. See "National School Celebration of Columbus Day: The Official Program" 1892. The description of the magazine is quoted from Paul 1992, 391. Paul, 392, reproduces the text from the *Companion* quoted below and a photograph of schoolchildren saluting the flag. For further information on *The Youth's Companion* see Guenter 1990, 120–32 and 227–29 (notes). Guenter, 197–200, reprints the complete text of the Official Program.

> Flag the military salute—right hand lifted, palm downward, to a line with the forehead and close to it. Standing thus, all repeat together, slowly: "I pledge allegiance to my Flag and the Republic for which it stands: one Nation indivisible, with Liberty and Justice for all." At the words, "to my Flag," the right hand is extended gracefully, palm upward, towards the Flag, and remains in this gesture till the end of the affirmation; whereupon all hands immediately drop to the side. Then, still standing, as the instruments strike a chord, all will sing AMERICA—"My Country, 'tis of Thee."

The author of the pledge's wording was New York Baptist minister Francis J. Bellamy of Rome, New York, who had also drafted the presidential proclamation of Columbus Day. Bellamy was employed at *The Youth's Companion*. The inventor of the saluting gesture was James B. Upham, junior partner and editor at the *Companion*.[10] Decades later Bellamy described the process by which he came upon the wording for the pledge. Upham's reaction to hearing the words for the first time was enthusiastic, and on the spur of the moment he came up with the gesture of the salute to accompany the pledge. As Bellamy put it:

> "Read it again," he said. I read it several times. Then I remember that he took the paper and read it himself; then coming to the posture of salute, he snapped his heels together and said, "Now up there is the flag; I come to salute; as I say 'I pledge allegiance to my flag,' I stretch out my right hand and keep it raised while I say the stirring words that follow." We went over the Salute in unison in that fashion several times to get the effect.[11]

Upham's snapping his heels imparts a military aspect to the salute. First schoolchildren and then adults adopted the Pledge of Allegiance as one

---

10. Miller 1976 gives a detailed account of Bellamy, Upham, *The Youth's Companion,* and the origin and early history of the Pledge of Allegiance. The book is written in the first person as if it were by Bellamy himself; on this cf. Miller, vi. She reproduces a photograph of the first appearance of the pledge in the *Companion* between pages 125 and 127 [*sic*].

11. Quoted from Miller 1976, 122. Cf. Rydell 1996, 21, for a slightly different version of what Upham said. See also Rydell, 25 note 19, for more on the authorship of text and gesture. Ellis 2005, 19–20, 44, and 115, confirms that it was Upham who invented the gesture accompanying Bellamy's words. Leepson 2005, 164, describes an earlier salute to the flag, named after Civil War veteran, teacher, and education official George T. Balch: "Balch's salute began with students touching their foreheads and then their hearts and saying: 'We give our Heads!—and our Hearts!—to God! and our Country!' The students then extended their right arms, palms down, and said, 'One Country! One Language! One Flag!'" Balch called this "The American Patriotic Salute."

of their most cherished national rites. Soon new American citizens pledged allegiance upon naturalization. Just as the words of the pledge underwent some changes, so did the gesture. Those pledging allegiance placed their right hands on their hearts during the words "I pledge allegiance"; on the words "to the flag" they extended their arms toward the flag and did not lower them until the end of the pledge.[12] This straight-right-arm salute to the flag, with palm up or down, continued until the early 1940s.[13] At that time the extension of the arm as part of this ceremonial salute was abolished because of its close similarity to the Fascist or Nazi salute.[14] The childhood reminiscences of G. Gordon Liddy, who was to become notorious in the 1970s in connection with the Watergate scandal, are worth quoting:

> After morning prayers at school, we all pledged allegiance to the flag. This ... required dignity and precision. We stood at rigid attention, facing the flag in lines straight enough to rival those of the massed SS in Leni Riefenstahl's *Triumph of the Will*.
> "I pledge allegiance ... " we began. At the words *to the flag* we shot out our right arms in unison, palms down, straight as so many spears aimed directly at the flag. It was the salute of Caesar's legions, recently popular in Germany, Italy, and Spain.
> ... I *enjoyed* the mass salute and performed it well, unexcelled in speed of thrust and an iron-shaft steadiness throughout the remainder of the pledge. That habit became so deeply ingrained that even today,

---

12. Cf. the 1899 photograph of schoolchildren's salute in Miller 1976, following 125 (bottom), hands over their hearts.

13. Miller 1976, 141, reprints the text of a leaflet entitled "How To Give the Salute to the Flag" and distributed by Upham to American schools. It begins: "Right hand lifted, palm downward, to a line with the forehead, and close to it." Then: "At the words, 'to my Flag,' the right hand is extended gracefully, palm upward, towards the Flag, and remains in this gesture."

14. Rydell 1996 twice refers to Romans in his characterization of the original saluting gesture but does not further discuss this supposed ancestry: "a modified version of the Roman gladiator's salute" (14) and "the Roman gladiator's gesture" (23). On the change in the gesture (mentioned by Rydell, 23) cf. especially the following representative articles from *The New York Times*: "New Flag Salute Ruled" (October 16, 1940; page 10: students in the New York City school system are required "to use the military type salute," i.e., right hand to forehead); "West Virginia Banishes 'Nazi' Salute in Schools" (February 2, 1942; page 17: no extension of the right arm); "Flag Salute Like 'Heil' Ends for School Pupils" (June 19, 1943; page 28: the same rule for students in the New York State school system). Cf. also Corcoran 2002, 146. The inside back cover of Baer 1992 carries a 1992 drawing of two schoolchildren raising their right arms, palms up, in salute. On this aspect of the American salute see especially Ellis 2005, 91, 113–20, and 251–52 (notes) in a chapter entitled "Making the Pledge Safe for Democracy" (i.e., different from Fascist and Nazi salutes). Ellis, 59–62 and 114, provides photos of schoolchildren giving various forms of the flag salute, including the raised-right-arm variant.

at assemblies where the pledge is made or the national anthem played, I must suppress the urge to snap out my right arm.[15]

The cinema here and later, as we will see, provides the most reliable evidence for this salute (and others). It is, in fact, more important than still photography because a film can show an action in motion. An example of the early form of the American Pledge-of-Allegiance ceremony may be found in George B. Seitz's epic film *The Vanishing American* (1925), a melodrama set on and around an Indian reservation in the American West before, during, and after World War I. It contains a school scene in which a white teacher leads her pre-teen Indian students in the Pledge. One student is holding the flag, and the teacher, reciting the pledge, first puts her hand to her forehead as in a military salute and then extends it toward the flag. This is the cue for the students to raise their right arms, palms down and not up, toward the flag as well. (Figures 8–10).

When the extension of the arm was superseded by the placement of the right hand over the heart, this gesture in turn found its way into historical cinema. Prominent examples, although by no means the earliest, are two epic films directed by Anthony Mann, one on a medieval, the other on a Roman subject. In *El Cid* (1961) Saracens use this gesture as a greeting, and in *The Fall of the Roman Empire* (1964) a martial variant—right fist on the heart—appears as the standard salute in the Roman army. Mann distanced his portrayal of ancient Rome from the Fascist overtones of earlier Roman films. (More on this film in chapter 7.) The fist-on-heart salute occurs elsewhere in the cinema as well. An example from among Italian films is Giorgio Ferroni's *Il colosso di Roma* (1965; *Hero of Rome*), in which Etruscans use it. (Roman senators express their consent to appointing Mucius Scaevola, the film's titular hero, to the supreme command over the Roman army by the raised-arm gesture, a kind of *acclamatio*.) The fist-on-heart salute also makes its way into high culture, occurring, for instance, in Lawrence Carra's ancient-dress video production of Shakespeare's *Antony and Cleopatra* (1983). Yet another military variant had appeared on American television in a modern-dress adaptation of Shakespeare's *Coriolanus* (1951): the open right hand, palm down, is put over the heart.[16]

In American popular culture the raised-arm salute, albeit with variations, survives without any political or historical connotations in other contexts as well. Again the cinema provides representative instances in

---

15. Liddy 1997, 4. Emphasis in original. The book was first published in 1980.

16. This one-hour version, adapted by Worthington Miner and directed by Paul Nickell for Westinghouse Studio One, was broadcast live by CBS-TV on June 11, 1951.

Figures 8–10. *The Vanishing American.* The pledge and flag salute. Famous Players-Lasky/Paramount.

Figure 11. *The Indian Fighter.* Indian chief greeting white officer. Bryna Productions/United Artists.

a film genre which is quintessentially American but in which viewers would not readily look for occurrences of raised-arm salutes. This is the Western. Scenes of greeting, mainly between Indians and whites, regularly display raised-arm salutes, if not always the kind associated either with modern history or with ancient Rome. In a scene of Raoul Walsh's *They Died with Their Boots On* (1941), an epic about George Armstrong Custer, no less famous a war chief than Crazy Horse raises his right arm to a brave whom he is sending away with an important message shortly before the battle at the Little Bighorn. But even the form of the raised-arm salute that is indistinguishable from the Fascist salute—or almost so—can occur on screen. A characteristic scene appears in Andre de Toth's *The Indian Fighter* (1955), in which an Indian chief so salutes an American army officer. (Figure 11) More famous is the ending of Sydney Pollack's *Jeremiah Johnson* (1972), when an Indian brave raises his right arm in a solemn greeting to the eponymous hero. (Figure 12) Jeremiah acknowledges it with the same gesture. Instances from other films could be added.

The American cinema, the most popular of all media, continued the tradition of visual presentations of antiquity that were first encountered on the late-nineteenth-century stage. Many of the gigantic spectacles presented in the American theater in the latter part of the 1800s were adaptations of best-selling novels, such as Edward Bulwer-Lytton's *The Last Days of Pompeii* (1834), Lew Wallace's *Ben-Hur: A Tale of the Christ* (1880), and Henryk Sienkiewicz's *Quo Vadis?* (1895). They provide their readers with edifying and exciting stories set during the Roman Empire. Stereotypically the empire is characterized by militarism, luxury, blood lust, and debauchery, a decadent culture which only the new religion of Christianity can rescue from all-pervasive spiritual emptiness. These

Figure 12. *Jeremiah Johnson.* Crow warrior saluting. Warner Bros.

popular works set the model for a whole series of such narratives well into the twentieth century. They were often adapted to the stage or provided the direct impulse for stage dramas on similar themes.[17] Wilson Barrett's *The Sign of the Cross* (1895) is a representative example of the latter, as is Lew Wallace's pseudo-Shakespearean tragedy *Commodus: An Historical Play,* first published in 1876 but never produced. In early-twentieth-century America stage adaptations of *Ben-Hur* were so popular with audiences that they played in ever bigger productions, replete with sea battle and chariot race, the latter being the show's main attraction. Over a twenty-year run *Ben-Hur* had more than twenty million viewers and was a huge commercial success.[18] Popular interest in ancient Rome had received an immense boost from the discovery of Pompeii in 1748 and from the city's subsequent excavations.[19] Paintings, stage plays, and novels set in Roman times took advantage of this renewed interest, moralizing on themes of empire, luxury, decadence, the conflict between paganism and Christianity, and the triumph of the latter over the former. The appeal of *The Last Days of Pompeii* and *Ben-Hur* and of their European and American imitators in print, on the stage, and later on film was near universal.

For visual representations of the Roman world, its surviving art and sculpture and the works of later imitators provided readily available mod-

---

17. On this subject see especially Mayer 1994.
18. On the stage play of *Ben-Hur* see Mayer 1994, 189–200. Its text is at Mayer, 204–90. The author of the adaptation was William Young.
19. Dahl 1956 provides a brief overview of the influence which the discovery of Pompeii had on art and popular culture before 1840.

els. For instance, classicizing sculpture took up the triumphal Roman iconographic tradition in both the Old World and the New. A representative example from the latter is Augustus Saint-Gaudens's equestrian statue in gilded bronze of American Civil-War general William Tecumseh Sherman, now in New York City. It is one of the most famous heroic monuments in American art. Begun in 1892 and completed in 1901, it had won a Grand Prix at the Paris Exposition of 1900 before it was unveiled in New York in 1903. The work shows the debt of American art to the art of imperial Rome. The victorious general is led by a winged Victory striding forth and holding up a large palm branch in her left hand. Her right arm is extended upward before her, her fingers slightly spread apart. The gesture is a loose example of what later becomes known as the Roman salute.

But where ancient Roman or later classicizing models are lacking for modern visual representations of the Romans, creative imagination must fill in the blanks. After all, the Romans' literary and historical record has left numerous gaps regarding specific details about their daily customs and their general way of life. This is a circumstance about Roman culture that becomes problematic to all creative artists who wish to bring the Romans back to life, either in literature or on stage and screen. The problem applies as much to the plot of a play or a film as to its sets and to the actors' costumes, diction, and gestures. Successful modern additions, however, are likely to acquire a life of their own in that they tend to become canonical for what is—or better: appears to be—"correct" because they have become familiar. In the cinema, the American Western is again a case in point. Over decades, standard Hollywood presentations of the West have become so iconic that any film that tries to achieve a higher degree of authenticity and to avoid the obvious historical errors or anachronisms found in innumerable other Westerns may, paradoxically, look wrong when audiences compare it to what they have come to accept as right from earlier films. The same is true for the genre of ancient spectacle, as an observation by Gore Vidal on the 1959 version of *Ben-Hur* makes evident. Vidal, himself a historical novelist, was one of the uncredited screenwriters for this film. He reports about its director: "William Wyler studied not Roman history but other Roman movies in preparation for *Ben Hur*."[20] Wyler had worked as an assistant on the silent *Ben-Hur* of 1925. This film and the 1951 *Quo Vadis* are most likely to have satisfied Wyler's curiosity about the history not of the Roman Empire but of Rome on film because they had been made by MGM, Wyler's own

---

20. Vidal 1992, 84. So also Vidal 1996, 303.

studio, and had been highly successful nationally and internationally. (All three films will be discussed in their contexts in later chapters.)

Regarding the visual side of social interaction of theatrical and cinematic Romans with their peers and superiors, archaeological and textual evidence from antiquity is insufficient to serve the purposes of producers and directors. Stage and screen stories must be specific, and where no useful information exists about how a certain moment should be represented, invention must close the gap. Classical scholars and ancient historians often are hired to conduct research for producers or to advise directors, but they may learn a sobering, perhaps even painful, lesson in the process.[21] The conclusions reached by P. M. Pasinetti, associate professor of Italian at a major American university and consultant to Joseph L. Mankiewicz's *Julius Caesar* (1953), a film adaptation of Shakespeare's play also for MGM, are telling. They apply to the stage as well:

> the producer knows very well that his historical reconstruction is not going to be exact and "scholarly" and, which is more important, that there is no reason why it should be so. A film is being made, not a contribution to a [scholarly] journal; the requirements are those of the film as an artistic whole.... [My] sort of research, whatever amount of it might be used, showed one crucial difference between scholarship and film making: while the former can afford to be vague in its results, the latter cannot. However uncertain the evidence, scanty the documents, and numerous the hypotheses, the decision had to be made as to how a piece of garment would be worn, a salute would be given, and so on.[22]

Much earlier observations on stage productions and theatrical acting bear out Pasinetti's conclusions. Robert Montgomery Bird, popular author of *The Gladiator* (1831), a play whose subject is the revolt of Spartacus, said about the practical side of acting:

> the education of an actor can only be acquired in the theater.... First he must learn "stage business," comprising the mechanical aspects of the actor's art, the management of voice, gestures, grouping, and so on. He must then learn to act with effect and to see in our great dramas "what it is that is effective."[23]

---

21. A recent example is Kathleen M. Coleman, "The Pedant Goes to Hollywood: The Role of the Academic Consultant," in Winkler 2004, 45–52.
22. Pasinetti 1953, 132 and 135.
23. Quoted from Dahl 1963, 51–52.

These words apply to all theatrical and cinematic productions, but nowhere are they more important than for the immense spectacles that had become all the rage on the late-nineteenth-century stage and that have well been characterized as anticipating the emergence of a new art form. The cinema was to eclipse its precursor through its almost limitless technological possibilities. The parallels between theatrical and cinematic spectacles, particularly when they both show a historical or pseudohistorical story, are an important link between the two media in the transitional era when the stage was forced to relinquish its hold over spectators' emotions and interest to film. The best study of this phenomenon is by Nicholas Vardac, who provides fascinating information about the rise and decline of melodrama and spectacle in the theater, the influence of early cinema on the stage, and the transition from one popular medium of visual storytelling to another.[24]

Vardac's observations on theatrical writing and acting, especially on styles of gesturing, pertain directly to our topic although he does not specifically mention the raised-arm salute. But he gives important information on the overall context in which these salutes occurred, first on the stage and then on the screen:

> Dialogue in many climactic scenes of the melodrama of this period was of secondary importance, and, as in the silent film, pictorial action, pantomime and business, dominated. Actors were unwittingly being trained for the silent film. There was no task here of creative interpretation or of dialogue. It was only necessary to carry out the action routine as outlined by author and stage manager. Drama depended essentially upon the sensational action, the spectacular scenic conceptions, and the cleverness of the overall episodic pattern.[25]

Hence Vardac's conclusion about audience expectations in general: "In the days which saw the fusion of stage and screen, drama was fancied in visual terms. . . . Audiences . . . had not come into the theatre to participate imaginatively . . . they had come to be shown."[26] By the same token a "style of pantomimic elaboration and overplay" comparable to and

---

24. Vardac 1949. My observations are greatly indebted to this classic work, unsurpassed until this day. A series of four books by Robert Grau (1909, 1910, 1912, 1914) also gives a detailed history of American theater and the popular stage in the nineteenth and early twentieth centuries and of the theater's connections with and eventual eclipse by the screen. Cf. further Booth 1981, 1–29 and 174–75 (notes; chapter entitled "The Taste for Spectacle"); Booth 1991, 70–98; Meisel 1983; Pearson 1992; Brewster and Jacobs 1997. Cf. also Verdone 1970.

25. Vardac 1949, 42–43.

26. Vardac 1949, 64 and 108.

deriving from "stage melodramatic spectacles" had been standard in early film acting.[27] Compare the following description of arm gestures from a late-nineteenth-century theatrical actors' training book:

> We may state that so long as in their movement the hands do not rise above the waist, they express sentiments of a quieter nature ... but so soon as the hands are raised above the waist, and therefore reach the chest ... their expression assumes much greater force, more intensity.[28]

Especially significant for gestures in acting are the stage directions that help cast members express their characters' feelings, attitudes, etc. As Vardac well puts it:

> Stage direction, both in its handling of individual character interpretation and in mass groupings, movements, and tableaux, supported and augmented the pictures achieved through scenery, lighting, costumes, and properties. The acting of Henry Irving and Ellen Terry was notable for its pictorial bias, its selection, and its emphasis of visual images, details of business or of pantomime.[29]

Stage business reinforces the chiefly visual appeal of theatrical spectacle. For example, the following was noted about Henry Irving's 1881 production of Alfred Lord Tennyson's *The Cup: A Tragedy*: "Gorgeously armoured Roman officers" had a "peculiarly strong" impact on the spectators.[30]

The tradition of spectacular productions reached its zenith with actor, playwright, and producer Steele MacKaye. MacKaye established on the American stage "a system of acting which arose out of and exploited a purely visual appeal." This method, developed in France by François Delsarte and "depending upon the pictorial values of body positions and attitudes ... was thoroughly in accord with the theatrical trends of the times." A contemporary reviewer observed about MacKaye's own acting style that it was "distinguished by a profusion of graceful but meaningless gesture and action, very much like a writing master's flourishes."[31] The

---

27. Vardac 1949, 218.
28. Garcia 1888, 61. This book's title page impresses readers with the author's academic credentials.
29. Vardac 1949, 246. Vardac devotes informative chapters to the acting and production history of famous impresarios David Garrick, Henry Irving, and David Belasco.
30. Quoted from Vardac 1949, 97.
31. Quotations from Vardac 1949, 144. Vardac, 265 note 237, gives the reference for the review he quotes. Pearson 1992, 22–23, provides a brief overview of Delsarte's method. For more

incredible stage effects which MacKaye developed for his new approach to large-scale theatrical storytelling led to his invention of a kind of stage that was utterly new in its technical advances over anything seen before; MacKaye aptly named it the Spectatorium.[32] The Spectatorium was to open at Chicago's Columbian Exhibition in 1893, but the project was too ambitious and expensive to become reality. MacKaye opened a smaller version, the Scenitorium, in 1894. "Acting . . . , of necessity, would become entirely pictorial" as a result.[33]

We may now apply this background information to the stage plays set in antiquity, which were among the most spectacular and thrilling ones in nineteenth-century theater history.[34] A number of them were duly filmed. (Cf. the next chapter.) The words of Bird and Pasinetti quoted earlier strongly imply that rituals of greeting between, for example, legionaries and their officers or between army commanders and the emperor are of special importance for visual stories set in Rome, since the theme of empire almost by necessity demands the presence of at least some military personnel. Audiences were then and are still familiar with highly elaborate and strictly circumscribed military rituals, particularly those of saluting. Scenes of militarism invariably occur in the story lines of Roman novels, plays, and films, but history does not reveal what the ancient equivalent of modern military rituals may have been in all circumstances. It is therefore dramatically necessary to invent something. The raised-arm salute readily offers itself as an immediately recognizable gesture, one that can be employed by the military and by civilians alike, especially when the latter form a crowd. On stage and screen it helps make for thrilling moments of spectacle, if accompanied by the exclamation "Hail Caesar!" The gesture, already established through the Pledge of Allegiance, can be traced on the American stage at the end of the nineteenth century, too. Photos of the New York City production of *Ben-Hur* provide the most important evidence.

---

details see Zorn 1968, a collection of texts by Delsarte and some close associates, with numerous passages on hand and arm gestures. Although saluting gestures are not specifically mentioned, we may compare, in part, the description of a gesture signifying authority: "Extend the arm and raise it in front a little higher than the level of the shoulder; then raise the hand . . . " (Zorn, 126). On the importance of gesture as stage business cf. Zorn, 157–59, a section entitled "Oratorical Value of Gesture," which contains statements such as "Gesture is more than speech" (157) and: "It is not ideas that move the masses; it is gestures" (158).

32. Vardac 1949, 146–49, describes the Spectatorium and discusses a number of MacKaye's special effects.

33. Vardac 1949, 149; cf. Vardac, 242.

34. For descriptions see Vardac 1949, 76–79 (*Quo Vadis?*), 79–82 and 230–32 (*Ben-Hur*), 109–11 (*Passion Play*), and 207–9 (*Judith of Bethulia*).

After Wallace's novel had become a publishing phenomenon, a theatrical adaptation opened on Broadway in November, 1899.[35] It, too, proved a sensational success. It was exported abroad and continued on Broadway in ever more spectacular stagings until April 1920, when it was closed down in anticipation of a film version. This film, however, was delayed until late 1925. The play was, in the words of someone who attended its opening night, "the most stupendous theatrical undertaking of this age."[36] Its success was unprecedented and unparalleled:

> *Ben-Hur* filled and overflowed the Broadway day after day, week after week, until it was obviously a unique phenomenon. People were entranced by its magnificence—sets, costumes, lighting, staging, music, and especially the chariot race. Nothing on this scale had been attempted before.... Written by a man with a strong theatric instinct, the play proved a "natural." It was destined to be performed 6,000 times, mostly in big cities and at high prices, a total of 20,000,000 persons were to pay $10,000,000 to see it. The itinerary for twenty-one years—with enlarged stages, S.R.O. signs, full-length seasons—is unequaled in the history of the theater.[37]

The New York production was accompanied by a classy souvenir album containing, among other things, numerous photographs.[38] Four of these are telling in different ways. Act II, Tableau 2 of the album is entitled "The Open Sea" and shows a scene with Ben-Hur and Quintus Arrius, the Roman tribune whose life he has saved during the sea battle, on the planks of a wrecked ship. Ben-Hur, kneeling, is supporting Arrius with his right hand; his left hand and open palm are stretched out and upward. The image is in itself inconclusive because it does not reveal the purpose of the gesture, which can be Ben-Hur's appeal to his god (or to a ship approaching outside the picture frame) or a promise or oath to save Arrius rather than to let him commit suicide. Act III, Tableau 3 ("Revels of the Devidasi") shows a mass of male and female revelers with one or both arms raised. (Figure 13) The Devidasi had been erroneously imported into Greco-Roman antiquity from East India by Lew

---

35. For the publishing history of the novel, the inspiration it provided to other authors for similar novels, and the history of its stage adaptations see McKee 1947, 164–88, and, in greater detail, Morsberger and Morsberger 1980, 297–312 and 447–66, with 517–18 and 528–29 (notes).
36. Quoted from Morsberger and Morsberger 1980, 460.
37. McKee 1947, 180.
38. *Souvenir Album: Scenes of the Play Ben-Hur* 1900, leaf 2: "Illustrations from flash-light photographs."

Figure 13. Souvenir program of stage production of *Ben-Hur*, Act III, Tableau 3. Author's collection.

Wallace in his novel and so reappear on the stage. Far more important is the second of two illustrations of Act IV, Tableau 1, both called "Dowar [i.e., tent] of Sheik Ilderim in the Orchard of Palms." In this photograph a standing Ben-Hur is greeting the seated sheik with his raised and outstretched arm, palm down. (Figure 14) Act V, Tableau 3 ("In the Arena") shows the crowd of spectators at the chariot race, with many arms raised.[39] One other image, not contained in the souvenir album, is of a small crowd so greeting Ben-Hur in his chariot.[40]

Three things are noteworthy about these illustrations. First, Wallace's novel had not contained a single instance of the raised-arm salute.[41] The same goes for the text of the theatrical production: no stage direction instructs any actor to raise his arm in greeting. Instead, we find directions such as these: "*Officer salutes and exits*" or "METELLUS *salutes and exits.*"[42] Similarly, Wallace's drama *Commodus* contains no stage directions for a raised-arm gesture.[43] Wallace and other authors of such plays are evidently unfamiliar with the raised-arm salute. A glance at any number of nineteenth-century stage plays bears out this conclusion.[44] The texts

---

39. Mayer 1994, 203, also shows this picture. The term "arena" (the site of gladiatorial combat) is inaccurate. The documentary *Ben-Hur: The Making of an Epic* (1993), directed by Scott Benson, traces the history of *Ben-Hur* from the novel to the 1959 film. It is accessible in the DVD editions of this version of *Ben-Hur* and contains some of the illustrations from the stage play's souvenir album and some footage from the 1907 film. All film versions of *Ben-Hur* will be discussed later.

40. This photograph is included in chapter 3 on the DVD edition of Benson, *Ben-Hur: The Making of an Epic*.

41. At least in part this is because Wallace did extensive research for his book. Although he had to take liberties with the plot, which freely mixes historical and fictional characters, he was aware that all else, e.g., his descriptions of Roman triremes and chariots, had to be as authentic as possible. As he put it in Wallace 1893: "Nor would the critics excuse me for mistakes in the costumes or customs of any of the peoples representatively introduced.... Of the more than seven years given the book, the least part was occupied in actual composition. Research and investigation consumed most of the appropriated time" (quoted from Wallace 1906, vol. 2, 932 and 934).

42. Quoted from Mayer 1994, 217 and 219. The same observation applies to all other stage plays anthologized in this book.

43. *Commodus* is best accessible in Wallace 1898, 81–168.

44. I have checked, in the modern editions cited, the following representative plays, either produced or unproduced, that are set in antiquity: Thomas Godfrey, Jr., *The Prince of Parthia: A Tragedy* (1765), in Moses 1918, vol. 1, 19–108; John Howard Payne, *Brutus; or, The Fall of Tarquin* (1818), and David Paul Brown, *Sertorius; or, The Roman Patriot* (1830), both in Moses 1918, vol. 2, 87–175 and 177–252; George Henry Boker, *Glaucus* (1885–1886, unproduced), in Boker 1940, 119–228; John Howard Payne, *Romulus, the Shepherd King* (ca. 1839, unproduced), in Payne 1940, 127–244; Royal Tyler, *The Origin of the Feast of Purim; Or, The Destinies of Haman and Mordecai, Joseph and His Brethren,* and *The Judgment of Solomon* (no dates given), all in Tyler 1940, 31–121; Julia Ward Howe, *Hippolytus* (produced 1864), in Russak 1940, 71–128. With the exception of those edited by Moses, the plays listed above are collected in volumes 3, 6, 15, and 16 of Barrett H. Clark 1940–1941.

Figure 14. Souvenir program of stage production of *Ben-Hur*; second image of Act IV, Tableau 1. Author's collection.

of neither Louisa H. Medina's adaptation of *The Last Days of Pompeii* nor Bird's *The Gladiator*, one of the most popular American plays of the early and mid-nineteenth century, make any mention of it.[45] Early handbooks on acting are likewise ignorant of the gesture.[46] The salute is evidently an addition intended to increase the audience's involvement and enjoyment of a grand spectacle by means of an effective piece of stage business. This is in keeping with the exaggerated style of acting in nineteenth-century theater, which in turn influenced the acting in silent cinema. The incorporation of new gestures, indeed their invention, is therefore not as remarkable as their very absence would be.

Second, comparison with the Fascist salute in the gestures from *Ben-Hur* described above are loose and unmilitaristic. They will remain so for quite a while in the theater and on film, as we will see. Third, the crowd employing them is ethnically mixed. (The scene of the chariot race is Antioch, capital of the Roman province of Syria.) This aspect, to be dealt with more extensively in the next chapter, reveals that the modern raised-arm gesture and salute were originally not limited to Romans. Indeed, in view of its twentieth-century Fascist use it is almost eerie to realize that Ben-Hur, a Jew, had used it not all that long before the rise of collective anti-Semitism propagated by political ideologies in Europe. With the popularity of such productions the gesture becomes a standard ingredient of ancient spectacles, first on the stage and later on the screen. In its early occurrences, of course, it does not carry the definite overtones or implications it was to acquire later.

Two films are of particular significance for this context. I therefore discuss them here, although this anticipates some of my later arguments. Both are prestigious works, carrying high-culture pretensions and even a measure of snob appeal. Both are based on plays by George Bernard Shaw. They are Gabriel Pascal's *Caesar and Cleopatra* (1946) and Chester Erskine's *Androcles and the Lion* (1952). The former is a British production with a screenplay credited to Shaw himself, boasting a stellar and expensive cast headed by Claude Rains and Vivien Leigh in the title roles and filmed in color, not a routine matter at the time. The latter, in black and white, was produced by Pascal but made and financed in the United States. Both exhibit the drawbacks of filmed theater, recapitulating, as

---

45. Medina (n.d.). The popularity of the story may be gauged from its parody: Reece 1850, which also has no mention of the salute. Bird's *The Gladiator* is most easily accessible in Richards 1997, 171–242. Actor Edwin Forrest, for whom Bird wrote the play as a star vehicle, played Spartacus "over a thousand times in his career" (Richards, 167). On the play's popularity see also Dahl 1963, 56–57.

46. Neither Siddons 1807 nor Barnett 1987 discusses or illustrates it.

it were, the transition from stage to screen that had made possible the silent epics to be discussed in chapter 4 and the rather uneasy mixture of modernity and antiquity that is unavoidable in such productions. (There are a number of anachronisms in both films.) But their most important feature for the present purpose is how they present their Romans saluting. As is to be expected by this time in the history of Roman films, civilians and military personnel employ the raised-arm salute. Civilians do so more loosely than soldiers and officers. In *Caesar and Cleopatra,* for instance, Caesar is so greeted by a contingent of soldiers who immediately afterward draw their swords and extend them toward him. "Hail Caesar!" is heard at the same time. The opening scene of *Androcles and the Lion* displays a raised-arm salute, too. But both films also show instances of the *modern* military salute, with the right hand, palm down, touching the greeter's helmet or, in one instance in the latter film, the bare head. In one scene of *Caesar and Cleopatra* a Roman officer delivers a message to Caesar. He puts his right hand to his helmet exactly as a modern soldier would do; before he leaves a few moments later, he gives Caesar a straight raised-arm salute. Modern military phraseology ("Yes, sir!" and "No, sir!") occurs in the two films as well. To anyone who pays attention to the military ceremonial and to the saluting gestures of cinematic Romans, all this is rather disconcerting. (The repeated instances of "Yes, sir!" and "No, sir!" in the opening sequence of Henry King's *David and Bathsheba* [1951] are especially jarring.) But it tells us that all the gesturing on the screen, here and elsewhere, has nothing to do with Roman or other ancient history and everything to do with modern staging and modern conventions, whether they are based on contemporary social customs or cinematic traditions. When both merge, as they do in these two films, the result is unintentionally revealing because it proves that historical accuracy is not to be expected on stage or screen.

four

Early Cinema

American and European Epics

THE CINEMA WAS the successor of stage spectacles and eventually usurped their popularity. With ever-advancing technology it proved to be capable of overshadowing and outdoing its older rival. Films set in antiquity, not least films concerning the life, passion, and resurrection of Jesus, were an integral part of earliest cinematic history. Hence the popularity of passion plays, which had a long theatrical and quasi-theatrical tradition going back to medieval mystery plays. From 1879 on, the first American passion plays had been produced for theatrical performances. They were not without controversy because they raised the religious concerns of clergymen and educators. The first film adaptations of passion plays were shown in 1897 and 1898. The earlier of the two, entitled *The Passion Play* and directed by Walter W. Freeman, was unusually long for its time, with an estimated length of about fifty minutes. The film was a cinematic record of the passion play performed that year in Höritz, Austria. Its producers were Marc Klaw and Abraham Lincoln Erlanger, the theatrical impresarios who two years later were to bring *Ben-Hur* to the stage with immense success. *The Passion Play* was "almost certainly ... America's first feature film with a storyline."[1] The second film, directed by Rich G. Hollaman and running to about nineteen minutes, was called *The Passion Play of Oberammergau;* it was produced as a successor to and rival of Klaw and Erlanger's film. Despite its title it was

---

1. On Klaw and Erlanger's film, which does not survive, see Niver 1976, 1–12, with an outline of the film's individual scenes on page 10. My quotation is from page 4.

not an adaptation of the Austrian passion play but an American recreation filmed on a rooftop in New York City.[2]

Both these films derived their social and religious respectability from the long tradition of European passion plays.[3] It is safe to say that the genre of cinematic spectacle was born with Klaw and Erlanger's film. As has rightly been observed: "Religious subjects in general were an important genre for the early film industry."[4] Religion, works of literature generally acknowledged to be masterpieces and taught in schools, and history were just the thing to lend social and cultural respectability to a new medium whose origins had nothing respectable about them since it had become popular at fairs and in low-class nickelodeons: "cheap places for cheap people," as the good citizens thought them to be.[5]

Films had thrived on sensationalism from the start. But spectacle films were based on culturally accepted subject matter such as European history or literature. They could impart status to the fledgling medium and avoid criticism from respectable citizens or institutions. The theater was of particular importance as a kind of role model for early cinema:

> The trend in favor of the theatrical story was initiated as early as 1908 by *Film d'Art,* a new French film company whose first production . . . represented a deliberate attempt to transform the cinema into an art medium on a par with the traditional literary media. The idea was to demonstrate that films were quite able to tell, in terms of their own, meaningful stories after the manner of the theater or the novel. . . . From the lower depths the cinema thus rose to the regions of literature and theatrical art. Cultured people could no longer look down on a medium engaged in such noble pursuits. . . . Producers, distributors, and exhibitors [in Europe and America] were quick to realize that Art meant big business.[6]

---

2. Niver 1976, 13–27, provides background information on this film. For an older account of the early passion plays see Ramsaye 1986, 366–78 (chapter entitled "The Saga of Calvary").

3. On the passion plays and their influence on early cinema see especially Musser 1990, 208–21. Musser also discusses Klaw and Erlanger's involvement in theatrical passion-play productions. On the cultural contexts of early biblical film epics see also Uricchio and Pearson 1993, 160–94 and 240–44 (notes), in a chapter entitled "Biblical Qualities: Moses."

4. Musser 1990, 219.

5. Hampton 1931, 61.

6. Kracauer 1960, 216–17. The 1908 French film is *L'assassinat du Duc de Guise,* whose production was supervised and whose screenplay was written by Charles Le Bargy, a member of the Académie Française (who also played the title part), and whose principal cast came from the Comédie Française. For a detailed outline of the representative process of cinema's cultural elevation and social acceptability, achieved primarily through epic films on ancient topics and

Generally, films on historical and literary topics are the best examples for the cinema's rise to respectability. In the United States the Bible and the plays of Shakespeare provided a ready supply of stories. Shakespeare's *Julius Caesar* and its early cinematic history is an instructive case.[7] So is the 1925 version of *Ben-Hur* (to be discussed in the next chapter). Its souvenir program book makes the cultural significance of the story's progress from novel to stage to screen explicit and emphasizes its public appeal and its edifying and instructive qualities—not without omitting the requisite advertising hyperbole. The souvenir book begins with a "Foreword: 1880–1925":

SINCE GENERAL LEW WALLACE wrote the last words of BEN-HUR forty-five years ago . . . that immortal story . . . has been the greatest of fictional themes. Eagerly read in every English-speaking community and translated into many foreign languages, millions of copies have been sold and the circulation during the period has been as great as that of the Bible itself. This tale of Bible times was blessed by His Holiness Leo XIII. . . .

MR. A.L. ERLANGER . . . realized the deep desire for a stage play based on the book. . . . The success was instantaneous. . . . The vogue of BEN-HUR was due not only to the theme, the spectacle and the admirable acting but equally to Mr. Erlanger's foresight and wisdom in maintaining the fine and reverential treatment of its grand subject by the author.

A FEW YEARS SINCE—in the newer art of the motion picture—Mr. Marcus Loew undertook the tremendous enterprise of visualizing BEN-HUR . . . and now presents it as a Metro-Goldwyn-Mayer picture. The direction of the work was entrusted to Mr. Fred Niblo, with the aid of the most distinguished players of the screen and Metro-Goldwyn-Mayer's unrivaled art and technical resources.

MR. NIBLO has handled the story of BEN-HUR in motion pictures with all the tenderness and delicacy and dramatic power that the subject matter calls for. The most casual reader of the book or former patron of the spectacle knows the richness of the material and the splendor

---

adaptations of literary masterpieces, cf. Abel 1999, 246–77, and Gunning 1991, 151–87 (chapter entitled "From Obscene Films to High-Class Drama"). For an introductory overview of early melodrama, especially in serial form, and its reputation see Singer 2001, 189–220 and 319–24 (notes; chapter entitled "'Child of Commerce! Bastard of Art!': Early Film Melodrama").

7. On this see especially Pearson and Uricchio 1990; rpt. in Uricchio and Pearson 1993, 87–95 (on the 1908 American film of *Julius Caesar*), and, with abridgments, in Grieveson and Krämer 2004, 155–68. Cf. further Decherney 2005.

and poignancy of the romance for picturization. It is now offered with the happy confidence that this immortal story has been filmed to the continual delight of millions of theatergoers in every part of the world where the newer art holds sway.

These points were apparently thought to be so important that they were made again. A few pages later, the next text section of the program book ("The Production of 'Ben-Hur'") is equally emphatic—and revealing even in its use of capital letters—about the transfer of respectability from stage to screen:

> TRADITION clusters around "Ben-Hur" as the most remarkable stage achievement of America. It is fitting that this well-grounded tradition is upheld by the Picture Spectacle, in its turn the capstone of the picturizing art.
>
> "Ben-Hur" [on the stage] effected epochal changes . . . the nature of its action and the fineness of its handling called to the patronage of the Better Drama millions of persons whose training hitherto had been sharply opposed to the theatre.
>
> . . . the causes of its vogue are not hard to seek, for it was great drama and great Spectacle in the historical setting of the birth of Christianity in the eastern half of the Roman Empire. . . . Throughout its stage career "Ben-Hur" was wisely maintained at the level of its original excellence, elaboration, and reverent spirit. . . .
>
> The Greater Ben-Hur exceeds the stage play, even as the Newer Art that has the whole world for its picturizing, exceeds the older one.[8]

So the new medium could present culturally accepted subjects that were educational, elevating, and even inspiring while not, of course, neglecting the audiences' demands for thrills or spectacle. It could also point to its own seriousness as a new art form. And what better subject than classical Greeks and Romans and their biblical "relatives" to achieve all this?[9] Consequently, the American *Julius Caesar: An Historical Tragedy* of 1908, to be discussed below, restages Caesar's assassination by imitating Jean-Léon Gérôme's painting *The Death of Caesar*. A well-known still

---

8. The quotations are from the inside front cover and pages 5–6 of the souvenir booklet (*Ben-Hur* 1926).

9. Bowser 1990, 128 and 255–56, respectively, mentions the 1910 version of *Elektra*, based on Richard Strauss's recent opera, and the Italian *Quo Vadis?* as examples of films that appealed to a better clientele, even though the production company of *Elektra* had advised distributors to "bill it like a circus."

from the film depicting the senate hall just after the assassination is an almost exact cinematic copy of Gérôme's painting, if in black and white rather than in color. The point is clear: educated filmmakers want the educated among their viewers to recognize the source they used and to appreciate the cultural—and cultured—representation of this decisive moment. Film, when done right, is artistic, uplifting, educating, inspiring. The cinema always remains a commercial product, but at the same time it is good for you.

The cinema naturally took over various traditions and conventions from the stage. Among them was the raised-arm salute, as may be observed in the earliest Italian and American films set in antiquity. During the silent era Italy and the United States were the chief and unrivaled producers of cinematic "spectaculars," as they were then called. Films successful in one country were usually exported, often with some changes, to another. In the U.S. the early Italian spectacles about ancient Rome became popular hits and influenced producers and directors.[10] Since silent cinema could convey information to its audiences only visually and, to a smaller extent, through intertitles, subordinates' reactions to commands, for instance, had to be expressed with gestures, just as greetings were more cinematic when actions replaced words. The use of title cards for the same purpose would merely have been repetitive and tiresome. So the raised-arm salute, already established on the stage and in American culture at large, as we have seen in the preceding chapter, was ready to make its debut on the screen.

The Passion Play of Oberammergau seems to have contained precursors of this soon-to-be-standard cinematic gesture. Scenes like "The Messiah's Entry into Jerusalem" and "The Crucifixion" include figures whose right arms are raised toward Jesus in greeting, as by members of the crowd during his entry, or as a sign of lamentation after the crucifixion.[11]

Of greater significance, however, is *La vie et la passion de Jésus-Christ, n. s.* [= *notre sauveur*, "our savior"; *The Life and Passion of Jesus Christ*], a French film begun in 1902 by Ferdinand Zecca, expanded in 1904, and, with Lucien Nonguet as director, expanded again in 1905 to a running time of about forty-four minutes. It is one of the earliest long films in history. This film depicts the story of Jesus in thirty-one tableaux. Well-known

---

10. Examples are the Italian imports *Quo Vadis?*, *Gli ultimi giorni di Pompeii*, and *Cabiria*, on which see, e.g., Bowser 1990, 210–12 and 258. Bowser, 266–72, examines the emergence of the perception of film as an art form immediately after her discussion of film as spectacle.

11. Musser 1990, 214–15, provides four stills from this film, including the two on which my observations are based. Regarding the latter, the figures important for my argument appear at the extreme lower left and right corners of the frame as reproduced in Musser's book.

works by Gustave Doré provided some visual inspiration to the filmmakers. In 1903 its production company, Pathé Frères, had developed a stencil process to add up to four colors to each print, and the eventual result looks ravishingly beautiful. (It still does in its restored edition.) The film became one of the biggest and longest-running hits of early cinema history, shown by theaters, missionaries, and traveling showmen in Europe, America, Asia, and elsewhere. As a result the film was instrumental in establishing the cinematic look of the New Testament. It is likely that the film also influenced the visual appearance of antiquity in general in the new medium.

As is to be expected, Zecca and Nonguet's color epic contains much gesticulating as a visual means of indicating characters' emotions and general excitement. Various kinds of raised-arm salutes are prominently on view. The most memorable instance occurs in the scene in which twelve-year-old Jesus has been left behind in the temple in Jerusalem. When Joseph and Mary find him among the learned doctors, Jesus rises from his seat, turns toward them, and greets them. At this moment he is standing sideways to the camera, his face in profile looking screen right. Jesus now raises his left arm to horizontal level, his hand bent upward an additional forty-five degrees, his palm facing out. Simultaneously he lowers his head and upper body while also moving his entire body slightly back and down by bending his knees. All this makes for a fluid, elegant, and elaborate gesture of greeting and deference toward his mother and foster father. (Figure 15) The gesture is a precursor of the politicized raised-arm salute that is to appear later. As will be seen in chapter 5, Cecil B. DeMille will resort to this kind of salute almost thirty years later in his film *Cleopatra* (1934), when a servant acknowledges Julius Caesar in virtually the same way, although, as a slave, he crouches far lower than Jesus does here. The reason that Jesus raises his left and not his right arm is due to the fact that he is facing to the viewer's right. Had the young actor playing Jesus been instructed to raise his other arm, part of his body and perhaps even his face might have been obscured momentarily. People facing screen left in this film raise their right arms when saluting.

When Jesus enters Jerusalem on Palm Sunday, we observe a small crowd raising and waving their arms, but one man greets Jesus with a straight raised-arm salute. After Jesus has died on the cross, the Roman soldier who pierces Jesus' side with his lance is, a moment later, so greatly overcome by emotion that he gives Jesus a raised-arm salute (with his right arm since he is facing screen left); then he sinks down on one knee and weeps. After Jesus has risen from the dead, his disciple John twice greets the angel found in the empty tomb with his right arm raised

Figure 15. *La vie et la passion de Jésus-Christ, n. s.* Jesus, age twelve, greeting Mary and Joseph in the Temple. Pathé Frères.

horizontally; he also bows slightly. Finally, in the tableau in which Jesus ascends to heaven, several of his disciples greet him with arms raised, the left one if they are facing right, the right one if they are facing the other way.

This early film is particularly instructive about salutes. It shows that gestures including those of arms raised in greeting, far from being based on an authentic Roman custom, are invented for the sake of visual activity on the screen; hence Jews and even Jesus himself can employ variants of the raised-arm salute. The film also makes evident that its makers did not consider the gesture to be specifically Roman. This becomes clear from another tableau. When we see Jesus before Pontius Pilate, a Roman soldier or officer in full armor, even wearing a helmet, acknowledges Pilate's command to lead Jesus away by inclining his head. This Roman-dominated scene would have provided an obvious occasion for a raised-arm salute if this gesture had indeed carried specifically Roman connotations at the time of the film's production. But nothing like such a salute occurs.

In 1907 Frank Oaks Rose and Sidney Olcott made a one-reel adaptation of *Ben-Hur* that provides another early example of the raised-arm salute on film.[12] It shows the gesture as a general way of greeting before

---

12. Niver 1985, 52 (s.v. *The Chariot Race*); McKee 1947, 186–87; and Morsberger and Morsberger 1980, 467–69, give information on this film. Mayer 1994, 298–99, also discusses it. Cf. further Ramsaye 1986, 459–64 (chapter entitled "Kalem and the First 'Ben Hur'"), and Solomon 2001, 202–3.

and after the chariot race, just as it had been on stage. That same year French film pioneer Georges Méliès produced, directed, and starred in the whimsical fantasy *Le Rêve de Shakespeare* (or *La Mort de Jules César;* English title: *Shakespeare Writing Julius Caesar*). Shakespeare sees in a dream Caesar's death and the events surrounding it, which appear in double exposure on the screen. Denying the conspirators' plea, Caesar raises his right arm, palm out; the gesture resembles the raised-arm salute but expresses Caesar's rejection.[13] The next year, however, the American *Julius Caesar: An Historical Tragedy*, a tableau-like adaptation of Shakespeare's play of about sixteen minutes' running time, contains several instances of the raised-arm salute. The two most important ones occur among senators entering the senate hall and in Caesar's house on the morning of the Ides of March, when Casca and others come to escort him to that fateful senate meeting.[14]

Also in 1908 American film pioneer D. W. Griffith made *The Barbarian, Ingomar* (sometimes referred to as *Ingomar the Barbarian* or simply *The Barbarian*).[15] This Roman-Empire one-reeler is significant for being, after Rose and Olcott's *Ben-Hur*, another important link between the popular stage and the cinema. Griffith, its writer and director, adapted parts of a play that had been highly successful on the London stage, Maria Lovell's *Ingomar, the Barbarian* (1851). Her play in turn was based on the German verse drama *Der Sohn der Wildnis* (or *Wildniss*, in its archaic spelling) by Friedrich Halm. When it was brought to the United States, Lovell's adaptation continued to be a great success and was performed in New York City in a variety of versions throughout the 1890s and until Griffith made his film. Two other companies produced film versions of the play

---

13. Ball 1968, 35–36, describes the film, presumed lost, and provides a still image of the moment here discussed (ill. 5). A clearer reproduction is in chapter 2 of the DVD *Landmarks of Early Films*, vol. 2: *The Magic of Méliès*. Cf. the illustrations of the assassination as staged in New York in 1871 by Edwin Booth and in London in 1898 by Herbert Beerbohm Tree in Shakespeare 1984a, 60 and 62 (ills. 3 and 5). Since Beerbohm Tree's sets were designed by Sir Lawrence Alma-Tadema, this moment is frequently reproduced, e.g., in Hesketh Pearson 1956, 99, and in Shakespeare 1988, 36 (ill. 11).

14. This film was most likely directed by William V. Ranous. Pearson and Uricchio 1990 discuss it as a cultural product of its time, focusing on the reasons for the extreme condensation of a complex model into a short film. On the Vitagraph films see also Ball 1968, 38–60; he discusses *Julius Caesar* at 48–50. The film is accessible on videotape from a print with German intertitles in the British Film Institute—and with a curious slip on a title card before the battle of Philippi, on which Octavius is called by a pseudo-Italian-plus-German version of his name ("Octavio Cäsar").

15. Niver 1985, 23, provides information about this film. Further details can be found in Usai 1999, 117–21 (no. 52; contribution by Scott Simmon and David Mayer).

in the same year. Film historians are convinced that the costumes worn in Griffith's film actually came from the stage.[16]

While it received high praise from critics in its time, a century later Griffith's film looks rather quaint, if not simplistic. This is especially true for the characters' gesticulations, which today appear excessive.[17] But they are in the tradition of popular theater. So the raising and waving of arms reappears in this film's ancient settings.[18] It is worth remembering that Griffith filmed *The Barbarian, Ingomar* in Connecticut, whose proximity to New York reinforces the likelihood that the costumes came from there. (If the stage play had not been a success, neither Griffith nor anyone else would have made a film of it.)

In 1912 Sidney Olcott, of earlier *Ben-Hur* fame, directed a famous and immensely successful drama about the life of Jesus. This was *From the Manger to the Cross,* for which Gustave Doré was again a source of visual inspiration. This epic film, shot on authentic locations in Palestine and Egypt under sometimes trying circumstances, had a running time of about one hundred minutes. Olcott's film is remarkable not for its use of the raised-arm salute but rather for the rarity with which this gesture occurs. It is seen clearly in only one scene, when the Three Wise Men meet each other in the desert en route to Bethlehem. Two of them raise their right arms, the third raises his left. No Roman ever does in this film. The gesture is obviously to be understood as a common ancient way of greeting, not a specifically Roman one.

The raised-arm salute regularly appeared in Italian cinema, too. In 1909 Luigi Maggi's *Nerone* opened with Nero greeting and being greeted in this manner; the gesture recurs no less than three times in the immediately following scene. Later the people greet Nero and Poppaea in the same way, bowing down in addition. (Figure 16) The gesture is no more than one of social etiquette.[19] Early films do not standardize the raised-

---

16. In Usai 1999, 119 and 120, Mayer twice mentions this circumstance. Apparently it was important. The same use of stage costumes in a film seems to have occurred with *Julius Caesar: An Historical Tragedy;* cf. Uricchio and Pearson 1993, 158.

17. Cf. Gunning 1991, 225–26, and especially Pearson 1992, 38–51 and 154–56 (notes), on "histrionic" vs. "verisimilar" acting styles in the theater and in Griffith's films, with the latter style beginning to supersede the former in the cinema around 1908–1909. The "extended bodily gestures of histrionic acting" (Gunning, 227) are still on display in Griffith's *Ingomar.*

18. There are some contradictions about the film's setting in the information provided in Usai 1999. The scene is Massilia (not "Massalia," as Mayer, 119–120, calls it), i.e., modern Marseilles, and its environs. But although the characters' names are Greek except for the Germanic Ingomar, the scene is not set in "ancient Greece" (118) or "Hellas" (117, the production company's bulletin) but in the Roman Empire, as Mayer, 120–21, states repeatedly.

19. The American release versions have *Nero and the Burning of Rome* or *Nero, or the Fall of*

Figure 16. *Nerone.* The opening tableau: Nero, far r., being saluted. Ambrosio.

arm salute nor make it exclusively Roman. In 1911 Enrico Guazzoni's one-reel *Bruto* (*Brutus*) employs salutes that are more in the nature of theatrical gesticulation, but the raised-arm salute appears as well. The film, about eight minutes long, shows the conspiracy against and assassination of Julius Caesar. When Caesar arrives in the senate on the Ides of March, he and the senators greet each other with raised arms while earlier, at home, Caesar and his wife Calpurnia had greeted each other the same way. Their black domestic servant uses the same gesture. After the assassination the conspirators employ the salute again.[20]

Guazzoni, now generally but undeservedly forgotten except by a few specialists in silent cinema history, was one of the pre-eminent Italian directors of large-scale epics. His work is of special significance for our topic. Guazzoni made numerous spectacles on ancient (Roman and Egyptian) and other historical subjects and was often in charge of producing, writing, or editing his films and of designing sets or costumes for them.[21] Given such close involvement in various aspects of production,

---

Rome for their title. Wyke 1997, 119, provides a description.

20. Ball 1968, 116–20, describes the film and reproduces (ill. 23) two stills. The second shows the raised-arm salute in a crowd scene in the Forum after Caesar's assassination.

21. For detailed information on Guazzoni see in particular Bernardini, Martinelli, and Tortora 2005, and, much more briefly, Prolo 1951, 52–56. Guazzoni's films on ancient Roman subjects besides those discussed here are *Agrippina* (1911), *Fabiola* (1918), and *Messalina* (1923;

the consistency and prominence of the raised-arm salute in his ancient films is of great importance. It may well have prepared the way for what was to follow with *Cabiria,* a film to be discussed in chapter 5. Guazzoni's *Quo Vadis?* (1913; some sources give 1912) is his most famous spectacle. This film, running for about two and a half hours, was to become one of the most influential early films ever made.[22] With it Guazzoni established the sweeping historical epic on the screen and imparted immense prestige to the cinema as purveyor of culturally accepted stories that were inspiring and instructive.[23] *Quo Vadis?* reveals Guazzoni's strong predilection for the raised-arm salute because the gesture occurs wherever possible. (Hearty handclasps occasionally do, too.) From its earliest scene, both high-ranking Romans and their servants or slaves (from Egypt, Africa, and Lygia—i.e., modern Poland) employ the raised-arm salute. Those of lower rank usually bow down from the waist as well. Left or right arms may be raised equally. A color poster advertising the film even features the raised-arm salute at a rather improbable moment: the Herculean Ursus, while wrestling with just his right hand the savage bull to which Lygia, the Polish princess and the story's noble heroine, has been tied, has raised his left arm in an appeal to Emperor Nero, whose box appears in the background,.[24] Assorted Christians even greet St. Peter with the raised-arm salute during a secret prayer meeting. Guazzoni was evidently fully aware of the high-class nature of his film, an adaptation of a Nobel Prize-winning novel, for he took care to be authentic in his depiction of the Roman world, e.g., with a flour mill copied from those excavated at Pompeii. Nor did Guazzoni neglect high art. His arena sequence is reminiscent of Gérôme's famous and influential painting *Pollice Verso* ("Thumbs Down"; 1872); Guazzoni even reproduces the exact moment of a gladiator's victory that is the picture's subject. And his heroine at one point looks as if she had escaped from modeling for a painting by Edward Burne-Jones.

Guazzoni's *Marcantonio e Cleopatra* (1913; *Antony and Cleopatra*) is a loose adaptation of Shakespeare's play.[25] It reveals that the raised-arm

---

The Fall of an Empress). Raised-arm salutes occur as expected; cf. Bertelli 1995, 61.

22. The following observations are based on the only version currently available. It runs ca. eighty minutes and seems to derive from a French adaptation. On the film see Wyke 1997, 120–28.

23. On its impact on American culture and cinema cf., e.g., Jacobs 1939, 91–93.

24. A reproduction of this poster is in Bagshaw 2005, 20. Its caption misidentifies Ursus as a gladiator. He is raising his left arm because it is the one further away (from the viewer's perspective) and in this way does not obstruct the scene's focus, which is on the foreground action.

25. Wyke 1997, 73–78 and 82–85, gives details about the film, its plot, and its overtones of contemporary politics. See further Ball 1968, 166–68 and 345–46, and, more recently, Wyke,

salute, standardized and already similar to the later Fascist salute, is firmly in place as part of the cinema's ancient iconography, although either the left or the right arm may be raised. Roman senators use the gesture in the senate and as a rhetorical flourish during their orations. Mark Antony first employs it while on his conquest of the East. The film is remarkable and differs from earlier and later films in that Guazzoni gives the salute only to Romans. Roman soldiers use it to acknowledge a command received, a function of the gesture that will become standard in cinema. Most of the film's plot takes place in Egypt, but the Egyptians use a different gesture to greet each other and their Roman conquerors. They raise their arm, palm held vertically and facing out, then bow low, taking the arm down with them. Both the Egyptian and the Roman salutes are visually striking and enhance the story being told. This is particularly true for one of the very last scenes of the film, when Octavian is standing over the bier of Mark Antony and gives his fallen foe the raised-arm salute. All this did not prevent Guazzoni from declaring, shortly before filming started, that he would make his film "in such a way that the smallest detail will be in conformity with the strictest historical truth."[26]

The year before, Guazzoni had directed the two-reeler *La rosa di Tebe* (*Rameses, King of Egypt*). In contrast to the later film and its restrictions of the raised-arm salute to the Romans, in this film he had frequently given it to Egyptians. The film's first large-scale scene, set among a crowd in the pharaoh's court, contains an uncanny premonition of what was to come, both on and off screen. Among the usual variations there also occurs one exact instance of what would become the Fascist salute.

Guazzoni's *Caio Julio Cesare* (1914) is a fictionalized epic biography of its subject.[27] This film shows so many instances of the raised-arm salute that an introductory text added in the mid-1940s to the film's American version by the evidently exasperated staff of the Museum of Modern Art complains of its "endless salutatory gestures." As is by now to be expected from Guazzoni, Romans use it in all manner of situations. Private ones: at an aristocratic social function (in the very opening scene), at home between father and daughter or husband and wife (Caesar and Cornelia) and during the latters' wedding ceremony in a temple (where ancient Romans did *not* get married). Public ones: in crowd scenes that visually foreshadow later Fascist rallies, as with the dictator Sulla's parade through the Forum and Caesar's triumphant return from his conquest of Egypt in the film's most elaborate set piece; in the senate (Pompey to the

---

"Caesar, Cinema, and National Identity in the 1910s," in Wyke 2006, 170–89.
    26. Quotation from Leprohon 1972, 28.
    27. On it Ball 1968, 208–10. Its usual English title is *Julius Caesar*.

senators, senators and Caesar to each other on the Ides of March, senators to Caesar's dead body as it is being carried away). Military use of the salute occurs repeatedly, as between Caesar and his officers and soldiers. Also remarkable are the instances of the salute by a Vestal Virgin to Sulla and by the soothsayer to Caesar. A bizarre case is that of a Valkyrie-sized priestess of the Gauls, who arrives at Caesar's door in Rome ostensibly to warn him off his Gallic Wars but really to assassinate him. Back in Gaul, her countrymen even greet her the same way.

Guazzoni's set for the Roman senate hall in which Caesar's assassination occurs is noteworthy as well. Positioned prominently in its center is a large statue of a male figure with his straight right arm stretched out horizontally, palm down. Around the wall behind the senators' benches we see a band decorated with figures of Roman cavalry and foot soldiers, among others. But immediately above them runs another band, this one giving a famous quotation from Roman literature (somewhat abbreviated). At its heart is this exhortation: TV ... ROMANE MEMENTO ... PARCERE SVBJECTIS ET DEBELLARE SVPERBOS ("you, Roman, remember: spare the conquered but defeat the proud"). These words occur at the climax of Book 6 in Virgil's *Aeneid* and are spoken in the Underworld by the shade of Anchises, the father of the Trojan prince Aeneas who is destined to become the ancestor of the Romans. Anchises ostensibly speaks to his son, but the words are really intended for the Romans of Virgil's own time, the beginning of the empire. They are among the most noble sentiments in all of Roman literature and have often been taken as an expression of Rome's "Manifest Destiny," as we may call it, to bring justice and civilization to conquered nations. But when we now, in retrospect, see them on prominent display in Guazzoni's film, and in close proximity at that with a (fictional) statue making an obvious gesture that was to be associated with a new and rather different kind of Roman Empire less than a decade later, as we will see in chapter 5, the effect is rather eerie.[28]

Other Italian directors show the salute, too, although they are not as taken with it as Guazzoni. The first scene in Mario Caserini's *Gli ultimi giorni di Pompeii* (1913; *The Last Days of Pompeii*) takes place on a Pompeian street and shows several instances in which Roman men and women employ this salute. (Figure 17) African slaves serving their Roman masters also use variants of it, as does even the Egyptian priest who is the story's villain. In Bulwer-Lytton's novel on which the film is

---

28. Bernardini, Martinelli, and Tortora 2005, 54, provide an impressive still of the senate hall in *Julius Caesar*. The full Latin quotation is Virgil, *Aeneid* 6.851–53.

Figure 17. *Gli ultimi giorni di Pompeii* (1913). The opening shot. A moment later, another woman entering the street screen left will raise her right arm in a salute as well. Ambrosio.

based, the raised-arm salute had never been mentioned. Caserini's film also reveals the strong influence of Alma-Tadema on the décor of its domestic scenes. Given this artistic and literary ancestry, the film is one of the best examples of the connections between elevated nineteenth-century culture and early cinema.[29]

In Giovanni Enrico Vidali's *Spartaco* (1913 or 1914) the Thracian slave Spartacus, now a gladiator in Rome, uses the raised-arm salute.[30] Somewhat unusually, he does so when meeting his sweetheart, the daughter of Roman general Crassus, in a moonlit garden.[31] Crassus, on his triumphal entry into Rome upon his return from Thrace, stands in his chariot and stretches out his arm in greeting to the crowd; he extends it again when entering the Circus Maximus to preside over the games. At his *pulvinar* he

---

29. Directional credits for this film vary. Sources also name Eleuterio Rodolfi as sole or co-director. A recently restored version opens with the allegorical figure of Father Time.

30. The film, which survives incomplete, is also known under its alternate title *Il gladiatore della Tracia;* its English titles are *Spartacus* and *The Revolt of the Gladiators.* On it see Wyke 1997, 44–46.

31. Cf. the illustration of a heroic Spartacus leading his men to battle in a 1916 edition of Raffaello Giovagnoli's novel *Spartaco* at Wyke 1997, 43.

repeats it no less than three times. Still later, when he takes command of the Roman army for his campaign against Spartacus, Crassus twice greets the senators the same way. By now the gesture is firmly established in the cinema, although it is not ubiquitous.[32] The American *Cleopatra: The Romance of a Woman and a Queen* (1912), directed by Charles L. Gaskill for its producer and star, theater actress Helen Gardner, had not employed the salute at all. When this Cleopatra raises her right arm, it is a theatrical gesture meant to convey emotion, but it is not a salute. However, the Babylonian story in Griffith's mammoth epic *Intolerance,* released in 1916 after an extremely complex shooting and editing process of about two years, shows some instances of the salute alongside a more frequent variant in which the palm is held outward vertically.

Another film about the life of Jesus, Giuseppe de Liguoro's *Christus* (1914), a feature-length spectacle with location filming in Egypt and Palestine, signals to its viewers its claim to high culture from its very beginning. It opens with a tableau of the Annunciation that imitates a painting by Fra Angelico, just as its Last Supper imitates Leonardo da Vinci. But it is also familiar with the iconography of the raised-arm salute. Early on we observe Emperor Augustus dreaming of empire and busy with the tasks of ruling; he then decides on the census that will lead to Jesus' birth in the manger. Augustus receives no fewer than three messengers who deliver scrolls containing apparently important information; each messenger salutes him in the accustomed manner and is so greeted by him in return (if less formally, as befits the man in absolute power). Facing screen right, the messengers raise their left arms; facing them, Augustus raises his right. But non-Romans use the same gesture as well. The salute recurs when the Three Wise Men and their entourage are in King Herod's court and when they find Jesus in Bethlehem. One of Herod's officers acknowledges the king's command for the Slaughter of the Innocents with the raised-arm salute. One of the Jews mocking Jesus as King of the Jews bows down before him in ironic submission; his raised arm and hand point first up and then down as he bends his body to the ground. Then he strikes Jesus across the face.

---

32. Released forty years later, Riccardo Freda's *Spartaco* (*Spartacus the Gladiator* or *Sins of Rome: Story of Spartacus,* 1953) is highly indebted for some of its sets to Piranesi's famous, if fanciful, images of the dungeons of Rome and to Vidali's film for its plot, but it has only very few raised-arm salutes, such as a perfunctory one given to Crassus. The fact that the Colosseum appears in one of the central sequences of Freda's film, which takes place about a century and a half before the Colosseum was built, reminds us that Italian filmmakers were and are just as unconcerned about historical accuracy as their colleagues in Hollywood. Spartacus' wholly invented romance with Crassus' daughter in the two films is another case in point. Vidali's Spartacus returns her affection, Freda's rejects it.

The year 1914 demonstrates conclusively the close ties among stage, cinema, and popular literature. The Universal Film Manufacturing Company released a prestigious remake of *Damon and Pythias* directed by Otis Turner, known as "the Dean of Directors." Turner had made the first version of the famous and edifying story about the two Sicilian friends and their enemy Dionysius, the fourth-century-B.C. tyrant of Syracuse, in 1908. A highly successful stage play on the subject by Irish poet John Banim had been first produced in London in 1821. In the United States this play had become the inspiration for the fraternal order of the Knights of Pythias founded in 1864 in Washington, D.C. By 1914, the year of Turner's second film version, the Knights of Pythias had grown to almost eight hundred thousand members. The following year the story was retold once again in a "dramatized novel," a "tie-in" as it would be called today, to Turner's film. It was illustrated with numerous film stills.[33]

Several of these still images are important for our topic because they show an instructive variety of raised-arm salutes and gestures.[34] "The Triumphant Return through Agrigentum after Vanquishing the Barbarians" shows a number of civilians, mainly women, waving at the victorious army and its chariot-driven leader. But at least two small figures visible in the center background employ the kind of raised-arm salute that would soon become standard. "The Wooing of the Maid Calanthe by Brave Pythias" has a middle-aged man raising his right arm toward the two self-absorbed lovers, whose backs are turned to him; the man's arm is horizontal, his palm down and fingers apart. "Then did the People Stand upon the Benches and the Clamor Deepened" is a standard crowd scene in a stadium; right arms are raised and presumably being waved about. The moment, at least in the appearance of this still image, resembles comparable scenes in later European films which have obvious political overtones. Immediately following it in the book is a still showing a political moment: "Knowing Damon is at the Wedding of Pythias, Dionysius arranges to be Crowned in the Senate." A number of Greek "senators" are raising their right arms, elbows bent, either at the moment of voting or in saluting or acclaiming Dionysius their new ruler. As do the clothing, armor, and architecture of the film, the caption's eclectic terminology also reveals that the film's view of antiquity is generic. (Romans, not Greeks, had a senate.) The same is true for the raised-arm gesture. This becomes

---

33. Terhune 1915. The book's illustrations are the most easily accessible images from Turner's film.

34. I identify them by their captions in Terhune 1915, following page 72, preceding page 96, between pages 128 and 129 (two stills), between pages 168 and 169 (two-page still), and preceding page 297.

evident in a two-page spread indicating a climactic moment in the story and on the screen: "Pythias Defeats Aristle [*sic*], the Best Charioteer of Sicily, and Claims the Prize." From his chariot Pythias greets the people in the grand box with his right arm raised high and straight; the crowd exhibits a variety of raised-arm salutes, right elbows bent or straight. A line of soldiers below the box have raised their right arms holding swords toward Pythias; their gesture is the gladiatorial greeting standard in Roman contexts. The last image in the book shows the redemption of the villain, his new bond of friendship with our two heroes, and the story's happy ending: "Dionysius, Tyrant though He Be, Will Never Sever Friendship Such as This." All three clasp hands; Dionysius' right arm is raised upward, palm out and elbow bent. The moment faintly echoes David's *Oath of the Horatii*.

Turner's film shows us a kind of summary of the development of the raised-arm salute from stage to screen up to this point. In retrospect it is remarkable that this should be so at just the moment when a watershed occurred in Italy with the production of the largest, longest, and biggest ancient spectacle ever undertaken so far. The year 1914 was to prove a milestone for the popular and later political history of the raised-arm salute, as the following chapter will show.

five

Cabiria

The Intersection of Cinema and Politics

IN 1914 the Italian cinema presented audiences with one of the most colossal spectacles in film history. Giovanni Pastrone's *Cabiria* was an epic of gigantic proportions, with an astonishing running time of over 150 minutes (varying according to the speed of projection, which was not standardized in the era of silent cinema).[1] The story of *Cabiria* is set before and during the Second Punic War and takes place mainly in North Africa. *Cabiria* sported color tinting throughout and had breathtaking sights like the eruption of Mt. Aetna, Hannibal's crossing of the Alps, and the Romans' siege and capture of Syracuse. A symphonic score by a famous composer deepened the impact of the images. Equally famous was the involvement of Gabriele D'Annunzio (or d'Annunzio), which made the film a gigantic success.[2] *Cabiria* was a phenomenon that caused

---

1. Some sources give *Cabiria* an incorrect release date of 1913. Sadoul 1951, 211, mentions an original running time of almost four hours. The original, 3370 meters long, is not known to have survived. The film was recently restored by the Museo del Cinema in Turin to 3300 meters, resulting in a length of about 152 minutes at current projection speed. On earlier restorations see Paolo Bertetto, "Il materiale di tournage di *Cabiria* e la messa in scena di Pastrone: ovvero come Piero Fosco vigilò l'esecuzione," in Bertetto and Rondolino 1998, 184–211, with data on surviving footage and restoration in notes 2 and 3. (Piero Fosco was Pastrone's pseudonym as director; he was primarily a film producer and studio head.) See further Paolo Cherchi Usai, "Alla ricerca della 'vittima eterna': Pastrone, D'Annunzio e l'edizione 1914 di *Cabiria*," in *Gabriele D'Annunzio* 1989, 229–43 ("The Eternal Victim" was D'Annunzio's earlier title for the film), and Umberto Ferrari, "Cabiria come prototipo estetico: Innovazioni tecniche ed influenze stilistiche dell'opera di Pastrone," in D'Anelli 2003, 79–84. A two-hour version of *Cabiria* is available on DVD.

2. Bertetto and Rondolino 1998 gives extensive information on various aspects of the

sensations in Europe and America and exerted an unprecedented influence on epic and historical cinema.[3] It was also a cultural and artistic event of the highest order. In Italy and wherever else it was shown, the film conclusively removed the stigma that had made cinema socially suspect from its earliest days as a form of low-level entertainment.

1. Gabriele D'Annunzio and *Cabiria*

Its success was mainly due to D'Annunzio, Italy's greatest and most famous man of letters at the time and a cultural and literary figure well

---

film, its origins, and its cultural and historical contexts. D'Annunzio's text for the film, first published in connection with the film's release under the title *Cabiria: Visione storica del terzo secolo a. C.* ("Cabiria: Historical Vision of the Third Century B.C."), is now better accessible in an augmented new edition (Pastrone 1977), which contains a still from each shot of the film in its 1931 reissue, including the card immediately following the title card that states "di Gabriele d'Annunzio 1913" (page 31), the portrait of D'Annunzio that appeared at the end of the film (page 186), all of D'Annunzio's writings on *Cabiria,* and other valuable textual and visual material. Chimirri 1986 provides an essay, some visual materials, and a reproduction of D'Annunzio's text for the film, often reprinted elsewhere, too, e.g. in D'Anelli 2003, 95–123. On Pastrone see Usai 1985, with extensive discussion of *Cabiria* at 45–84. See further the accounts by Sadoul 1951, 206–18; Prolo 1951, 67–71 and 111–12 (notes); and Brunetta 1993, vol. 1, 97–102 and 173–77. More recently Solomon 2001, 47–49; De España 1998, 206–11; and Maria Wyke, "Screening Ancient Rome in the New Italy," in Edwards 1999, 188–204, discuss the film in some detail. Wyke also examines other Italian films set in ancient Rome in connection with *Cabiria* and contemporary political contexts, as do in greater detail Rondolino 1980a and de Vincenti 1988. On D'Annunzio and cinema cf. Claudio Quarantotto, "Cinema di D'Annunzio e cinema dannunziano (1908–1938)," in Perfetti 1993, vol. 2, 169–97, with further references and a discussion of *Cabiria* at 180–84, and Valentini 1995. The youngster in the title of the last item is cinema itself; the phrase is D'Annunzio's, adapted from Gordon Craig (Valentini, 39 note 24). Valentini reprints D'Annunzio's film texts, including the one for *Cabiria* (45–59, with synopsis and some stills). Redi 1999, 140–53 (chapter entitled "I letterati"), outlines the involvement of literary figures in Italian film, beginning with D'Annunzio (140–42). D'Annunzio's son Gabriellino had become closely connected with cinema even before *Cabiria;* cf. Valentini, 10–13. He was Georg Jacoby's co-director and co-scenarist of the 1924 version of *Quo Vadis?*

3. *Cabiria* had deep focus, split screen, and double exposure. Griffith's *Intolerance,* mentioned in chapter 4, owes much to *Cabiria,* not least its famous Babylonian statuary of elephants rampant, whose cinematic ancestors were the Carthaginian elephant statues on display in *Cabiria*. Cf. Sadoul 1951, 217–18. In particular see on this Fausto Montesanti, "Pastrone e Griffith: Mito di un rapporto"; Davide Turconi, "G. P. & D. W. G.: Il dare e l'avere"; and Adriana Belluccio, "'Cabiria' e 'Intolerance' tra il serio e il faceto," all three in Cincotti 1975, 8–16, 33–39, and 53–57. More famously, *Cabiria* introduced camera movement independent from the movement of on-screen characters, a technique that came to be known as "Cabiria movement." On this see Bordwell, Staiger, and Thompson 1985, 228–29. Cf. further the relevant works cited above in note 1. For the first time in the history of marketing, an airplane was used to advertise a film. For its opening in Rome a pilot flew across the city four times and dropped leaflets announcing that *Cabiria* would be shown that evening (Prolo 1951, 111 note 7).

known throughout Europe. In Italy D'Annunzio was generally referred to simply as "the Poet" (*il Poeta,* with a capital letter). Another of his honorific titles was *il vate* (a term meaning "the seer-poet") or *vate nazionale.* The term *vate* is derived from the Latin *vates* and indicates the stature of a poet who is as visionary as he is accomplished and who is beloved by his readers. In ancient Rome Virgil and Horace, among others, had been such exemplary *vates.* In contemporary Italy and beyond, D'Annunzio was another:

> il nome di D'Annunzio, notissimo in Italia e all'estero, simbolo vivente della "grande poesia" contemporanea, [era utilizzato] per dare lustro a uno spettacolo cinematografico che si annunciava grandioso, magniloquente, di vaste proporzioni, in cui fatti e personaggi, ambienti e situazioni drammatiche si collocavano sullo sfondo della storia, con Cartagine, gli elefanti di Annibale, la seconda guerra punica, e tutti i miti nazionalistici e i ricordi scolastici ad essi collegati.

> D'Annunzio's name, extremely well known in Italy and abroad, living symbol of contemporary "grand poetry," [was used] to give luster to a filmic spectacle that was announced as grandiose and grandiloquent, of vast proportions, in which actions and characters, settings and dramatic situations were placed on the background of history, with Carthage, Hannibal's elephants, the Second Punic War, and all the nationalist myths and school memories connected with them.

This immense international prestige was the very reason why Pastrone, who chiefly occupied himself with the production and distribution of films and only occasionally directed any, wanted D'Annunzio to be involved in his upcoming super-production. His contract with Pastrone, for example, required D'Annunzio to be present when *Cabiria* would open in different countries. Its simultaneous premieres in Turin and Milan on April 18, 1914, followed by the one in Rome four days later, indicate the level of cultural, social, and hence political importance that was being accorded a film for the first time:

> Era la chiamata a raccolta della intellettualità italiana di maggior prestigio cultural-mondano per nobilitare il cinema come spettacolo non più soltanto per le "masse," ma anche e sopratutto per la borghesia. Di qui il richiamo alla tradizione storigrafica colta, alla grandiosità della messinscena, alla letterarietà delle didascalie, all'uso della musica appositamente composta.... Di qui la necessità di presentare il film in un

teatro abitualmente impiegato per concerti sinfonici e opere liriche. Di qui l'attesa e poi la soddisfazione del pubblico e della critica.

It was the rallying cry of the Italian intellectuals with a major reputation in the world of culture to confer nobility on the cinema as a spectacle no longer only for the "masses" but also and above all for the middle and upper classes. Hence the call to the venerated tradition of historiography, to the grandeur of the production, to the high literary level of the intertitles, to the use of music expressly composed [for the film]. . . . Hence the necessity to show the film in a theater usually reserved for symphony concerts and lyrical operas. Hence the high expectation and then the approval of the public and of the critics.

Indisputably, cinema had arrived as an art form. "Ah, quel D'Annunzio!" ("Ah, that D'Annunzio!") was one reviewer's ecstatic outcry in a Turin newspaper the day after the opening.[4] It helped that D'Annunzio had some interest in cinema, although he believed himself vastly superior to this new art with its distasteful mass appeal. A film historian has put the case well: "D'Annunzio, with his Latin exuberance, his facile lyricism, and his fondness for éclat and pathos, was the missing link between the two art forms [of stage and screen]; not unaware of the fact, he became interested in the cinema from the start."[5] As has been observed recently, "D'Annunzio was the first and most influential figure [in Italy] to formulate what looked like a full-fledged idea of cinema."[6] His collaboration with Pastrone had begun in June 1913:

---

4. This and the preceding two quotations are from Rondolino 1980a, 7–8. See further Sadoul 1951, 207–9; he quotes (208) from Pastrone's 1949 account of his meeting with D'Annunzio. The most famous piece of music written for *Cabiria* was Ildebrando Pizzetti's *Sinfonia del Fuoco* ("Symphony of Fire") that accompanied the human-sacrifice sequence.

5. Leprohon 1972, 22–23.

6. Giorgio Bertellini, "Dubbing *L'Arte Muta*: Poetic Layerings Around Italian Cinema's Transition to Sound," in Reich and Garofalo 2002, 30–82; quotation at 43. D'Annunzio expressed his awareness of the connections between ancient Roman literature and the cinema in February 1914, in an interview published in *Il Corriere della Sera*; the text is reprinted in Oliva 2002, 278–85. He was greatly taken with Ovid's *Metamorphoses* in this regard—*Ecco un vero soggetto cinematografico* ("There you have a true cinematic subject")—and particularly with Ovid's story of Daphne (282); cf. Usai 1985, 52. D'Annunzio's first original work for the screen was the 1912 script for the melodramatic love story *La rosa di Cipro* ("The Rose of Cyprus"). For further details see Aldo Gamba, "Trucco, trucchi, truccherie: Letteratura e cinema nel primo Novecento," in D'Anelli 2003, 65–78 (the title phrase is D'Annunzio's, quoted on page 69), and Gambacorti 2003, especially 58–61, 84–85, 111–12, 114–16 (all on *Cabiria*) and 329–31 (bibliography on D'Annunzio and cinema). See further Ciani 1999.

He set to work revising a silent film already shot in large part and taken from the original novel by Emilio Salgari, *Cartagine in fiamme* (Carthage in Flames); D'Annunzio altered the title to *Cabiria,* changed the names of some of the characters, and rewrote the captions, using much more grandiloquent expressions than those initially employed by Pastrone. In effect D'Annunzio assumed responsibility for the screenwriting, and pocketed a cool 50,000 lire for his pains.[7]

D'Annunzio's participation in the film was considered to be so important that the title card proudly identified the final product as his intellectual property upon its release: "Gabriele D'Annunzio's *Cabiria.*"[8] Even earlier, D'Annunzio had disingenuously claimed to be the film's true creator and the inventor of its plot.[9]

The period of Roman history that *Cabiria* revisits is a crucial and famous part of Rome's rise to hegemony in the Western Mediterranean and her eventual achievement of world empire. Scipio Africanus the Elder, Rome's most famous general before Julius Caesar, overcomes the Punic menace with his victory over Hannibal in North Africa. Scipio's invasion of Africa, the turning point of the Second Punic War, and its aftermath were topical in Italy before *Cabiria* was produced. Ancient Libya had become a Roman province after the defeat of Hannibal. In 1911 Italy had occupied Tripolis in modern Libya. Local resistance had been and remained fierce even after Italy bought Tripolis from Turkey by treaty in 1912. Film historian Georges Sadoul observes about Pastrone's choice of just this subject for his film:

> Ce choix lui avait été suggéré par la guerre Tripolitaine, qui passionnait alors l'Italie et qui avait été pour les nationalistes l'occasion d'évoquer la conquête de l'Afrique par Scipion et d'excuser le revers de l'expédition coloniale de Libye en évoquant les victoires sans lendemain d'Annibal. L'imperialisme italien d'autant plus bouillonnant et désordonné qu'il était jeune et débile parlait hautement de transformer à nouveau la Méditerranée en une *Mare Nostrum.*

---

7. Woodhouse 1998, 268. D'Annunzio at this time was in financial troubles and was living in Paris in a kind of self-imposed exile, so the money he earned for *Cabiria* was more than welcome.

8. Bertetto and Rondolino 1998 reproduces three color plates of posters which name only D'Annunzio. Two such posters appear in Bagshaw 2005, 10 and 22. On the film's title see also De España 1998, 208; he reproduces (207) the title page of the 1931 score of the film when *Cabiria* was reissued with a music track ("Cabiria di Gabriele D'Annunzio ... ").

9. In the interview published in *Il Corriere della Sera;* see Oliva 2002, 283.

This choice had been suggested to him by the Tripolitan war, which then raised Italy's passions and which had given the nationalists the opportunity to recall Scipio's conquest of Africa and to excuse the setback of the colonial expedition to Libya by recalling the short-lived victories of Hannibal. Italian imperialism, so much more boiling and disorderly for being new and weak, spoke highly of transforming the Mediterranean anew into a *mare nostrum* [lit., "our sea," the Romans' term for it].[10]

Variations of the raised-arm salute occur throughout *Cabiria* on the part of Romans and Africans. Scipio uses the gesture once. Furius Axilla, the story's fictitious hero, twice employs it as a farewell greeting to his hosts, although in an entirely nonmilitary manner and context. (Figure 18) The Numidian king Massinissa, guest of the Carthaginian Hasdrubal, raises his right arm in greeting and is so greeted in return, as he is once by the strongman Maciste, Axilla's loyal servant. Princess Sophonisba and King Syphax mutually greet each other with great ceremony by raising their right arms while inclining their bodies. (Figure 19) Non-Romans in general tend to lower their heads and bend their upper bodies when saluting in this way. The ethnic and gestural variety of its occurrences in *Cabiria* is once again proof that the salute is a modern invention to demonstrate to viewers the exotic nature of antiquity.

Pastrone was no newcomer to ancient subjects. He had co-directed, in 1911, another giant spectacle, *La caduta di Troia* (*The Fall of Troy*). So he knew well enough that the use of the raised-arm salute went back to the early history of epic filmmaking and was practically required to appear in *Cabiria*. But he also knew that the excessive gesturing that came with classical topics and settings was part and parcel of this tradition, even if it was already beginning to look antiquated by the time of *Cabiria*. Georges Sadoul considers it this film's greatest weakness. But Sadoul quotes a fascinating defense by Pastrone of this exaggerated style of acting. It was necessary, Pastrone declared in retrospect, because it afforded *Cabiria* the status of a work of art rather than that of a mere commercial commodity:

> On a pu me reprocher une mimique exagérée, une sorte de déclamation muette. Mais rappelez-vous l'époque. C'était celle de Sarah Bernhardt avec ses maquillages excessifs, sa gesticulation grandiloquente. Mon film

---

10. Sadoul 1951, 207. For a contemporary account (and defense of the invasion) see, e.g., Cottafavi 1912.

Figure 18. *Cabiria.* Furius Axilla taking his leave from his hosts. Itala Film.

Figure 19. *Cabiria.* Sophonisba and Syphax formally saluting each other. Itala Film.

n'aurait pas été retenu comme une oeuvre d'art si (comme j'avais utilisé le nom de d'Annunzio) je n'avais pas, avec l'interprétation d'Itala Almirante Mazzini, payé un tribut à Sarah Bernhardt.

Cette concession une fois faite à l'"élite" du public, je me suis efforcé pour les autres interprètes d'obtenir un jeu plein de dépouillement et une grande simplicité.

I could be reproached for an exaggerated sign language, a kind of mute declamation. But remember the period. It was the time of Sarah Bernhardt, with her excessive make-up, her grandiloquent gesticulations. My film would not have remained a work of art if (just as I used the name of d'Annunzio) I had not, with Itala Almirante Mazzini's performance, paid tribute to Sarah Bernhardt.

With this concession once made to the "elite" among the public, I was forced to obtain, for the other performers, an acting style full of restraint and a grand simplicity.[11]

With an acting style in the long-approved manner of one of Europe's most famous and revered stage personalities for its main female role, combined with the renown of D'Annunzio's name and reinforced by hours of the most stupendous sights ever put on the screen by means of pioneering technical innovations, *Cabiria* could not fail to be both popular and prestigious. We see once again, but with special clarity, that actual Roman culture had precious little to do with how antiquity was portrayed on cinema screens.

2. Fiume: The Roman Salute Becomes a Political Symbol

It was, however, Gabriele D'Annunzio and not Giovanni Pastrone who was to exert the greatest and longest-lasting influence that *Cabiria* was to obtain on modern history. Poet, lover, dandy, and World War I aviation hero—D'Annunzio was all of this. As a historian observed:

> D'Annunzio the poet, novelist, dramatist, and aesthete, lived for sensations, gloried in violence, revelled in speed, power and adventure.

---

11. The quotation is from Sadoul 1951, 212–13. He provides no source reference for this French version of Pastrone's words (but cf. 208 note 1). According to Edmond Rostand, Sarah Bernhardt was the queen of posture and princess of gestures; cf. Joannis 2000. This book's title quotes Rostand's famous dictum.

Theatrical and flamboyant in both his private and public life, he offered his public fascinating tales of brutality, voluptuousness and Nietzschean supermen. Often he took as his themes the martial tradition of Rome. . . . he educated a whole generation . . . to dream of a new Italy, assertive, masterful and imperial.[12]

Another historian aptly summarized D'Annunzio's character in the terms of cinematic melodrama: "D'Annunzio's life was like the spectacle films such as *Cabiria*."[13] That such verdicts are not exaggerated became evident in 1919, when D'Annunzio became an unexpected political and military force and acquired another famous epithet, that of "soldier-poet" (*poeta-soldato* or *poeta-condottiere*).[14] D'Annunzio now turned into a small-scale precursor of two of the most influential shapers of history in twentieth-century Europe. He had already been a close associate of young Benito Mussolini, on whom he exerted considerable influence, if only for a time.[15] On September 12, 1919, D'Annunzio, at the head of about two thousand men, invaded and occupied the Yugoslav city of Fiume, today's Rijeka in the Republic of Slovenia, which he declared part of Italy and held until December 1920.[16] This episode, a turning point in Italian, European, and even world history, was intimately connected with D'Annunzio's flamboyant character as poet and man of refined sensibilities. His close friend and private secretary Tommaso Antongini, who was with D'Annunzio in Fiume for several months, wrote years later:

---

12. Seton-Watson 1967, 350.
13. Landy 1986, 120. For further information on the subject see Casadio 1989. On D'Annunzio in World War I see especially Martinelli 2001. D'Annunzio had won gold, silver, bronze, and other medals and honors in the war. His airplane was called *Asso di picche* ("Ace of Spades") and so decorated on its sides; a photograph is at Martinelli, 21. The ultimate conclusion reached by Martinelli, 309, is that D'Annunzio was *non imitato e inimitabile* ("not imitated and inimitable").
14. Cf. Cesare Rossi 1958, 113.
15. Neville 2004, 40, gives a summary of the relations between D'Annunzio and Mussolini. Seton-Watson 1967, 542, notes that "Mussolini . . . made himself D'Annunzio's chief spokesman in Italy" after the latter's invasion. A brief summary of D'Annunzio's character appears in Bosworth 2006, 110–15.
16. Detailed accounts of D'Annunzio's invasion of Fiume and its social and political contexts are numerous. The most extensive, if hagiographic, one is Chiurco 1929, the first two volumes of a four-volume history covering the years until Mussolini's acquisition of power in 1922. See further Antongini 1957, 492–540. Modern scholarship includes Woodhouse 1998, 315–52; Ledeen 2002; De Felice 1978, especially 3–104; Andreoli 2000, 557–82. Among others, Lyttelton 1973 gives a detailed overview of early Fascist history. For a contemporary voice cf. Giovanni Gentile 1929, now accessible in English (Gentile 2002). Pfaff 2004, 153–86 (chapter entitled "The Mediterranean Superman"), gives a brief survey of D'Annunzio's life, with emphasis on Fiume.

No one but a poet could have wrought such a miracle, and the fact that the rest of the world has been painfully slow to understand his gesture [i.e., the invasion] is only the most convincing proof of the immense spiritual importance of the audacious expedition on which he embarked, for its very grandeur is beyond the comprehension of the average individual.... The city itself, enchanted, and in ecstasy before its conqueror, gave itself to Gabriele D'Annunzio as a passionate woman gives herself to her lover, and lived as contentedly as if it had been assured of the protection of millions of bayonets.[17]

A major part of D'Annunzio's political strategy was to strengthen the ties among himself, his men, and the population of Fiume. In this he was entirely successful. One important part was D'Annunzio's custom of addressing the people in a manner that was to set a pattern for dictators in the 1920s and 1930s:

Nearly every day the *Comandante* harangued the mob from the balcony of the Palace. The spiritual communion between him, the Legionaries and the people was complete. His words nourished his listeners, who had been starved of hope; they constituted a sort of miraculous sustenance.... Thus the life of Fiume became daily more paradoxical and more sublime.[18]

It fits in with this elevation of D'Annunzio into the sphere of the superhuman hero—not to say, of the demigod—that he was accorded a more than human accolade when people referred to or addressed him. Religiously charged terms like *Salvatore* ("Savior") or *Redentore* ("Redeemer") had no trace of irony about them.[19] In this D'Annunzio found himself

---

17. Antongini 1938a, 520, in a chapter entitled "D'Annunzio, King of Fiume" (520–36; the title is not meant ironically). This is the English version of Antongini 1938b.

18. Antongini 1938a, 527. The anti-Fascist politician Emilio Lussu even reports that D'Annunzio "harangued the populace four times a day"; cf. Lussu 1936, 8. This book is an expanded version of Lussu 1945. The poet-soldier's political writings done at Fiume are collected in D'Annunzio 1974, with an extensive introduction by the editor on D'Annunzio's seizure of Fiume (vii–lxxviii). For D'Annunzio and the crowds of Fiume see, e.g., the two photographs reproduced in Andreoli 2003, 50. D'Annunzio was already experienced in this sort of thing; for illustrations see the photographs of him and the crowds in Rome from May 1919, in Salierno 1988, figs. 3–4 (unnumbered). On Mussolini's appearances before huge crowds see, e.g., Galeotti 2000, 49–50, with reference to the aptly named documentary film *Balconi e cannoni: I discorsi di Mussolini* (1996).

19. The honorifics—capitalized, of course—occur in the proclamation that made D'Annunzio a citizen of Fiume on March 18, 1920, the name-day of the Archangel Gabriel. The text of the proclamation, with comments, may be found in Gerra 1974, 272–73.

in a direct line extending back to Roman emperors, some of whom received divine titles and cults, and extending forward to Mussolini and Hitler, who both were accorded quasi-religious status.[20] D'Annunzio's reign at Fiume has been vividly described in the following terms:

> Fiume became a symbol of patriotic fervour and youthful vitality. Futurists, ex-servicemen, Nationalists, syndicalists, anarchists and adventurers flocked there from all over Italy. They swaggered round in cloaks and daggers (literally), bullied the local citizens, and enjoyed themselves immensely. The regime was a permanent *festa,* full of processions and ceremonies, of dancing and slogans. D'Annunzio's idea of democratic decision-making was rather like Mussolini's later: long rhetorical speeches from balconies to the eager crowds below, punctuated by massive acclamations. D'Annunzio also invented many of the other trappings of the later Fascist regime, including the militia, the 'Roman salute,' the compulsory castor-oil 'purgation' for dissidents, and even the meaningless war cry 'Eia, eia, alalà.' However, D'Annunzio's Fiume was not just comic opera.... The '*Comandante*' issued proclamations *urbi et orbi.*[21]

Closely connected to D'Annunzio's custom of regularly appearing before the people is his introduction of the raised-arm salute into his political and military protocol. In imitation of early epic films, not least *Cabiria,* D'Annunzio appropriated the raised-arm salute for his own purposes. Now a more rigid—and rigorously observed—form of the salute became a propagandistic symbol for D'Annunzio's political aspirations and later for those of all Italy, to which Fiume by this time belonged. The memory of the glorious Roman past played a large part in all this. That D'Annunzio had himself been a war hero also helped. He was now called Consul, and

---

20. For the religious aspects of Fascism see especially Emilio Gentile 1993 or, in English, 1996b, a fundamental work. See further Galeotti 2000, with the texts of numerous Fascist "Ten Commandments." The book's main title ("Mussolini Is Always Right") is one such commandment. The following are particularly telling examples of the divine nature of the Duce: *Mussolini è Dio* ("Mussolini is God") and *un nuovo Gesù* ("a new Jesus") and the school creed which begins *Io credo nel sommo Duce* ("I believe in the highest Duce"); quoted from Galeotti, 19 and 31, who gives the source references. If Mussolini was a new Jesus, D'Annunzio was considered by many to have been the John the Baptist of Fascism. Emilio Gentile 1990 gives a summary in English. That the quasi-religious nature of Fascism was considered to accord well with pagan Rome becomes evident from the following Fascist statement quoted by Emilio Gentile 1996b, 80: "Rome . . . knew how to impart a mystical value to its very name, which was no longer that of a city but that of a divine entity; being a citizen of Rome meant partaking of that divinity." The Nazi equivalent of this will be dealt with in chapter 6.

21. Clark 1996, 204–5.

his soldiers, many of them *arditi* from the Great War, were called Legionaries—the *Federazione Nazionale dei Legionari Fiumani*—or Praetorians.[22] As such, they needed a sign to distinguish them visually from their political adversaries, one that was readily comprehensible even to outsiders as being (supposedly) ancient. So D'Annunzio and his legionaries adopted the raised-arm salute, long familiar to all and sundry from the screen and now declared to be *il saluto romano,* i.e., the real thing:

> They also invented a new salute, the raised right arm, chosen from among the many gestures of Greco-Roman orators. It was clearly superior to the humble bow or bourgeois handshake; its limits seemed the sky. At the same time it seemed, symbolically, to thrust a dagger into the throat of an invisible enemy.[23]

The metaphor of the dagger is apropos because it reminds us of the earlier salute of the *arditi,* who used to raise their arms holding their naked daggers. But as we now know, raised-arm salutes are even older, although they are not among the gestures of ancient orators. D'Annunzio's introduction of raised-arm salutes at Fiume vividly illustrates that a gesture from stage and screen, one that had previously functioned equally well in various invented situations—private and public, political and military—can be adopted for a specific ideological purpose. Through appropriation for a new political reality it became thoroughly militarized. As a result it could never again be perceived as a harmless or innocent gesture. But in the process of this appropriation the salute also lost the wide variety of arm movements that had been possible before. It became rigid and from now on *had* to be performed in a snappy and pithy manner to achieve the visual impact it was intended for. So it remained and remains an aspect of spectacle, although of a spectacle much different in nature from the comparatively innocuous and naïve spectacles presented on stage and screen earlier. The gesture's new contexts are serious determination, force,

---

22. On the close connections between D'Annunzio's troops at Fiume and veterans of World War I, especially the *arditi,* see the standard work by Cordova 1969 and the more recent study by Marco Rossi 1997. Cordova, 66, quotes D'Annunzio stating in 1921 that three quarters of his legionaries at Fiume had been *arditi.* On the *arditi* cf. also my Introduction.

23. Rhodes 1959, 212. Cf. Bosworth 2002, 123–44 (chapter entitled "The First Months of Fascism"), and Farrell 2003, 75–109 (chapter entitled "The Birth of Fascism"). Bosworth, 145, reports that Cesare Rossi, an important figure in early Fascism, localized the first use of the Fascist salute in Verona; see Cesare Rossi 1958, 103. Regrettably, Rossi provides no details. On Rossi and his subsequent fate see the summary in Bosworth 2006, 137–38. On the Fascist salute and the initial resistance to it as replacement of the traditional handshake see Galeotti 2000, 50–52.

and hostility, all aimed at subjugating enemies or dissenters. Small wonder that such a gesture should later appeal to the Nazis. Their political and highly military system of power bent on conquests far exceeded anything ever envisioned by D'Annunzio or his Italian imitators.

Modern historians have provided only little information about the origin of the Roman salute as adopted by D'Annunzio and his men and then by the early Fascists. The most noteworthy account comes not from a professional historian but from a contemporary eye-witness, who was also one of the leading figures of Italian literature and culture in the early twentieth century. This is Giuseppe Antonio Borgese, a novelist, poet, essayist, and literary critic and historian.[24] He had been an admirer of D'Annunzio, about whose work he published an appreciative study in 1909, replete with D'Annunzio's portrait and signature: *Gabriele D'Annunzio: Con bibliografia, ritratto e autografo*.[25] But later Borgese became an anti-Fascist: "In his essays published in [the newspaper] *Il Corriere della Sera*, he . . . openly defied Benito Mussolini and his Fascist propaganda."[26] Borgese went to the United States in 1930, where he lived and worked as an academic until 1948. He had not returned to Italy earlier in order to preserve his intellectual independence from Fascist totalitarianism. In 1937 Borgese published, in English, his book *Goliath: The March of Fascism*, simultaneously a study of the origins of Fascism and an indictment of it. *Goliath* became "one of the most famous and best-received denunciations of Mussolini's dictatorship" and was translated into numerous languages.[27] Unfortunately it now seems to have been excluded from scholars' reading lists.

The specific passage that is important for our topic is Borgese's detailed and vivid description of the new ritual that D'Annunzio instituted for his addresses to the assembled people of Fiume. Borgese also gives his explanation of the origin of the raised-arm salute. His description of D'Annunzio at Fiume is so visual, even cinematic, that it deserves to be better known. It must therefore be quoted in its entirety.

Borgese begins by summarizing a poem by Italy's famous writer Giosue Carducci in which peaceful country folk take up arms to defend themselves against "the Hun or the Slav." In this poem the following words appear: "In the name of Christ and Mary—I order and will that

---

24. Parisi 2002 gives an introduction to Borgese's life, works, and thought.
25. On Borgese and D'Annunzio see Parisi 2000, 31–32; D'Alberti 1971, 42, 46, and 69–73, the latter passage on Borgese's book about D'Annunzio; Orvieto 1988, 111–39; and Pasini 1994, 50–76 and 96–115. Cf. also Mezzetti 1978.
26. Parisi 2002, 59.
27. Parisi 2002, 71. On *Goliath* see also Parisi 2000, 82–84.

this among the people be.—*Raising their hands the people said: Yes."* The poem also refers to the rural population's "little senate." (The term here does not, of course, mean the senate of classical Rome.) Borgese then describes, with occasional sarcasm, the reality analogous to Carducci's poem that could be observed in Fiume when D'Annunzio spoke to the people:

> This delightful poem, together with a few high-school reminiscences from pages of Greek and Roman historians in which Pericles or Caesar addressed, outdoors, the citizens or the legionaries, provided the foundation of d'Annunzio's political system, which in turn was to be the foundation of Mussolini's and Hitler's regimes.
>
> The people and the soldiers convened in the square beneath the palace of the government. The poet, in his over-medalled military uniform, appeared, conveniently flanked by some of the staff, on the balcony, which looked like a baldachin. There he delivered an elaborate harangue, more or less pertinently moulded according to the rhetorical rules of Graeco-Roman public speaking. At the end he bolstered up as best he could his penetrating but rather effeminate voice, and asked the people for consent.
>
> The people raised their right hands and arms, and answered: Yes.
>
> The gesture of the raised right arm, which was to be sooner or later the Roman and, unbelievable but true, the German salute, had been picked at random from classical museums, from gestures of Graeco-Roman orators and rulers, and perhaps also from the medieval romance of Carducci. In antiquity it had been occasionally an attitude of oratorical vehemence, or of command, or even of pardon. It may also have been seen, occasionally, as a salute from the distance, which happens nowadays as it always has, whenever people at the railway station or on the pier bid farewell to departing friends. It never had been the ordinary salute in the streets of Greece and Rome, where the free citizens shook hands or affectionately clasped each other's wrist, while no doubt the slave, meeting his master, saluted with the raised right arm, almost to show that his hand was disarmed and his obedience defenceless. A salute of slaves; such indeed was the gesture of Fiume to become, sooner or later, in Italy and Germany.
>
> D'Annunzio and the Fiumani liked it because it seemed straight and strenuous, incomparably more dignified than the humble bow of the civilian baring his forehead, and more powerful, also, than the military salute stopping at the képi level, midway between the hero's torso and the sky, his limit. The dash of the fully swung arm in Fiume seemed,

on the contrary, to plunge right away a dagger into the throat of an invisible enemy, gladiator-like. It spread, at least symbolically, future and blood in the elastic air; and since no Hun or Slav threatened battle it incidentally was a kind of exercise. Several might have seen the equestrian monument which represented Garibaldi sighting Palermo from the surrounding mountains and showing the golden city to a comrade as he, the red-shirted liberator, raised the right arm and promised: "Nino, tomorrow in Palermo." D'Annunzio, at the balcony or on horseback, imitating the posture, was likely to mean: "Boys, tomorrow we sail toward the world." But it is even possible that at times he would add a vague allusion to some sort of episcopal or papal benediction, which solemn gesture he much enjoyed in the all-embroiling stew of his imagination.

The crowd, surging and raising hundreds of right arms, answered, no matter what he had said: Yes. But they also often—and more often in the process of time—yelled or sang: *Eya! Eya! Alalà!*

These syllables, which were soon to become the Fascist outcry, had also been concocted by d'Annunzio, from obscure recollections of Homeric poetry with a dash of the Kaiser's hip-hip-hurrah and of the hunter's hallali and tallyho.[28]

In his references to ancient Rome Borgese is not quite accurate when he assesses the gesture and concludes that it is not a true revival of a classical Roman custom. But anybody interested in the origin of the Fascist and German salutes must be indebted to him. Indeed Borgese's comparison of the raised-arm salute to a dagger thrust did exert some influence on modern scholarship, as when it was revived more than twenty years later, as we have already seen.

Despite its usually pithy appearance the raised-arm salute allowed for a certain measure of variation, as a contemporary description tells us:

> The whole arm is raised forward and upward at an angle of about forty-five degrees, the palm of the hand out straight and stiff. Sometimes the salute is performed with grace and dignity, but usually it is either excessively vigorous and awkward or slovenly and formless. The former attitude is common among the boys, the latter is conspicuous among politicians and officials. Doormen, porters, etc., in public employ have taken up with the custom and are apt to carry it to ridiculous lengths.

---

28. Borgese 1937, 158–59. The following pages are also instructive. For an indication of the value of Borgese's description of D'Annunzio at Fiume cf. Farrell 2003, 87, a passage that is clearly indebted to Borgese.

The salute is most effective when made by soldiers in mass formation or by a large crowd at a public gathering.[29]

3. From D'Annunzio to Mussolini

In this way there began, in the Fiume of 1919, what Eric Hobsbawm has termed the invention of a tradition.[30] After D'Annunzio the raised-arm salute and its Roman connotations caught on immediately, not only within Italy. Nazi Germany is the most prominent example. As Borgese and other contemporary and recent scholars have stated, Mussolini and Hitler followed D'Annunzio's model. The importance of the raised-arm salute for their new political systems is not to be underestimated. How seriously the Fascist party hierarchy took it becomes evident from the role the salute played in the ideological education of Italy's youth.[31]

D'Annunzio had imperial designs and modeled himself on Julius Caesar. For example, he began a letter written to Mussolini on the day before his seizure of Fiume with the words: *il dado è tratto* ("the die is cast"), an allusion to Caesar's famous *Alea iacta est*.[32] As early as 1935 a historian sarcastically described D'Annunzio's vision of himself as a new Caesar:

> He revelled in instituting analogies between himself and Caesar. Like Caesar, he was middle-aged and bald, but, like Caesar, he would conceal his baldness with a laurel wreath. Like Caesar, he had been obliged to remain for years outside the frontiers of Italy owing to financial troubles, financial troubles which an ungrateful Government had refused to solve for their greatest poet. Like Caesar, too, he had had numerous love affairs, and like Caesar he had never allowed those love affairs to hamper

---

29. Schneider and Clough 1929, 192.
30. Eric Hobsbawm, "Introduction: Inventing Traditions," in Hobsbawn and Ranger 1983, 1–14. On D'Annunzio as quasi-mythical figure in connection with contemporary politics see Paolo Nello, "Natura e funzione del mito dannunziano nel primo fascismo," in Perfetti 1993, vol. 1, 141–62.
31. Cf. the text of the relevant section of the Opera Balilla handbook in appendix 2. See also Heller 2008, 109–17.
32. Salierno 1988, 25, provides the text of this letter and of another one by D'Annunzio to a different recipient that begins with the same sentence. D'Annunzio's letter to Mussolini is quoted in a rather free English version ("The dice are on the table") in Mussolini 1998 (vol. 1: *My Rise*), 79. This book is a one-volume reprint of Mussolini, *My Autobiography* (1928) and *The Fall of Mussolini: His Own Story* (1948). According to Farrell 2003, 479 note 2 to chapter 2, *My Autobiography* was written chiefly by Mussolini's brother Arnaldo; differently Richard Lamb in his "Introduction" to the 1998 reprint.

him in his career as a literary man and a soldier. And, unlike Caesar, who had been merely a poetaster, he was the world's greatest poet!!![33]

The *faux*-Roman legions of the soldier-poet provided an effective starting point for political rituals: "He held a procession of parades, meetings at which he distributed medals, and other public events designed to appeal to the Italian love for the theatrical."[34] But D'Annunzio's influence was not limited to Italy. As has been observed more recently about his influence on European Fascism:

> D'Annunzio anticipated the aesthetics of fascist mass politics with rituals such as the speech from the balcony, the call-and-response dialogue and the mystical fusion of leader with crowd, the Roman salute, and the ritual cry—in other words, a politics of *spectacle*.[35]

George Seldes, an American journalist expelled from Fascist Italy in 1925, was more sarcastic on the grand theatrics of D'Annunzio and Mussolini.

---

33. Griffin 1935, 171.
34. The quotation is from Hoyt 1994, 49.
35. Witt 2001, 34, with references in note 5. On Italian Fascism as "pyrotechnics" of political spectacle cf. Cesare Rossi 1958, 103 (*pirotecnica*); Barzini 1996, 133–56 (chapter entitled "Mussolini or the Limitations of Showmanship"); Cannistraro 1975, especially 273–322 and 395–405 (notes), a chapter on cinema; Jens Petersen, "Mussolini: Wirklichkeit und Mythos eines Diktators," in Bohrer 1983, 242–60, especially 248–51; and, more recently, e.g., Eric Hobsbawm, "Foreword," in Ades 1995, 11–15; Falasca-Zamponi 1997; Jacqueline Reich, "Mussolini at the Movies: Fascism, Film, and Culture," in Reich and Garofalo 2002, 3–29; and Fogu 2003, especially chs. 3 ("Historic Spectacle") and 4 ("The Historic Imaginary and the Mass Media"). As Barzini 1996 makes clear on numerous occasions, spectacle has been a regular feature of Italian history and politics. On D'Annunzio see, in this regard, Antonio Spinosa, "La teatralizzazione della vita di D'Annunzio," in Perfetti 1993, vol. 2, 151–56. The strategy to present politics as spectacle had reached an earlier climax in France; cf. Horne 2004, 51 ("Napoleon I at [his coronation] . . . had vested himself in the pomp and circumstance of power comparable only to that of the Roman caesars [*sic*], of Charlemagne and of the Holy Roman emperors"), and especially Bierman 1988. On Napoleonic aspects of Mussolini's Italy cf. further Patrizia Minghetti, "Mussolini e/o Forzano nel segno delle sconfitte 'momentanee' di Napoleone e di Cavour," in Renzi 1992, 53–66, and the following summary by Neville 2004, 119: "Much of this [Roman] symbolism seemed grotesquely inappropriate to critics of the régime, but it was part of an attempt to mobilise the people to Fascism's cause. Just as Napoleon had recognised the importance of baubles and decorations, Mussolini saw the potential in florid uniforms (a feature of Fascism) and high-sounding titles." On Caesar, Napoleon, Mussolini, and Fascism see now also Jane Dunnett, "The Rhetoric of *Romanità:* Representations of Caesar in Fascist Theatre," and Oliver Benjamin Hemmerle, "Crossing the Rubicon into Paris: Caesarian Comparisons from Napoleon to de Gaulle," both in Wyke 2006, 244–65 and 285–302. Giovacchino Forzano was the author of the Mussolini-inspired stage play *Campo di Maggio* (1930), which he filmed under the same title in 1935. (An alternate Italian title of the film is *Cento giorni;* its American title is *100 Days of Napoleon*.) Casadio 1989, 32–33, has basic information on the film. Bertelli 1995, 21, reports that Mussolini himself was the author of the stage play. Cf. now Dunnett, 257–61.

In his book *Sawdust Caesar* he commented on the invasion of Fiume as follows:

> Comic opera as this may seem today, the attack and its success led directly to the making of the Fascist movement and the advent of Mussolini in Rome. The poet had supplied the black shirts, the black fezzes, the slogans, the spirit of armed adventure, the ideal of force triumphant and the salutes, yells, and claptrap of Rome of the time of the Caesars. A shrewder man knew how to employ them on a national scale.[36]

The name "Fascism" (in Italian, *fascismo*) derives from the term *fascio di combattimento* ("bundle of combat"), which had first appeared in 1919 as a name for Mussolini's troops. From these, D'Annunzio took over the term for his men in Fiume.[37] D'Annunzio's initial spectacular success only reinforced Mussolini's own ambitions, and he quickly adopted D'Annunzio's Roman rituals and terminology. Robert Paxton's recent comments are a concise summary of the connections between D'Annunzio and Mussolini but also of their differences in political shrewdness and foresight:

> In September 1919, D'Annunzio led a band of nationalists and war veterans into the Adriatic port of Fiume, which the peacemakers at Versailles had awarded to the new state of Yugoslavia. Declaring Fiume the "Republic of Carnaro," D'Annunzio invented the public theatricality that Mussolini was later to make his own: daily harangues by the *Comandante* from a balcony, lots of uniforms and parades, the "Roman salute" with arm outstretched, the meaningless war cry "Eia, eia, alalà."
> As the occupation of Fiume turned into a national embarrassment for Italy, D'Annunzio defied the government in Rome. . . . D'Annunzian Fiume became a kind of martial populist republic whose chief drew directly upon a popular will affirmed in mass rallies. . . .
> Mussolini uttered only mild protests when [Prime Minister Giovanni Giolitti] negotiated a settlement with Yugoslavia in November 1920

---

36. Seldes 1935, 73; cf. 73–75 on D'Annunzio's penchant to dress in various uniforms and style himself on famous figures from different eras of history. Cf. further Bosworth 1998, 58–81 (chapter entitled "Mussolini the *Duce:* Sawdust Caesar, Roman Statesman or Dictator Minor?"). Cf. Farrell 2003, 84–89 (section entitled "If d'Annunzio's March on Fiume Was Comic Opera, Mussolini's March on Rome Was *Opera Lirica*").

37. Cf. Salvemini 1973, 126. Original texts on the *fasci di combattimento* and the Fascist *squadrismo* are collected in De Felice 2001, 11–70. Cf. also Silone 1934, now easily available in an Italian edition which reprints (Silone 2002, 89–91) the text of the "Program of the Italian Bundles of Combat" of August 28, 1919 (*Programma dei Fasci Italiani di Combattimento lanciato il 28 agosto 1919*). On the corporations and associations in Italian and German Fascism see the detailed study by Reichardt 2002.

that made Fiume an international city, and then sent the Italian navy at Christmas to disperse D'Annunzio's volunteers. This did not mean that Mussolini was uninterested in Fiume. Once in power, he forced Yugoslavia to recognize the city as Italian in 1924. But Mussolini's ambitions gained from D'Annunzio's humiliation. Adopting many of the *Comandante*'s mannerisms, Mussolini managed to draw back to his own movement many veterans of the Fiume adventure....

D'Annunzio ... was more interested in the purity of his gestures than in the substance of power.... D'Annunzio's failure is a warning to those who wish to interpret fascism primarily in terms of its cultural expressions. Theater was not enough.[38]

It is no exaggeration to say that the founding father of Fascism was D'Annunzio and that his most observant disciple was Mussolini. This is the result:

Many [of D'Annunzio's] legionaries now [i.e., 1921] joined the fascist militia, which provided the best prospects of 'action,' and accepted Mussolini's leadership. But though the Fascist party broke with D'Annunzio and Fiume radicalism, it showed that it had learnt much from the Fiume adventure. The uniforms and the black shirts, the 'Roman salute,' the 'oceanic' rallies, the party hymn, *Giovinezza* ["Youth," the song of the *arditi* in World War I]; the organisation of the militia into cohorts and legions, commanded by consuls; the weird cries of *Eia Eia Alalà!*, the demagogic technique of 'dialogue' between orators and massed audiences; all the symbolism, mystique and 'style' with which the world

---

38. Paxton 2004, 59–60; notes omitted. (The cover of the 2005 reprint edition shows a photograph with a straight-arm salute.) D'Annunzio had first introduced his air squadron to the cry *Eia, eia, alalà* in 1917 during the bombardment of Pola; he revived it at Fiume. It, too, is an example of D'Annunzio's (pretentious?) veneration of classical antiquity and of his appropriation of its cultural standing for his own purposes; cf. Giardina and Vauchez 2000, 214–15. The words—Greek, not Latin—are not quite as meaningless as Paxton believes since they are attested in the works of dramatic and lyrical ancient poets. *Eia* (something like "Up! On! Away!") appears in Aeschylus, Euripides, Aristophanes, and Plato; it is not "di origine latina," as Cavazza, "Saluto romano," in de Grazia and Luzzatto 2003, 579, has it. *Alalà*, deriving from the ancient Doric dialect (in Attic: *alalé*), is an onomatopoetic term for a loud cry, especially a war cry, and occurs in Euripides and Pindar, with Aristophanes' variant *alalaí*. Pindar even personifies Alale as Daughter of War. D'Annunzio, a famous dramatist and lyrical poet, saw himself in a line with the great authors of an idealized classical past. Cf. Green 1991, 133, on the Macedonian battle line: "At the same moment, every man of the phalanx beat his spear on his shield, and from thousands of throats there went up the terrible ululating Macedonian war cry—*'Alalalalai!'*—echoing and reverberating from the mountains. This sudden, shattering explosion of sound ... completely unnerved [the enemy]."

was later to grow so familiar, were plagiarised from D'Annunzio, who in this sense too could justly claim to be one of the spiritual fathers of fascism.³⁹

Now a new version of the imperial and military spectacles that the Italians for many years had loved to watch on the screen about their mighty ancestors, the Romans, was turning into a kind of reality, for legions and leaders were again on the move in Rome and in the cities and towns of Italy. D'Annunzio was a kind of father figure for Mussolini, to be emulated at first but then to be discarded:

> D'Annunzio had conceived the idea of the uniforms with their black fezzes, the assemblies, the slogans, the administration of castor oil to political opponents, and the claptrap of a Fascist regime. He had appealed to chauvinism, to the adventurous spirit of youth, to the desire of the masses for colorful pomp, and to the ideal of force. Mussolini, who had hitherto relied on inflammatory rhetoric and journalism, was clever enough to see that these meretricious devices of political pageantry could be developed and usefully applied to his own wider purpose.⁴⁰

It was a shrewd strategy on D'Annunzio's part to strengthen his military, political, and social influence throughout Italy by an extensive appeal to most people's inclinations toward ritual, history, and a vague but powerful quasi-religious ceremonial, in all of which ancient Rome played a significant part. As a modern historian summarizes it: "People and nation were bound up in a thick web of symbols, which embraced town- and landscape, machines and monuments, art and costume, dress and gesture, and which stamped on every thing and in every place, from the weapons of the state to roadside milestones, the emblem of the lictor's fasces."⁴¹ Another historian observes: "Virtually the entire ritual of Fascism came from the 'Free State of Fiume.'"⁴²

In an autobiographical reminiscence writer Italo Calvino commented on the evolution of Mussolini's appearance in contemporary art. He observed:

---

39. Seton-Watson 1967, 596.
40. Kirkpatrick 1964, 90. On Mussolini and Caesar cf. Seldes 1935, 370–72. Cf. Farrell 2003, 87: "D'Annunzio like Mussolini wanted to transform Italians into heroes and Italy into a reincarnation of the heroic Roman empire."
41. Gentile 1996b, ix.
42. Ledeen 2002, vii. On Fiume and its connections to Fascism see, e.g., Perfetti 1988, who reprints a number of documents from 1921 and 1922. Cf. Gumbrecht 1996. On the ideological differences between D'Annunzio and the Fascists cf. Emilio Gentile 1996a.

Radio and cinema were the principal media not only of the dissemination but also of the very formation of this [i.e., the classic] image [of Mussolini] . . . in the cinema the leader's image was more effective and tangible than when it was seen directly by the crowd underneath that balcony. . . . The audio-visual media of the time were, in short, an essential component of Mussolini's Roman cult.[43]

An autobiographical sequence in Federico Fellini's *Roma* (1972) that is set in a local film theater during the Fascist era exemplifies Calvino's point. In general, Mussolini was Italy's most popular film star (*divo*):

Considering the ubiquity of . . . newsreels and documentaries during the 1920s and 1930s, it is necessary to recognize that the most widely viewed figure of the Italian cinema for almost twenty years was Benito Mussolini . . . it is film . . . that did most to convey [his] personality through heroic, larger-than-life images, that enabled greatest public access to him (even live, he was often seen from afar), and that still serves as the most vivid record most people have of him.[44]

The influence of *Cabiria* on Mussolini's public image is extensive. The film had given cinema one of its most enduring heroes—the strongman Maciste, whom D'Annunzio had named for his parallels to Hercules,

---

43. Italo Calvino, "The Duce's Portraits," in Calvino 2003, 207–20; quotation at 212.

44. Hay 1987, 222 and 224, in a section entitled "Mussolini as Divo" (222–32); cf. Brunetta 1993, vol. 2, 110–21 (section called "Il divismo mussoliniano"). See also Gili 1985, especially 80–86. This book is the most extensive recent account of Italian cinema during the Fascist era. In general see Cardillo 1983 and Gori 1988. "Luce" (or L.U.C.E.) in the title of the former book is the acronym of *L'unione cinematografica educativa*. On the importance of cinema, both newsreels and fiction films, for Fascism and Nazism in general see especially the various contributions in Renzi 1992. Giovanni Spagnoletti, "'Gott gibt uns das Brot—Er bereitet es uns und verteidigt es': Bild und Mythos Mussolinis im Film," and Stephan Dolezel and Martin Loiperdinger, "Hitler in Parteitagsfilm und Wochenschau," both in Loiperdinger, Herz, and Pohlmann 1995, 111–34 and 77–100, provide overviews. Spagnoletti, 116, quotes Mussolini's motto that film is the most powerful weapon: *La cinematografia è l'arme più forte*. On Mussolini's love for theater and film see the interview with his son Vittorio Mussolini, "Mio padre amava, semmai, il teatro," ed. Dario Zanelli, in Renzi 1992, 43–47. The famous Cinecittà studios outside Rome, the *Centro sperimentale di cinematografia*, and the *Istituto nazionale Luce* were all created under Mussolini's auspices. Cinecittà, still the pre-eminent Italian film studios, had been opened in 1937 with a grand ceremony on April 21, the date on which the Fascists celebrated the birth of Rome. On the importance of cinema for Fascist propaganda see also Malvano 1988 and Argentieri 2003. Cf. further M. B. Jampol'skij, "Potere come spettacolo del potere" (i.e., "Power as Spectacle of Power"), in Renzi 1992, 129–54 (on Stalin and Soviet film). For a comparative study cf. Kertzer 1988.

Maciste's mythical ancient precursor.[45] Maciste eventually became the hero of a whole series of popular muscleman films down to the 1960s.[46] Maciste could even leave the ancient world and battle evil wherever and whenever it occurred. (The same was to be the case with Hercules in the films of the 1950s and later.) In the Fascist era Mussolini appeared like a modern and real Maciste. Not the least reason for this was that the Duce bore a strong physical resemblance to Bartolomeo Pagano, the actor who had played Maciste for Pastrone and who shortly after had begun appearing in commercially successful Maciste films with contemporary settings. When we first see him on the screen in *Cabiria,* Maciste, with his nude torso and his arms folded over his chest, has a posture and facial expression that uncannily foreshadow Mussolini's. (Figure 20)[47] Maciste,

---

45. Cf. Alberto Farassino, "Maciste e il paradigma divistico," in Bertetto and Rondolino 1998, 223–32, on the origins of heroic stardom on celluloid in the case of Maciste. Bertellini in Reich and Garofalo 2002, 45, only surmises that D'Annunzio named Maciste after Hercules. But we can be more precise. Chimirri 1986, ill. 38, reproduces a page handwritten by D'Annunzio on which he changes Pastrone's original name of the hero from Plinio (Plinius) to Fulvio (Fulvius) Axilla and that of his *compagno strapotente* ("extraordinarily strong companion") from Ercole (Hercules) to Maciste. D'Annunzio adds that Maciste is *del paese prode dei Marsi* ("from the valiant land of the Marsians," an old Italic tribe whose ancestry predates even that of the Romans and who were renowned for their old-time simplicity and hardihood) and that his name is *un antichissimo soprannome del semidio Ercole* ("a most ancient epithet of the demigod Hercules"). This latter statement is based on the mention by the ancient geographer Strabo of a temple of Macistian Herakles (in Latin, *Macistus Hercules*) in his *Geography* 8.3.21; however, the town of Makiston or Makistos (Latinized to Macistus), which is mentioned by several ancient authors (e.g., Herodotus, *Histories* 4.148), is on the Peloponnesus in Greece and not in Italy. The late-ancient scholar Stephanus of Byzantium derives the town's name from an obscure figure in Greek mythology: Makistos (Latinized: Macistus), son of King Athamas and brother of Phrixus; see Stephanus of Byzantium 1849, 428, lines 11–15. Herodotus, *Histories* 9.20, mentions Masistios, a famous Persian cavalry commander whom some Greeks called Makistios; Herodotus says nothing about his physical prowess. Another, if less probable, explanation of the name Maciste is its derivation from the Greek *mechane* (cf. Latin *machina*), which points to its bearer's strength. In all likelihood D'Annunzio let his imagination be his chief guide. He seems to have taken part of the name of Maciste's master (Fulvius) from Virgil, *Aeneid* 7.279; cf. Usai 1985, 53.

46. Elley 1984, 185–86, lists the most popular Maciste films. Cf. also Cammarota 1987, 67–86 (chapter on Maciste films). The year after *Cabiria* Maciste advanced to his own place among cinematic heroes, even having a film, again directed by Pastrone, named after himself: *Maciste* (English titles: *Maciste of Turin, Marvelous Maciste, The Perplexities of Maciste*). In this film a young girl watches *Cabiria* in a theater and begs Maciste to help her out of a predicament; so he does. In 1916 *Maciste alpino* was co-directed by Pastrone, Luigi Romano Bargnetto, and Luigi Maggi, the last-mentioned a major director of ancient epics in his own right, as we have seen; this film has Maciste as a hero in World War I. He is still being played by Pagano, who was Maciste in well over twenty films made until 1926. On Maciste and Fascism cf., e.g., Brunetta 1975, 22–23.

47. In a late scene of *Cabiria* the victorious Roman general and consul Scipio, helmeted and in full uniform, converses with his friend and confidant Laelius. When he appears in profile, Scipio's face resembles Mussolini's. This is not the only moment in which an uncanny analogy

Figure 20. *Cabiria*. Maciste foreshadowing Mussolini. Itala Film.

too, employs the raised-arm salute in Pastrone's film, a circumstance that has caused a modern commentator to call the actor an actual stand-in for Mussolini.[48] For propaganda purposes Mussolini liked to appear as a kind of heroic laborer in the midst of his people. Stripped to the waist to show off his muscles, he worked in the fields at harvest time as part of his *battaglia del grano* ("battle of wheat"), an endeavor to increase Italy's grain yields and decrease the necessity of imports. Such occasions were duly recorded on film.[49]

In Fascist Italy the historical screen spectacle was "one of the most powerful means of cementing popular culture. Through the authority of

---

becomes evident. On Scipio and Mussolini see below.

48. Bertelli 1995, 42 ("la controfigura di Benito Mussolini"). Bertelli's first illustration (facing page 192; the same as Figure 20 here) shows Pagano wearing a kind of toga draped over one shoulder, in a heroic leader-like pose (*modello per un condottiere di popoli,* reads the caption). All this is despite the fact that Maciste in *Cabiria* was not even a Roman and that the film's screenwriters claimed in an article published that year in the film journal *Bianco e nero* "not to have changed in any way ancient values but simply to have compressed, in a necessary dramatic synthesis, historical matter" (*di non aver in nulla alterato i valori storici, ma semplicemente di aver costretto, in una sintesi drammatica indispensabile, la stessa materia storica;* quoted from Bertelli, 44).

49. E.g., in the 1925 documentary *La battaglia del grano*. Brunetta 1975, 33, quotes Curzio Malaparte's 1926 dictum that Mussolini's artistic masterpiece was not Fascist Italy but Mussolini himself. Much of this "art" derived from the cinema.

historical film's realism and mass audience recognition, history seemed to write itself."[50] Carmine Gallone's epic about Scipio Africanus (*Scipione l'Africano*, 1937) is the most instructive as well as visually explicit example. The film returns to the same time of Roman history and the same historical figure that *Cabiria* had already immortalized on celluloid.[51] *Scipione l'Africano* even features a score by the composer who had written the famous "Symphony of Fire" for *Cabiria*.[52] It also uses the same raised-arm salute. But this time its appearances on the screen are different. Now the salute is Gallone's chief visual means to make Mussolini an explicit analogy to Scipio in the context of modern Italy's campaign in Abyssinia. The film, made with government support, was Italy's most expensive production to date. Mussolini's son Vittorio served as executive producer, although without screen credit.[53] The raised-arm salute occurs from the outset and with such abandon that Gallone's film rivals those of Guazzoni discussed in the preceding chapter. The salute looks most contemporary in scenes with huge crowds filmed in long shot: "the masses are shown like the Red Sea parting for their hero and saluting him in a scene reminiscent of Mussolini's relationship to the masses."[54] (Figure 21) When Scipio appears among them, he is usually in

---

50. Hay 1987, 179. Cf. also the chapter on film in Ben-Ghiat 2001, 70–92 and 235–42 (notes).

51. The film is now available on DVD in an English-dubbed version as *The Defeat of Hannibal*. This version's running time is less than eighty-five minutes, omitting as much as thirty minutes of the original footage. On the film see Gili 1985, 149–55; Landy 1986, 194–200 (Massinissa, however, is not "a Roman officer," as Landy, 197, calls him); Casadio 1989, 22–23 and 27–29; and De España 1998, 211–13. Elley 1984, 84; Hay 1987, 155–61; and Wyke 1997, 21–22, have further discussions and quotations from contemporary sources and place the film into the historical context of its making. See now also the extensive analysis by Pasquale Iaccio, "*Scipione l'Africano:* Un *kolossal* dell'epoca fascista," in Iaccio 2003, 51–86; the title of this essay collection indicates that Gallone's name has gone down in cinematic and cultural history because of this one film. The book (bottom of plate 15, unnumbered) provides a revealing photograph of the Barberini cinema in Rome taken on October 27, 1937, in which the building's façade is decorated with Italian flags alternating with Swastika flags. In 1960 Gallone would make *Cartagine in fiamme* (*Carthage in Flames*), the only film about the destruction of Carthage by Scipio Africanus the Younger at the end of the Third Punic War (148–146 B.C.).

52. Roberto Calabretto, "Un gran brutto pasticcio: Pizzetti e la colonna sonora di *Scipione l'Africano*," in Iaccio 2003, 87–117, links Pizzetti's music for the film to his composition for *Cabiria* and to the context of musical culture under Fascism in general. Dalle Vacche 1992, 27–52, discusses Pastrone's and Gallone's films side by side.

53. Vittorio Mussolini was his father's personally appointed expert on historical films (Bertelli 1995, 21).

54. Landy 1986, 196. Brief excerpts of this film's crowd scenes, replete with arms raised, are intercut into *Messalina* (*The Affairs of Messalina*, 1951), Gallone's second film set in ancient Rome, presumably to save money on hiring huge numbers of extras. Straight-arm salutes like those on display in the earlier film recur, but Gallone includes a few variations. Apparently the

Figure 21. *Scipione l'Africano.* Scipio (center background, behind row of lictors) and the crowd. Ente Nazionale Industrie Cinematografiche.

an exalted position, towering above the crowds. Such scenes, in combination with massive architecture on view in numerous shots, present a clear visual analogy to Leni Riefenstahl's *Triumph of the Will,* a film to be discussed in chapter 6. So does a night scene in which the Romans conduct a torchlight procession to celebrate their victory over Hannibal. When Scipio delivers a speech in the senate, Gallone even has the actor resort to a gesture of the kind that Mussolini had made familiar to his viewers. And like Mussolini himself, this Scipio is rather short and stout and not at all the handsome young hero audiences might expect in a historical epic. Before the decisive battle at Zama, Scipio announces to his army that the Roman battle cry will be "Victory or Death!" This is the kind of pithy slogan with which Fascists (and Nazis) were familiar. Well-known examples are D'Annunzio's motto *Italia o morte* ("Italy or death") at Fiume and Mussolini's *O Roma o morte* ("Either Rome or death") at his march on Rome.[55] The kitschy choirs on the soundtrack of

---

cinematic tradition is still exerting its influence although Gallone no longer attempts to evoke Mussolini's Italy.

55. This in turn echoes "Rome or Death" (*Roma o morte*), Giuseppe Garibaldi's oath to his supporters of 1862. The oath is quoted, in English translation, in Pick 2005, 75; an illustration, replete with raised arms, appears in Pick, 94. D'Annunzio paid homage to the hero after his death with *La canzone di Garibaldi.* On Mussolini's imitation of Garibaldi see, e.g., Passerini

Gallone's epic which underscore the momentous nature of some scenes are also in the spirit of the Fascist, not the Roman, times. All this bears out the observation made in 1939 by influential Italian film director Alessandro Blasetti:

> An historical film can re-create moments perfectly analogous to those that we live, or rather those with which we can readily identify; they can convey warnings, they can excite, they can induce realizations that serve to maintain or to reinforce today's popular consciousness.[56]

So it is appropriate that a chapter on Gallone's film in a critical study of Fascist cinema should be entitled, somewhat sarcastically, "Benito l'Africano."[57]

Despite its obvious political intentions, however, the film does not serve Italy's imperial master all that well. Its Scipio is a bland presence on screen, so much lacking in charisma as a leader that he is no match for its Hannibal. It is also ironic that the actor who plays Scipio (Annibale Ninchi) is named after Hannibal and that those who portray the African leaders Hannibal (Camillo Pilotto) and Syphax (Marcello Giorda) bear names of great Roman heroes: Camillus, the legendary early savior of Rome, and Marcellus, general in the Second Punic War. Even the raised-arm salute is not as exclusively Roman as the overall Fascist nature of the film could lead modern viewers to believe. When the scene switches from Rome to Africa, for example, we are surprised to see that the Carthaginians, too, employ raised-arm salutes. While the Romans executing their salutes keep their bodies upright and their right arms straight, the Africans usually have a somewhat different posture: they tend to incline their heads and upper bodies and to bend their elbows. A particularly noteworthy example of this occurs when Hannibal dismisses a messenger from his tent. (Figure 22) This is the first instance in the film's English-language version in which someone who is not a Roman so salutes. In a combination of acknowledgment and greeting, the messenger raises his right arm and simultaneously lowers his body backwards by bending one knee but keeping the other leg straight before him. His posture at this moment is reminiscent of that employed by courtiers in films set in the

---

1991, especially 94 and 193. Cf. Pick, 214–16 and 255–56 note 5, and Riall 2007, 6. The Fascists' black shirts were meant as a kind of homage to Garibaldi's red shirts.

56. Blasetti 1939, here quoted from Hay 1987, 179, who supplies the original text of the quotation at 267 note 34.

57. Carabba 1974, 52–64. He provides a photo of Mussolini looking through the camera during the filming of *Scipione l'Africano* (ill. 36).

Figure 22. *Scipione l'Africano.* Hannibal saluted by messenger. Ente Nazionale Industrie Cinematografiche.

royal or aristocratic courts of feudal Europe. No doubt the unusual position of his body is intended to show up the difference of his salute from that of the Romans, which appears more heroic and less servile. Except for some nobility in the character of Hannibal, the Carthaginians in *Scipione l'Africano* are barbarians and on a noticeably lower level of culture and manners than the Romans. Massinissa, king of Numidia, also employs the raised-arm salute, if more in the manner of the film's Romans. Clearly the cinematic tradition which had introduced the raised-arm salute as a key visual aspect of antiquity accounts for the fact that in a highly political film like Gallone's even enemies of Rome employ what is firmly established in contemporary reality as the Roman or Fascist salute.

At this point in our study of how the Roman salute developed in history, film, and modern culture at large, it is appropriate to look back once more on the way modern scholarship has attempted to understand and interpret this gesture. Two European historians write:

> Il saluto fascista . . . , usato originariamente dai legionari fiumani di D'Annunzio, trovava riscontro in un vasto repertorio iconografico romano, anche se non mancavano numerose attestazioni di un saluto identico nell'arte greca. Nella società romana, i significati di questo gesto, che non era l'unico né il più diffuso gesto di saluto, erano molte-

plici e variavano a seconda dei contesti. Prevale tuttavia, nella scultura come nelle raffigurazioni monetali, un significato augurale, del tutto privo di risvolti politici. Nel rituale fascista esso adunse invece una forte connotazione politica e ideologica, perché indicava un'appartenenza partitica intrisa di marzialità. Esso veniva anche esaltato, oltre che per la sua maggiore igienicità, per la sua rapidità, che esprimeva bene il dinamismo fascista.

The Fascist salute ..., used originally by D'Annunzio's legionaries at Fiume, found its correspondence in a vast repertory of Roman iconography, even if numerous attestations of an identical salute were not lacking in Greek art. In Roman society, the meanings of this gesture, which was not the only nor the widest-spread gesture of salute, were manifold and varied according to their contexts. Nevertheless, in sculpture as in representations on coins, a benevolent meaning prevailed that completely lacked political aspects. In Fascist ritual, on the other hand, it assumed a strong political and ideological connotation because it indicated a party-political feature soaked in everything martial. It also came to be elevated, other than through its greater hygienic value, through its rapidity, which well expressed the dynamism of Fascism.[58]

This assessment is inaccurate about antiquity and about D'Annunzio at Fiume, but the description of the ritual and martial aspects of the Fascists' understanding of the gesture is illuminating. Both the ritualized and the warlike sides of the straight-arm salute become more pronounced in the political and cinematic culture of Nazi Germany, at which we will take a closer look next.

---

58. Giardina and Vauchez 2000, 215.

six

Nazi Cinema and Its Impact on Hollywood's Roman Epics

From Leni Riefenstahl to *Quo Vadis*

THE PSEUDOHISTORICAL model of empire provided by Italian Fascism found ready imitation in Germany. *Italia docet* ("Italy teaches"), as one German intellectual—and coiner of the phrase "The Third Reich"—had put it in 1922.[1] So the question arose: Who would be Germany's Mussolini?[2] The answer came in January 1933, when Adolf Hitler was appointed Chancellor of Germany. The Nazis' *Dritte Reich*—i.e., "Third Empire"—succeeded the Wilhelmine empire that Bismarck had brought about in 1871 after the Franco-Prussian War and in turn harked back to the most famous German empire in history. The Holy Roman Empire of German Nation (962–1806) had managed to exist for well over three quarters of the time that the new Nazi empire was supposed to last. Even earlier, Charlemagne had been crowned Roman Emperor. To make the Nazis' view of historical continuity plausible, the period between the fall of the Western Roman Empire in 476 A.D. and Charlemagne's coronation in 800 A.D. had been explained as a mere suspension of Roman history. So in 1933 the new rulers of Germany could claim long-standing connections to ancient Rome and a Roman-influenced imperial ancestry,

---

1. Arthur Moeller van den Bruck, "Italia docet!," in Moeller van den Bruck 1932, 123–24; first published in *Gewissen* (November 6, 1922). His most influential book, first published in 1923, was entitled *Das dritte Reich* (Moeller van den Bruck 1923) and went through several editions and reprints in the 1930s and 1940s. It was translated into English in a condensed version in 1934 (Moeller van den Bruck 1934). The copy of its first edition now in the Library of Congress belonged to Hitler. Cf. now Schieder 1994, and Schieder, "Fatal Attraction: The German Right and Italian Fascism," in Mommsen 2001, 39–58. See further Schieder 1983.

2. Jens Petersen, "Mussolini: Wirklichkeit und Mythos eines Diktators," in Bohner 1983, 242–60, at 255.

and they did.³ In his 1878 essay *Was ist deutsch?* ("What is German?") Richard Wagner, Nazi Germany's favorite composer and one of its chief cultural figureheads, had anticipated a historical development he was not to witness himself:

> in der Sehnsucht nach "deutscher Herrlichkeit" kann sich der Deutsche ... gewöhnlich noch nichts anderes träumen als etwas der Wiederherstellung des römischen Kaiserreiches Ähnliches, wobei selbst dem gutmütigsten Deutschen ein unverkennbares Herrschergelüst und Verlangen nach Obergewalt über andere Völker ankommt.
>
> in their longing for "German grandeur" Germans can ... commonly not yet dream of anything other than something similar to the restoration of the Roman Empire. In this even the most good-natured German is seized by an unmistakable lust for domination and a craving for supreme power over other peoples.⁴

Wagner made these observations following a brief discussion of the Holy Roman Empire. A revealing if rather sardonic, even grotesque, visual statement of the connections between Wagner and Hitler on the one hand and the Romans on the other appears in Hans-Jürgen Syberberg's seven-hour filmic meditation *Hitler—Ein Film aus Deutschland* (*Hitler: A Film from Germany* or, more loosely, *Our Hitler;* 1978), in which Hitler rises from Wagner's grave wearing a toga. To Syberberg, Hitler represents the unavoidable end point toward which German and European history and culture have been moving. The abyss awaits.

Hitler's own views on the ancient Romans fit all these perspectives. Two of his informal statements give us a representative summary: "The Roman Empire is a great political creation, the greatest of all." And: "The Roman Empire never had its like. To have succeeded in completely ruling the world!" So the Romans were a natural model for the new Germany. As such, they had to be integrated into Nazi ideology. How could this be done? By postulating that Aryan Indo-Germanic settlers had actually brought about the civilizations of the ancient Mediterranean. In Hitler's words: "It was in Greece and Italy that the Germanic spirit found the first terrain favourable to its blossoming."⁵

---

3. Appendix 3 lists the relevant scholarship on this and closely related issues.

4. Richard Wagner, "Was ist deutsch?" in Wagner 1983, vol. 10, 84–103; quotation at 88. In the immediately following sentence Wagner states that the Romans and their politics had been highly detrimental to the German tribes.

5. The three quotations are taken from Trevor-Roper 2000, 10 (July 21–22, 1941), 111 (November 2–3, 1941), and 289 (February 4, 1941). With the last of these cf. the chapter on the

In the German appropriation of Fascist rituals, the raised-arm salute and the accompanying words "Heil Hitler!" had become part of what now was called the "German Salute" (*deutscher Gruß*).⁶ Its words followed the pattern of "Ave Imperator," Italy's Latin greeting for Mussolini. But since the Italians had already claimed the straight-arm gesture as their own not least through its very name, it clearly would not do to adopt the gesture and preserve its foreign name. A new term was necessary to establish the Germans' independence from the Italians and to lay claim to the gesture as being innately German. Hitler himself traced its origin to earlier periods in German history:

> On parades, when mounted officers give the military salute, what a wretched figure they cut! The raised arm of the German salute, that has quite a different style! I made it the salute of the Party long after the Duce had adopted it. I'd read the description of the sitting of the Diet of Worms, in the course of which Luther was greeted with the German salute. It was to show him that he was not being confronted with arms, but with peaceful intentions.
>
> In the days of Frederick the Great, people still saluted with their hats, with pompous gestures. In the Middle Ages the serfs humbly doffed their bonnets, whilst the noblemen gave the German salute. It was in the *Ratskeller* at Bremen, about the year 1921, that I first saw this style of salute. It must be regarded as a survival of an ancient custom, which originally signified: "See, I have no weapon in my hand!"
>
> I introduced the salute into the Party at our first meeting in Weimar. The SS at once gave it a soldierly style.⁷

Roman Empire as Nordic creation in Gehl 1940, 72–122, a history textbook for high school (*Gymnasium*) and related schools and only one of such pseudo-historical Nazi statements that could be adduced here. On Hitler and antiquity, with extensive quotations and references, see in particular Karl Christ, "Reichsgedanke und *Imperium Romanum* in der nationalsozialistischen Ära," in Gabba and Christ 1991, 17–42, rpt. in Christ 1996, 255–74; Lorenz 2000; and Alexander Demandt, "Hitler und die Antike," in Seidensticker and Vöhler 2001, 136–57, and Demandt 2002. On Nazi ideology and imperialism and their sources—cf. such terms as *Weltpolitik* and *Lebensraum*—see, e.g., Smith 1986, especially 231–58 and 304–8 (notes; chapter entitled "Nazi Imperialism").

6. Cf. Franz-Willing 1974, 127. The origin of the words accompanying the German Salute is unrelated to the gesture and for that reason excluded from the present study. On the verbal greeting see Hamann 1999, 243 and 252, and Fritzsche 2008, 19–24; for a study dating to shortly before the Nazis' seizure of power see Prause 1930, 2 (diagram), 123–26, and 180.

7. Trevor-Roper 2000, 172–73 (January 3–4, 1942). Allert 2008 is a sociological study of the German salute and its uses and implications; see especially Allert, 30–53 and 102–3 (notes; chapter entitled "An Oath by Any Other Name") and 93–100 (on its survival after 1945). The SS (*Schutzstaffel*) was originally Hitler's bodyguard but became an independent and paramilitary force in 1925.

Hitler's mention of the SS reinforces what we have observed earlier about D'Annunzio, the militarization of a previously rather innocuous gesture adopted for a specific ideological purpose. Hitler's explanation of the origin of the "German" salute, attributing to it some vague Germanic past, only reveals his lack of historical knowledge.[8] It is also unconvincing. Anyone in ancient, medieval, or modern times can show someone else an open palm but still be armed and dangerous. Nazism has made the "soldierly style" even more famous—or infamous—internationally than its Italian precursor had managed to do. There is also a noteworthy variant: the man in absolute power most often employed a salute in which his right arm was raised but bent back at the elbow, sometimes so far back as to make the palm facing up horizontally. This *Führergruß* ("Leader's salute") set Hitler apart from his minions—*they* want to show their eagerness to him by snappy salutes, *he* does not have to do so to them—but it was also employed in situations when there was insufficient space to extend a straight arm.[9]

The Nazi salute's close similarity to that of the Italians was the chief reason why the NSDAP, the Nazi party, was often called a Fascist party, although the Fascist and Nazi ideologies were closely related to begin with.[10] In his overview of Western European peoples cultural historian Luigi Barzini attributed the Germans' propensity to imitate others to their innate "blotting-paper capacity at all times to absorb and improve alien conceptions," a characteristic part of their *Deutschtum*. He then went on to ask rhetorically:

> Was not nazism (among other things) a thoroughly perfected and efficient copy of disorganized and ramshackle fascism, down to the Roman salute? (Nobody really knows if the Romans saluted each other and the emperor by raising their right arms. The salute was probably invented at the beginning of the century by the forgotten director of a silent movie version of *Quo Vadis* or *Fabiola*.)[11]

---

8. The SS played a major part in what was called *Ahnenerbe* ("ancestral legacy"), in which German historians and archaeologists were involved to more or less decisive degrees. So were classical scholars, some of them well known, although the Nazis' main focus was on Germanic, not on Greco-Roman, history and culture. On this topic see especially Kater 2006.

9. Heller 2008, 30 (ills. 28–29), reproduces illustrations from a guidebook on proper salutes, including ones with bent elbows.

10. So Mussolini himself said on his visit to Berlin in 1937; the text of his speech, delivered in German, may be found in Mussolini 1951–1981, vol. 28, 248–53.

11. Both quotations are from Barzini 1984, 88. The book's original British title was *The Impossible Europeans*.

For reasons that are by now clear to us, Barzini was right in his skepticism about the Roman ancestry of the Fascist or German salute but not quite right with his surmise about early cinema. Nevertheless his observation deserved—and deserves—more attention than it has received.

More recently John Toland, author of the most widely read biography of Hitler in English, correctly maintained that Hitler took much of his political inspiration from Mussolini and that "he claimed that the stiff-arm salute at least was German." Toland next quoted the passage from Hitler's table talk given above. But even as astute and careful a scholar as Toland followed the common misperception about the salute when he stated, just before the words quoted above:

> Audiences were always properly prepared for his [Hitler's] virtuoso displays by pagan-military pageantry. In addition to stirring music and flying banners, new features had been added—Roman-type standards that Hitler had designed himself and a Roman-style salute. Perhaps he had borrowed both from Caesar by way of Mussolini. . . . [12]

Historically speaking, it is doubtful that Julius Caesar was Hitler's source for the Nazi standards, although these were indeed modeled on the *vexilla* (flags or standards) of the Roman legions. But these had existed long before the days of Caesar. And the salute has nothing to do with either Caesar or any other Roman. Even so, close ties between Italian Fascism and Nazism did exist in many regards, ranging from ideology, anti-Semitism, militarism, and others to parts of their rituals. The German army's goose step, which goes back to the Prussian army of centuries earlier, is a case in point. Mussolini introduced it in 1938, after being "greatly impressed by the Nazi parades he had witnessed" on his state visit to Berlin the year before.[13] At that time Italian-German relations were so close as to make the origin of the new step obvious to all Italians. Nevertheless it, too, was officially propagated as a Roman custom and accordingly called the *passo romano* ("Roman step").[14]

---

12. Toland 1976, 147. Cf. Franz-Willing 1974, 126–27. Spotts 2002, 50 and 51, reproduces Hitler's sketch of the party standard's design and a photograph of its first public display in 1923. Spotts, 50, quotes Toland's phrase "Caesar by way of Mussolini" without comment.

13. Quoted from Parks 2005, 58. Neville 2004, 148, speaks of Mussolini's "love affair" with Nazi Germany.

14. See, e.g., Giardina and Vauchez 2000, 259–61, and Luca Scuccimarra, "Passo romano," in de Grazia and Luzzatto 2003, vol. 2, 335–36. In a speech given on October 25, 1938, Mussolini said that the Italians were the only people in the world in whose history geese had played an important part and told the early Roman legend of the geese on the Capitoline Hill which had saved the city from the Gauls. The text is accessible in Mussolini 1951–1981, vol. 29, 185–96,

One German film set in antiquity provides an eerie anticipation of Hitler's commanding role as *Führer* of a Germany rising to new prominence and power after the defeat and misery following World War I. The film also anticipates what Gallone would do later with his analogy of Scipio Africanus and Mussolini. This film is *Die Hermannsschlacht* ("Hermann's Battle"; 1922–1923 or 1924), directed by Leo König.[15] Its subject is the battle in the Teutoburg Forest in 9 A.D., in which Arminius the Cheruscan—Hermann is his German name—defeated and destroyed three entire Roman legions, three cavalry squadrons, and six auxiliary cohorts. Quinctilius Varus, the Roman commander, committed suicide; no one in the Roman army survived.[16] According to the Roman tradition this was the second worst defeat the Romans ever suffered after the one Hannibal had inflicted on them at Cannae more than two centuries earlier. According to German tradition Arminius had liberated Germany from Roman rule. Since his victory had depended on an alliance of several German tribes, popular historical tradition also made him the first leader to achieve a unified Germany. The foreign occupation of the Ruhrgebiet after World War I was seen as the modern equivalent of the Roman occupation of German territories east of the Rhine. Just as Hermann got rid of foreign overlords in the first century, so Hitler was to do in the twentieth, some years after the release of this film. Hermann is a German leader and liberator. After the premiere of König's film the audience is said to have sung the *Deutschlandlied* ("Deutschland, Deutschland über alles ... ") with great enthusiasm.

Of central importance for the iconography of the raised-arm salute in both political ideology and popular culture during the second third of the twentieth century are two artistic documentary films designed and directed by Leni Riefenstahl. These are *Triumph des Willens* (1935; *Triumph of the Will*) and *Olympia* or *Olympische Spiele* (1938), a two-part epic filmed during the 1936 Olympic Games in Berlin. The former celebrates the 1934 Nazi party rally at Nuremberg; its title, the rally's official motto, was chosen by Hitler himself.[17] This may well be the most controversial

---

with the Capitoline geese at 188–89. In a much earlier speech (April 3, 1921) Mussolini had rejected the thought that in their marches the Fascists were copying the Germans who, after all, had only been copying the Romans. The text is in Mussolini 1951–1981, vol. 16, 239–46, at 244. Ironically, the German term for the goose step (*Stechschritt*, i.e., "stabbing step") has nothing to do with animals.

15. Some of my information here comes from Lindner 1999, 527–28 note 26.

16. The principal ancient sources about this defeat are Tacitus, *Annals* 1.60–62, and Cassius Dio, *Roman History* 56.18–22. The site of the battle was discovered some years ago at Kalkriese near the city of Osnabrück.

17. Leiser 1974, 135 and 137. The well-known essay by Susan Sontag, "Fascinating Fascism,"

film ever made. It shows numerous examples of the raised-arm salute on the part of Hitler, high-ranking party officials, and the masses, both party affiliates and the German people in general. The film went on to be shown on a regular basis in German theaters until the end of the Nazi regime, often in truncated versions.[18]

The first spectacular sequence of *Olympia* shows the opening ceremony of the Olympic Games on August 1, 1936. The national teams enter the Olympic stadium and greet Hitler, their host country's head of state, as they file past his reviewing stand. We see a number of teams do so with the raised-arm salute, but it is not always clear to a viewer whether they mean this to be the political salute—German or Fascist—or the Olympic salute. The latter, in which the raised arm is extended either to the front or to the side, had become familiar with the 1924 Olympics held in Paris.[19] French athlete Georges André had delivered the Olympic oath with his right arm raised in a manner indistinguishable from the Fascist or Nazi salute; the poster for that year's games and French stamps

---

in Sontag 2002, 71–105, is a good introduction to the continuing popular appeal of Fascism and Nazism and to Riefenstahl's career and reputation.

18. It exists in various editions, most of them cut from its original running time of 110 minutes. The best version currently available is a "special edition" on DVD of the complete film, published in 2000 with a historian's audio commentary. The DVD also contains an incomplete version of Riefenstahl's 1935 film *Tag der Freiheit: Unsere Wehrmacht* ("Day of Freedom: Our Armed Forces") on that year's party rally. Her film of the 1933 rally, *Sieg des Glaubens* ("Victory of Faith"; "faith" in a quasi-religious sense), long believed lost, survives in one print that is now in the Filmmuseum der Stadt München (Municipal Film Museum, Munich). *Leni Riefenstahl: Die Macht der Bilder*, a three-hour 1993 German-French documentary directed by Ray Müller, is available in English as *The Wonderful Horrible Life of Leni Riefenstahl*. It includes detailed information about the making of *Triumph of the Will*, Riefenstahl's cinematic artistry, and her comments on Hitler and Nazism. Critical studies of Riefenstahl and of her association with National Socialism have proliferated in recent years, especially in Germany; the following are the most informative or important ones: Loiperdinger 1987, the most detailed study of the film; Barsam 1975, on which, however, see the footnote at Sontag 2002, 82; Infield 1976, 3–11 and 73–112; Taylor 1998, 162–74 and 235 (notes; chapter on *Triumph des Willens*); Hinton 2000, 19–46; Kinkel 2002, 45–61 and 319–22 (notes) on *Sieg des Glaubens*, 62–88 and 322–25 (notes) on *Triumph des Willens*, and 89–95 and 326–27 (notes) on *Tag der Freiheit*; Giesen 2003, 18–34 and 268–69 (notes), 220 on *Sieg des Glaubens*, 223 on *Tag der Freiheit*, and 224–25 and 255–56 on *Triumph des Willens*; Trimborn 2007, 105–30 and 298–301 (notes) on *Triumph des Willens* and *Tag der Freiheit* and 278–80 on Müller's documentary; Bach 2007, 115–22 and 322–24 (notes) on *Sieg des Glaubens*, 123–40 and 324–27 (notes) on *Triumph des Willens*, and 287–90 on Müller's film. Cf. also Rother 2002, 45–76 and 190–200 (notes) on *Sieg des Glaubens, Triumph des Willens,* and *Tag der Freiheit*. Cf. further Martin Loiperdinger, "'Sieg des Glaubens'—Ein gelungenes Experiment nationalsozialistischer Filmpropaganda," in Herrmann and Nassen 1994, 35–48, with additional references. Riefenstahl describes *Triumph of the Will* in Riefenstahl 1995, 156–66 and 208–9. Older but still useful work on German cinema includes Kracauer 1947 and Leiser 1974. Leiser, 134–42, provides documents on Riefenstahl's films.

19. On this salute see Alkemeyer 1996, 395–96.

commemorating the games display it as well.[20] But the raised-arm gesture had already been adopted at the opening of the 1920 games in Antwerp, when the ceremony of the Olympic oath had been introduced.[21] A stylized variant could be seen again during ceremonies at the 2004 games in Athens, when classicizing "statues" of nude athletes raised their *left* arms, with a slight bend at their elbows, presumably to avoid exact political parallels.[22] A photo of the moment in which one athlete, as representative of all, delivers the Olympic oath from an elevated platform during the opening of the Paris games is revealing: he is holding his right arm up and out in exactly the manner soon to become familiar from political contexts.[23] But a clear distinction between the Olympic and the Fascist or Nazi salute seems to be impossible.[24] A larger-than-life bronze sculpture of a nude male athlete that was commissioned for the Amsterdam Olympic stadium in 1928 gives the Olympic salute but extends his arm to the front.[25] (Figure 23) Publicity for Nicola Fausto Neroni's film *Maratona* ("Marathon," 1929), a contemporary drama, showed a stylized figure of

---

20. Kluge 1997, 483, reproduces this poster. The photo archives at the International Olympic Committee's Internet site (www.olympic.org) show the poster, stamps, and the moment of the Olympic oath being taken. A cinematic recreation of the 1924 games, replete with their poster, appears in Hugh Hudson's film *Chariots of Fire* (1981).

21. Large 2007, 125, states that the Olympic salute was introduced in 1924 and describes the gesture slightly incorrectly ("right arm forward and horizontal from the body"). On the introduction of the Olympic oath see, e.g., Callebat 1988, 198–99 (with reference to ancient athletes' oaths), and Eyquem 1966, 229–30. On the connections between the early modern Olympic Games and the spectacle tradition see MacAloon 1981, 128–38 (section entitled "True Tests and Living Pictures: The Exposition Tradition"). The Olympics of 1900, 1904, and 1908 were "amalgamated to world's fairs" (MacAloon, 138); their founder, Pierre de Coubertin, had visited the Chicago World's Fair in 1893 (MacAloon, 164–65).

22. At least in its early days the Fascist salute could be given with the left arm, too. Heller 2008, 84 (ill. B2) provides an example from 1923.

23. The photograph may be seen in Eyquem 1966, facing page 208. Its caption reads: *Géo André prête le Serment olympique aux Jeux de Paris.*

24. Cf. Large 2007, 250, on the confusion of the Nazi salute and the Olympic salute during the opening ceremony at the 1936 Winter Games. That the gesture may appear in the most unlikely places is shown by the 1922 painting "Colossus of Rhodes (City)" by Czech artist Frantisek (or Frank) Kupka, now in the National Gallery, Prague, which shows the gigantic statue of Helios (cf. chapter 1) facing away from the viewer and giving the salute with his raised right arm. Since neither any trace nor any conclusive description of this famous statue has survived, all reconstructions, of which there have been many since the Renaissance, are more or less fanciful. Kupka's painting, perhaps the most anachronistic of all modern imaginations of the statue's appearance, is reproduced in a small black-and-white image in Vachtová 1968, 298 (catalogue no. 42), and in a cropped full-page color image in Romer and Romer 2000, plate 7 (erroneously attributed to "M. Kupka").

25. Cf., on the IOC's website, the photographs from the 1928 games with Olympic salutes being given by athletes on a train and of an onlooker who, gazing straight into the camera, seizes the moment of having his picture taken with the winner of the marathon race.

Figure 23. Statue of athlete in front of the Amsterdam Olympic stadium, 1928. Author's collection.

an athlete, running and giving the Olympic salute, that is based on the bronze statue of Mercury by Giovanni Bologna (Giambologna) of 1576. The Olympic salute was on prominent display again at the 1932 games held in Los Angeles, when, for instance, American athlete George Charles Calnan took the Olympic oath in this fashion.[26] The Italians naturally brought the Fascist salute to the games.[27] In a 1936 photograph taken at the ancient site of Olympia, athletes swearing the Olympic oath are extending their right arms before their bodies at a horizontal or nearly horizontal angle; their gesture is reminiscent of the oath of the Horatii in David's painting. In another photograph from the same year, presumably taken in Hungary during the journey of the Olympic torch from Olympia to Berlin, five young men are saluting the Olympic flame with right arms raised in a manner almost indistinguishable from the Fascist or Nazi salute.[28] The relay race of the Olympic torch from Greece was introduced in 1936 and appears in the prologue of Riefenstahl's film.[29]

---

26. The IOC website shows a photograph of this moment as well as another one with three victorious Japanese athletes giving the Olympic salute, if in a more relaxed manner.

27. So Bosworth 2006, 229.

28. The latter two photographs described are in Kuron 1936, a commemorative picture book on the journey of the Olympic torch from Greece to Germany, with captions in German, English, French, Spanish, and modern Greek. Only the introductory text is paginated. The English captions of the photographs in question are "Saluting the Fire" and "The Olympic Oath before the start."

29. The official report, published in 1937, of the games by the organizational committee—*XI. Olympiade Berlin 1936: Amtlicher Bericht,* 2 vols. in continuous pagination—provides a

Olympia shows numerous scenes of Hitler, German spectators and officials, and several victorious German and Italian athletes giving the raised-arm salute.[30] But the opening ceremony displays the most arresting sights of raised-arm salutes in Riefenstahl's film, whether they are Olympic, political, or both. Noteworthy are the range and variety of the salutes, not only from the countries we expect (Italy, Germany, Austria), but also from several others. Among the teams prominently shown giving the raised-arm salute are those from Greece and France, both countries that would come to suffer heavily from German occupation in the course of World War II.[31] The comments by a modern historian on the opening ceremony are worth quoting:

> The march of the athletes in 1936 was complicated by an existing, though rarely used, "Olympic" salute which resembled the Nazi "Heil" except that the open hand, palm down, was held off to the side. In a few delegations the salute was plainly Olympic; among others the gesture was clearly a tribute to the new boss of Europe. The Austrians greeted Hitler in a Nazi fashion and moved the vast crowd to love and grateful applause. The small team of Bulgarians ... caused a sensation when they offered a smart Nazi salute and dipped their flag to trail its tip in the red cinders—all the while doing a snappy goose step. The Germans expressed their pleasure loudly, though this performance was, in fact, for the king of Bulgaria who was at the Tribune with Hitler. Then another generous, indeed almost fervent, ovation for the French team's 250 members.... Some Frenchmen later claimed that their salute was Olympic, but it looked like obeisance to Hitler, as with arms raised they passed the dais upon which the beaming recipient was placed....

---

detailed description of all aspects of the games, with numerous photographs. An account of the relay race, with several instructive photos of raised-arm salutes, may be found in vol. 1, 512–37. It is impossible to tell if the salutes are meant as political or Olympic gestures; most probably, they are a combination of both. The photograph at vol. 1, 483, shows several members of the International Olympic Committee, civilian spectators, and one person in Nazi uniform giving the raised-arm salute in virtually identical form.

30. Such moments in Riefenstahl's film may be supplemented by photographs of victorious athletes saluting their national flags in *XI. Olympiade Berlin 1936,* vol. 1, 629 (a Canadian), and vol. 2, 665 and 945 (a Hungarian and three U.S. athletes, respectively, giving the raised-arm salute but with palms held vertically.)

31. Alkemeyer 1996, 396, describes the historical background (French-German relations after the German occupation of the demilitarized Rhineland earlier in 1936, French opposition to Berlin as site for the games) and contemporary connotations of the French team's salute. On Riefenstahl's film see especially Downing 1992; Graham 2001; Rother 2002, 77–90 and 200–203 (notes); Kinkel 2002, 107–72 and 328–35 (notes); Trimborn 2007, 131–52 and 301–3 (notes); Bach 2007, 123–63 and 327–32 (notes); and Large 2007, 295–315 and 373–75 (notes).

The Italian Fascists, grinning, ebullient, and giving the salute which they originated, got a warm reception. . . . Somehow the few Turks who emerged from the tunnel maintained the saluting position all around the track. The crowd was appreciative.

The last team to enter was Germany's: "Almost the entire stadium rose instantly to freeze into the 'Heil Hitler' position and to stay that way."[32]

Similar scenes had occurred at the opening ceremonies of the Olympic Winter Games held in Garmisch-Partenkirchen earlier that year: "The Italians . . . rais[ed] their right arms to Hitler in a brotherly fascist salute," but

> most of the other national team members opted for the "Olympic greeting." . . . Needless to say, this saluting business was the source of some confusion, for it certainly *looked* as if the athletes of the world were honoring the German Führer with a Nazi salute. Many in the crowd of sixty thousand interpreted the gestures in this fashion, which is why they screamed in delight when the French athletes held out their right arms on passing the reviewing stand.
>
> The only foreign team receiving a louder ovation than the French squad was the large Austrian contingent, whose raised-arm salute was gleefully interpreted as a sign that the Austrians were anxious to "come home to the Reich." (The head of the Austrian delegation insisted later that the gesture in question had been the Olympic greeting.) Some German spectators claimed to have heard members of the Austrian team

---

32. Both quotations are from Mandell 1987, 148–49 and 150. Cf. also Hart-Davis 1986, 156–57, and Large 2007, 194–95. A detailed report of the opening ceremony, with numerous photographs of salutes, is at *XI. Olympiade Berlin 1936*, vol. 1, 544–76. Noteworthy photos of the teams are at 548 (Greece, Afghanistan), 550 (Bulgaria), 551 (Colombia, Estonia), 552 (France), 553 (Italy), 554 (Canada; arms held far to the side), 556 (Monaco, Austria, Peru; the last of these with arms held sideways only), 559 (Hungary; male athletes with their arms sideways but holding their hats in their hands), and 560 (Germany). A photo on the next page (561) shows the German spectators greeting the teams entering with their own raised-arm salute. On Riefenstahl's rearrangement of parts of the opening ceremony for greater visual and emotional impact in her film and on the French team's salute and its political background see especially Loiperdinger 1988, 44. During the opening session of the International Olympic Committee in Berlin on July 29 a Nazi functionary had even invented the short-lived greeting "Heil Olympia!" Höfer 1994, 163 and note 502, provides textual quotation and source reference. On the cultural and political background of the 1936 Olympic ceremonies see Henning Eichberg, "Thing-, Fest- und Weihespiele in Nationalsozialismus, Arbeiterkultur und Olympismus: Zur Geschichte des politischen Verhaltens in der Epoche des Faschismus," in Eichberg, Dultz, Gadberry, and Rühle 1977, 19–180, at 143–53 (section entitled "Weihespiele und olympisches Zeremoniell") and 178–79 (notes).

yell "*Heil Hitler!*," although Austrian officials vehemently denied this as well.[33]

The only film produced in Nazi Germany that is set entirely in classical antiquity is the 1935 musical comedy *Amphitryon (Aus den Wolken kommt das Glück)*. This film is a witty and irreverent updating of *Amphitryo*, a comedy by the Roman playwright Plautus. In the tradition of both cinematic depictions of antiquity and Fascist and Nazi iconography this film shows Albert Speer-inspired architecture and a crowd comparable to those in *Triumph of the Will*.[34] But its director, Reinhold Schünzel, was partly Jewish. He succeeded in undercutting all the surface enthusiasm for the Nazis that audiences would have expected by now, especially in mass scenes.[35] Two hundred members of the *Leibstandarte Adolf Hitler*, the personal guard of the Führer, played Theban soldiers in the film. When an overweight big shot is being carried through the crowd, it seems obvious that any resemblance of this character to Hermann Göring is purely intentional. More importantly, not a single raised-arm salute occurs in the entire film. Instead, crowds raise both their arms at moments of acclamation. Such scenes do not imitate contemporary practice or political ideology. Schünzel had some problems with censorship over this film, but the following year his film *Land der Liebe* made work in Germany impossible for him.[36] He left the country in 1937 and went to Hollywood. Ironically, there he sometimes played Nazis, as did other expatriate Germans.

A curio of Nazi cinema is *Ewiger Wald* (1936; *Enchanted Forest;* literally, "Eternal Forest"), directed by Hans Springer.[37] It appears to have

---

33. Both quotations are from Large 2007, 125–26. Austria's "return" to the Reich occurred with the *Anschluß* in March 1938.

34. On this film see Cadars and Courtade 1972, 262–63; De España 1998, 418–21; Witte 1995, 88–93; and especially Kreimeier 1996, 231–33. Kreimeier, 233, points to visual connections of Schünzel's film to *Triumph of the Will* and juxtaposes stills from both (ills. 7–8, between pages 280 and 281). Cf. also Witte, 93.

35. Witte 1995, 88, speaks of Schünzel's dismantling of power in this film. *"Beim nächsten Kuß knall ich ihn nieder!,"* a 1995 semi-documentary biography of Schünzel directed by Hans-Christoph Blumenberg, shows how Schünzel managed to get his satire of Nazi pomp and rhetoric past the censors. The title of this film is a quotation of a line of dialogue from Schünzel's next film, *Land der Liebe* ("Land of Love").

36. On Schünzel's relation to the Nazis and in particular to Josef Goebbels, who had provided Schünzel with a kind of patronage but then turned against him, and on the reasons for and circumstances of Schünzel's self-inflicted exile see Jörg Schöning, "Zur Biographie," in Schöning 1989, 50–63, at 58–62; and Helmut G. Asper, "Reinhold Schünzel: im Exil," in Schöning 1989, 64–79, especially 64–69. Schöning, 59, gives samples of dialogue that had to be cut from the screenplay of *Amphitryon*.

37. Some sources also name Rolf von Sonjewski-Jamrowski and Wilhelm Georg Siehm as co-directors. On the film cf. Lindner 1999, 527–28 note 26; Cadars and Courtade 1972, 56–58

been intended as a kind of artistic "documentary" with obvious ideological purposes and was marketed as a "symphonic film poem" (*Symphonische Filmdichtung*) and a "hymn to the unity of people and forest" (*Hohelied auf die Einheit von Volk und Wald*). This side of the film is reflected in its alternate title *Ewiger Wald–Ewiges Volk* ("Eternal Forest—Eternal People"). The infamous Nazi ideology of *Blut und Boden* ("blood and soil") finds a pure expression in this remarkable film, although it is couched in historical storytelling. The second of its eight episodes, which extend from pastoral prehistory to the Nazi era, shows the Romans' expedition, already mentioned, into Germany in A.D. 9. Even nature rebels at the Romans' intrusion onto sacred German soil, for a number of gigantic trees in the forest primeval come crashing down on the Roman troops. Audiences could learn from such thrilling action scenes that Providence, a major if rather nebulous pseudoreligious concept in Nazism, had destined Germany for National Socialism and its attendant greatness all along. An off-screen narrator intones the following lines as accompaniment to the screen images:

> Ihr Zeichen der Fremde, Standarten der Römer,
> was sucht ihr im Lande, was sucht ihr im Wald?
> Wer fremd deinem Boden, Wald, fremd deiner Art,
> dem bleibt nicht erspart
> unsagbares Leid.
>
> Legionary standards of Rome, you foreign emblems,
> what is your business in this land, in this forest?
> Those foreign to thy soil, forest, foreign to thy kind
> will not be spared
> inexpressible suffering.

These vaguely poetical lines were hardly necessary to convey the film's ideological message. Ironically, Goebbels and Hitler are said to have disliked the film. The raised-arm salute is absent from this episode of *Ewiger Wald* chiefly because the Romans are the enemy of the very people whose descendants will later adopt this gesture.

In the wake of, first, the entire iconographic tradition of silent films about antiquity, in particular the immense impact *Cabiria* had on historical

---

(with plot outline); Ulrich Linse, "Der Film 'Ewiger Wald'—oder: Die Überwindung der Zeit durch den Raum: Eine filmische Umsetzung von Rosenbergs 'Mythus des 20. Jahrhunderts,'" in Herrmann and Nassen 1994, 57–75; and Giesen 2003, 35–37 (a description with quotations) and 192 (filmographic information).

epics, and, secondly, of the renewed interest in the Roman Empire on the part of Fascist Italy and, to a smaller degree, Nazi Germany, the raised-arm salute had become a regular part of Roman iconography in Hollywood films, too.[38] Notable examples are Fred Niblo's version of *Ben-Hur* (1925) and Cecil B. DeMille's *The King of Kings* (1927), a reverent epic about Jesus Christ. In Niblo's *Ben-Hur* comparatively few raised-arm salutes appear, usually without political significance. After the sea battle Arrius publicly announces that Ben-Hur has saved his life and is now his adopted son; he raises his arm in a loose gesture, and so do others in reply. Here and in a later scene among the evil Roman Messala and his friends, the salute is not yet formalized. In *The King of Kings* the first raised-arm salute, if with the fingers of the right hand held apart, occurs when Caiaphas, arrived to denounce Jesus to the Romans, greets Pontius Pilate: "Hail, Roman!" Pilate's reply ("Hail, priest!") is highly condescending in order to convey to viewers the power of the empire he represents. Sitting on a throne-like seat before an immense eagle statue, Pilate only languidly raises his right arm at the elbow from his chair's arm rest. Later salutes on the part of Roman soldiers are much more what we expect, although elbows can still remain somewhat bent. Even in his two sound films set in classical antiquity, *The Sign of the Cross* (1932) and *Cleopatra* (1934), DeMille does not thoroughly fix the execution of the gesture.

A little-known short film of the same year corroborates this view. In Roy Mack's *Good Morning, Eve!,* an unsubtle but effective musical comedy that revels in its ravishing color photography, mankind's first couple travels down an abbreviated timeline of history from Paradise to modern America. En route they stop by antiquity. Their first encounter is with Mercury, a kind of divine postman who leaps about and keeps raising his right arm. Next comes Nero and his court: "Rome 100 AD," we are informed; historical accuracy is not the issue in such comedies. The raised-arm salute duly appears, as when Nero so greets—you guessed it—Adam and Eve. No political statement is intended, not least because most of the comedy derives from the fact that Romans and other

---

38. And occasionally elsewhere. A generally unknown instance occurs in Erich von Stroheim's *The Merry Widow* (1925), a remarkable (because primarily tragic) adaptation of the famous operetta. At one moment the leering villain, crown prince of the Balkan kingdom of Monteblanco, ironically greets his cousin and amatory rival, the film's romantic hero, with a raised-arm salute but keeps his elbow bent. The gesture must have appeared rather out of place among the Austro-Hungarian uniforms and operetta-land costumes and settings, as must have been the case with the classical Greek motto on the royal coat of arms among all the other signs, notices, etc. in Cyrillic letters.

historical figures are only thinly disguised Americans. But if you present ancient Romans, you had better include "their" salute.

The following year, however, Ernest B. Schoedsack took specific recourse to Fascist Italy and its Roman trimmings for *The Last Days of Pompeii*. An educational guide accompanied the release of this film and asked the following questions: "What form of salute was used by the Romans? In what countries are similar salutes now demanded by the government?"[39] Throughout this film the raised-arm salute occurs in private and public settings. In military contexts it is an analogy to the modern salute in which the right hand touches the helmet or cap. When a soldier acknowledges receiving a command from Pontius Pilate or an officer acknowledges the command of the prefect of Pompeii to open the games, they respond with the raised-arm gesture. In a French film made the same year, Julien Duvivier's *Golgotha* (sometimes called *Ecce Homo* or *Behold the Man*), Pilate repeatedly addresses the Jerusalem masses during the trial of Jesus with the raised-arm salute, attempting to calm them down. And a large statue of a male nude stretches out its right arm horizontally to the front, an example in which the same gesture lacks any particular context. Presumably this statue owes its existence to a conflation of Roman statuary of orators and the cinema's own use of raised-arm salutes.

Not long before Niblo's *Ben-Hur,* DeMille had made the first of two film versions of a story that was to come to be intimately associated with him: *The Ten Commandments*. The earlier version appeared in 1923, the later, DeMille's last and most colossal film, in 1956. The silent film contains an especially noteworthy example of the right-arm gesture because with it one of the Hebrews reproves Aaron, who is engaged in making the Golden Calf. The moment again shows that the raised right arm is an almost unavoidable ingredient in films with ancient settings.

One of DeMille's lesser-known films is *Manslaughter* (1922), a contemporary melodrama whose rather preachy attitude toward modern manners and morals does not make it appealing today. But the film is quintessential DeMille, demonstrating to good effect his hallmark of titillating his audiences and simultaneously moralizing to them. The film's story shows the recklessness of the Jazz Age with champagne parties, high-society flappers, fast cars, and the inevitable fall from morality. Twice DeMille interrupts this modern story with flashbacks to the Roman Empire in the throes of, first, orgiastic decadence—we observe an imperial Bacchanal that now looks embarrassingly tame—and, second, the

---

39. Quotation from Wyke 1997, 178. She also discusses analogies to monumental Fascist art in the film and believes that the destruction of Pompeii in this film exorcizes the American fear of Fascism.

Figure 24. *Cleopatra* (1934). Cleopatra saluting Caesar. Paramount/Universal.

price to be paid for this. Barbaric-looking German invaders encounter no resistance when they enter the Roman palace in which worn-out orgiasts are sleeping off their debauch and have to suffer the fate history has held in store for them all along. The leader of the Germanic horde gives a raised-arm salute to his men. The Romans in the film never once use this gesture. Perhaps they are too enervated.

DeMille's Roman films are instructive for their variations of the raised-arm salute and for other forms of greeting that occur where we might expect the "Roman" one. At the beginning of *The Sign of the Cross* Praetorian Prefect Tigellinus greets Emperor Nero with a completely different gesture; at Tigellinus' headquarters fictional Marcus Superbus, Prefect of Rome and the film's hero, is received with quite a variety of raised-arm salutes. Once Nero even greets Tigellinus with a raised-arm salute although his henchman had *not* greeted him that way. Gladiators in the arena salute Nero by raising and stretching out their right arms holding weapons. This manner of greeting, examined in chapter 1, recurs regularly in arena sequences. Several examples in DeMille's *Cleopatra* conform to the same loose usage. In Alexandria Cleopatra, fresh out of her carpet and without missing a beat, greets Julius Caesar with the raised-arm salute upon their first encounter. (Figure 24) They take their last farewell in Rome on the fateful Ides of March the same way, prematurely hailing each other as "Emperor!" and "Empress!" Then, ascending the steps to the senate hall, Caesar, being hailed by an arm-waving crowd, turns around and gives them a raised-arm salute. More important is the scene already referred to in chapter 4: a servant or slave arrives and kneels before Caesar, his right arm stretched out horizontally. The same gesture and posture recurs in DeMille's second version of *The Ten Commandments* as a salute to the queen of Egypt. The fist-on-heart salute appears in this film as well. So DeMille does not closely distinguish between or among ancient peoples in the ways he shows them saluting. One year after *Cleopatra*, for instance, the gesture and posture of Caesar's servant finds an almost identical analogy in DeMille's *The Crusades* when a servant kneels before Sultan Saladin to bring him the news about the advancing crusaders. Earlier, Saladin had addressed the assembled Christian kings. The herald who has just announced him gets down on one knee and bends his upper body forward and down. At the same time—he is screen left, facing to the right—he extends his right arm, open palm down, but holds this arm pointing toward the ground in deference. Except for this angle, his arm gesture is identical to the familiar raised-arm salute.

DeMille's *Cleopatra* is, however, even more instructive about cinematic salutes than the moments from it that have been mentioned so far. It contains a scene that shows the clearest proof that the creative artist must invent something dramatic when historical evidence is lacking. The scene in question is an important moment that foreshadows the fall and suicide of Mark Antony. It involves Antony's most loyal follower, Domitius Enobarbus—to give his name Shakespeare's spelling, since DeMille's screenwriters took this incident from the bard.[40] Enobarbus deserts Antony and goes over to the winning side of Octavius Caesar. In Shakespeare's *Antony and Cleopatra* his desertion takes place off-stage and is reported to Antony by a messenger. This news affects Antony deeply and calls forth his nobility of character: he sends Enobarbus' "treasure" together with "gentle adieus and greetings" after him. This in turn makes Enobarbus realize the ignoble nature of his act, and in due course he dies, most likely of remorse.[41]

By contrast, DeMille puts the moment of Enobarbus' desertion on the screen. To emphasize to his viewers its fateful nature, DeMille has

---

40. On Shakespeare's conflation of two separate historical figures (mentioned in Plutarch, his source) into his Enobarbus see the comment in Shakespeare 1995, 87.

41. The quotations appear in *Antony and Cleopatra* 4.5.12 and 14. Enobarbus is overwrought ("I am alone the villain of the earth.... This blows my heart"; 4.6.31 and 35) and appears to die in Act IV, Scene 9, although cf. the editor's note to 4.9.26 in Shakespeare 1995, 246. DeMille's Enobarbus does nothing of the sort. He can be seen in the company of the Romans who come upon Cleopatra's dead body in her palace in the film's final moments.

Enobarbus, armed and wearing full military regalia, chide Antony for not abandoning Cleopatra and reclaiming his power in Rome. But, Enobarbus adds, "for what you might have been I give you my last salute." Without any more words he draws his sword with his right hand, blade upright, and moves it first to the left and next to the right side of his chest. Then he leaves.

This scene looks impressive but has no basis in fact. It is pure invention, as a moment's thought will reveal. Enobarbus' gesture is far too clumsy to have been a military salute; it is also rather dangerous to the tip of the saluter's nose. But it is intended to replace what viewers would expect in a modern drama although it would be an anachronism here: a military officer's formal hand-to-cap salute. The modern mindset underlying this scene is evident from the fact that Enobarbus wears on his chest insignia commemorating his campaigns with Antony and their heroic deeds together—another invention, the equivalent of modern medals. The scene in the film is unhistorical, but it plays memorably. And that is the only point that matters.

Confirmation for such a view will occur a quarter century later in the most famous of all Roman films. During the triumph sequence of William Wyler's *Ben-Hur* (1959) Consul Quintus Arrius, resplendent in full military regalia, approaches Emperor Tiberius striding up a huge flight of steps, his left hand on the hilt of his sword. (In this, the grandest version of the story, Arrius is no longer a mere tribune.) Before Tiberius, he gives the raised-arm salute. A few moments later and in closer proximity to the emperor, who is now addressing him, Arrius snaps to attention, even audibly clicking his heels. When Tiberius awards him a "baton of victory," Arrius again stands at attention, again clicks his heels, and dramatically puts his hand on his sword's hilt at the same time. All this military ceremony looks most impressive and effortlessly draws the audience, which recognizes Arrius' "body language," into the proceedings. But all of it is invented.[42]

We can easily understand why if we contrast a verbal exchange given in yet another film. William Castle's *Serpent of the Nile: The Loves of Cleopatra* (1953) begins with the assassination of Julius Caesar by Marcus Brutus and his fellow-conspirators and the battle of Philippi before it turns to the story of Antony and Cleopatra. At Philippi a Roman captain in Brutus' army is looking for his commander. He asks the guard outside Brutus' tent "Is the general here?" and receives the answer "Yes, sir." This verbal

---

42. The baton, however, is an exception; it corresponds to the Roman *scipio eburneus,* an ivory staff with an eagle on top that was carried by triumphators.

exchange reproduces twentieth-century military language verbatim and for this reason is far more jarring than many of the visual anachronisms in this and other historical films. If Wyler had had his Arrius respond to Tiberius' award of the baton with similar language—e.g., with "Thank you, your majesty!" or with a simple "Yes, sir!"—he would only have undermined his grand moment. To express a modern idea, in this case a military salute, in invented visual terms that make it appear ancient is the best cinematic procedure, even if it is unhistorical.

Now back to the era of Fascism and Nazism. How far the Roman salute had become a standard symbol in 1930s films to denote imperial power or tyranny in any exotic setting becomes evident in an unlikely context. In 1936 Frederick Stephani and Ray Taylor co-directed the thirteen-part science-fiction serial *Flash Gordon,* one of the best-known campy films of all time. It was made on Hollywood's Poverty Row, but with gleeful abandon and a disarming disregard of its own artificiality. Its eponymous hero battles the forces of evil in outer space, but some of these forces look suspiciously ancient, at least in some ways. An example is King Vultan, a winged human dressed in vaguely Roman armor. His minions carry not only futuristic beam shooters but also antiquated spears. The raised-arm salute is their sign of acknowledging their sovereign's power. Past (ancient Rome), present (e.g., contemporary art deco sets and dialogue), and future (science fiction) all converge.

That same year images of the Olympic Games and of Italian and German political rituals, all including the salute, appeared frequently in photographs in American magazines and newspapers and in the newsreels shown in film theaters. Then, during World War II, scenes of German, Italian, and Japanese mass rallies reappeared on American screens in some of the seven parts of *Why We Fight,* a series of propaganda films that Hollywood produced in 1942 and 1943 in cooperation with the Office of War Information's Department of Motion Pictures. Director Frank Capra was the general supervisor of these films, each roughly an hour long and consisting largely of enemy footage. They were required viewing for all American soldiers, intended to enhance their historical and political education and their fighting morale.[43] Part One of the series, *Prelude to War* (1942), and Part Three, *Divide and Conquer* (1943), focused on the rise of Fascist Italy and Nazi Germany and prominently contained footage from

---

43. On the production history of the series see Capra 1997, 359–95. His book is notoriously unreliable, and his account should be supplemented by David Culbert, "'Why We Fight': Social Engineering for a Democratic Society at War," in Short 1983, 173–91, and McBride 2000, 455–82. On the inclusion of nondocumentary footage in the *Why We Fight* films see McBride, 479–82. Capra, 362–68, refers to Riefenstahl's *Triumph of the Will* as inspiration for his approach to the *Why We Fight* series, but see McBride, 466–67.

Triumph of the Will. Through these films in particular Americans became closely familiar with images of dictators addressing vast masses of people. The raised-arm salute played a major part in such scenes.

Parallels to modern history in the image of imperial Rome became most pronounced in Hollywood films made after World War II. During and after the time that the United States, now itself expanded into a world empire, had been fighting no less than three aggressive empires more or less simultaneously—Germany, Italy, and Japan—the major films set in the Roman Empire reflect an awareness of the ideology of the two twentieth-century Fascist empires that traced their roots directly back to the Romans. In this way the standard image of Rome's empire as a cesspool of vice, luxury, debauchery, bloodlust, and religious persecution becomes much more pointed. In particular the Roman Empire can now be identified with a specific modern one: Nazi Germany. Hollywood's first grand postwar Roman spectacle, MGM's *Quo Vadis* (1951), directed by Mervyn LeRoy, is the best example of all. To indicate in its very title how seriously the studio took its responsibilities for what it claimed to be historical authenticity, the question mark that had been part of the title of Henryk Sienkiewicz's novel and had been preserved in all earlier film adaptations was now dropped because Romans had not used it, either. Ironically, this epic extravaganza was filmed at Cinecittà, Mussolini's studios. After the defeat of Italy and Germany Hollywood could update the standard negative view of the Roman Empire by presenting it as a precursor of its fiercest recent enemy empire, replete with scenes of mass rallies, triumphal processions, and the Fascist salute. Fascist totalitarianism is, in fact, the very starting point of *Quo Vadis*. For this reason the film deserves a more detailed treatment here than other films have received or will receive, excepting *Cabiria*. *Quo Vadis* supplies us with the clearest evidence of the anachronistic modern view of the Romans as proto-Nazi imperialists. Several moments in the film are highly instructive for our understanding of how the filmmakers updated this oft-filmed tale by explicit visual and verbal references to recent history.[44]

The film opens with shots of the victorious Roman army returning from abroad, while an omniscient narrator describes to the audience the totalitarian system:

> Imperial Rome is the center of the empire, an undisputed master of the world. But with this power inevitably comes corruption. No man is sure of his life, the individual is at the mercy of the state, murder replaces justice. Rulers of conquered nations surrender their helpless subjects to

---

44. The following discussion of *Quo Vadis* is taken from that in Winkler 1998.

bondage. High and low alike become Roman slaves, Roman hostages. There is no escape from the whip and the sword.

Images of prisoners of war pulling wagons heaped with booty and either being whipped on by Roman soldiers or collapsing and being trampled into the dust accompany these words. The narrator then rises to a rhetorical height of condemnation ("this pyramid of power and corruption, of human misery and slavery") before identifying Nero as the "Antichrist" at the prologue's climax.

Religious and political conflicts are intended to illustrate the moral decline of Rome which foreshadows the eventual fall of its empire, an analogy to the recent fate of Nazi Germany. Throughout the film we can observe such analogies both visually and verbally. Its hero, the Roman commander Marcus Vinicius, will eventually renounce his immoral pagan ways and embrace Christianity, an obligatory process for a cinematic hero in this type of story. As long as he is an unregenerate pagan, however, his militarist language points directly to the Fascist rhetoric with which American audiences had become familiar during the war: "Just as long as there's money to pay the army, Rome will stand forever. That I'm sure of." And: "Conquest. . . . It's the only method of uniting and civilizing the world under one power—you have to spill a little blood to do it." Nothing like these words, a clear reminiscence of the Nazis' *Blut und Boden* ideology, appears in Sienkiewicz's novel. After World War II Hollywood presented the "civilizing" mission of Rome as that of a master race imposing its rule and ideology on other nations by force of arms. "A man must be a soldier," Vinicius will say later.

The first grand epic sequence in *Quo Vadis* shows Vinicius' triumphal procession through the Roman Forum before Nero and his court. It contains obvious analogies to Fascism. The novel had contained no scene of triumph. Its hero was not a commander but a military tribune and, as such, neither a victorious conqueror nor eligible to hold a triumph. After the fall of the Roman republic only an emperor, or an emperor together with an associate as in the case of Vespasian and Titus in A.D. 71, could celebrate a triumph, even if he had not been in the field himself. This is because the emperor was commander-in-chief of the legions, and he alone held the power and authority of office, the highest *imperium,* which was a prerequisite of the *triumphator,* the man to be honored.[45] A cinematic triumph such as the one in *Quo Vadis* is therefore an inaccurate

---

45. See Livy, *From the Foundation of the City* 28.38.4; Valerius Maximus, *Memorabilia* 2.8.5. On Roman triumphs see now Beard 2007.

rendering of Roman practice.[46] But it is an accurate rendition of the spirit of Fascism as it manifested itself in mass assemblies and parades.

The long and spectacular sequence is closely modeled on Nazi rallies, replete with martial fanfares, Nazi-like architecture resembling that on view in *Triumph of the Will,* and the closest imitation of the Nazi salute ever put into a film set in the distant past. The victorious legionary commander gives his emperor the snappiest raised-arm salute of any film set in antiquity. (Figure 25) He is rewarded by Nero with a version of the salute that is patterned on Hitler's own way of greeting: more relaxed, as becomes the man in ultimate power, and with his arm first straight (Figure 26) and then slightly bent. There is a noticeable discontinuity in the editing between the straight-arm salute and the *Führergruß* variant, as if LeRoy wanted to emphasize the Nazi analogy by combining two different takes of the moment. As Hitler did on occasion, this Nero also looks bored. The influence on *Quo Vadis* of Riefenstahl's films and of other documentary footage from Germany makes for a particularly effective portrayal of the Roman Empire as a precursor of the Third Reich and turns Nero into a close analogy of Hitler. *Quo Vadis* thus gives its viewers the most explicit presentation of the Roman Empire as a Fascist military state and contains the most important examples of the Roman salute. No wonder the American Falangist Party was still enamored of the film decades later.

The huge mass of people present on the screen during the triumphal sequence of *Quo Vadis* is meant to evoke viewers' memories of newsreel and documentary footage of Fascist assemblies and parades. It is instructive to juxtapose scenes from *Triumph of the Will* and *Quo Vadis.* As Italian and German film documentaries, newspapers, and magazines had done regularly, both these films prominently feature the appearance of dictators at a window or balcony above the crowd.[47] If the triumphal rally as depicted in *Quo Vadis* is a historical impossibility, it is also an architectural one. The Forum Romanum at the time of Nero was far too much built up and too small to accommodate the immense mass of people seen in a panoramic shot on the screen through an obvious special effect, nor did the city possess any other suitable space in the vicinity of the imperial

---

46. Bertelli 1995, 61–62, describes Fascist analogies in several cinematic triumph sequences and dismisses all of them as lacking any foundation in history.

47. An especially telling photograph with Mussolini on a podium looking over a sea of people, *faux*-Roman legionary standards topped by eagles, and lictors, appears in Emilio Gentile 1996b, ill. 7. The photo, from October 1935, is a close visual analogy, albeit a static one, to corresponding moments in *Triumph of the Will.* Cf. also Gentile, ill. 10. Illustrations in this book, unnumbered, are between pages 52 and 53.

Figure 25. *Quo Vadis* (1951). Marcus Vinicius, holding his triumph, saluting Nero. Metro-Goldwyn-Mayer.

Figure 26. *Quo Vadis* (1951). Nero returning salute. Metro-Goldwyn-Mayer.

palaces which would have been large enough. But documentary footage of German, Italian, and Japanese mass rallies taken before or during World War II makes clear that Fascist assemblies are the inspiration for the triumph in *Quo Vadis*. A mass scene such as this visually represents the triumph of the Fascist will. In 1951 none of the adults in the audience could have overlooked the implications of Nero's repeated raised-arm salute to the people, to the troops, and to their commander, particularly since they follow closely on an appearance, a little earlier, of the *fasces* on either side of Nero's throne and of the sculpture of a huge eagle hovering above it.[48] On the cinema screen Roman eagles and Nazi eagles could equally appear as symbols of imperialist or dictatorial power. And after 1945 the standard exclamation "Hail Caesar!" in Hollywood's Roman films will have echoed the familiar German "Heil Hitler!" even in the linguistic similarity of both expressions.

But *Quo Vadis* refers its audience to Hitler's Germany in more than this one sequence. Not least the popular perception throughout history of Nero as Antichrist reinforces this.[49] To Americans the reincarnation of the Antichrist in the first half of the twentieth century was Hitler, their archenemy in World War II. The ubiquity of Nazis in American mass media on any level long after the war attests to the lasting American fascination with Nazi Germany as archetypally evil. Throughout the 1950s and 1960s Hollywood turned out large enough numbers of grand-scale World War II films alongside its Roman epics to satisfy any audience's demands for huge spectacles and hissable villains. Evil Romans and ice-cold Nazis are kindred cinematic spirits.

In *Quo Vadis* yet another parallel to Nazism may be found in the cult of the emperor. Throughout the film Nero is regarded as a son of Jupiter, addressed as "Divinity," and treated accordingly; moreover, he believes himself to be a god on earth as well. But this aspect of Neronian culture is unhistorical, too. Roman emperors, including Nero, did not as a rule consider themselves to be gods while they were alive and did not receive or encourage divine rites in their honor at Rome. (Exceptions were the bad emperors Caligula and Domitian.) But American soldiers learned in 1942 and 1943 from some of the *Why We Fight* films that divinities were back in earthly power. The narrator of *Prelude to War* informs his audience that "to the Japanese people the emperor is God. Taking advantage of their fanatical worship of the god-emperor, it was no great trick to take away what little freedom they had ever known." Later he summarizes the

---

48. On the Roman *fasces* as a major aspect of public spectacle see Marshall 1984.

49. On Nero as devil see Gwyn 1991, 430, 443, and 451–52. On Nero as Antichrist see Gwyn, 452–53; McGinn 2000, especially 45–54; Fuller 1995, 28–29; and Wright 1995, 16.

German perspective on this over footage of Josef Goebbels and infamous fanatic Julius Streicher presumably expounding their creed: "Our Führer is the intermediary between his people and the throne of God. Everything the Führer utters is religion in the highest sense." Shortly afterwards a grade-school teacher leads her students in a new song which contains their pledge to obey the Führer, their god, unto death: *Für den Führer bis zum Tod, denn er ist, er ist unser Gott.* And in the next installment of the series, *The Nazis Strike,* the narrator observes that the Germans' "passion for conquest reached its historical climax when Adolf Hitler enthroned himself as god and the German Führer."[50] Whereas in pre-War cinema the cult of the emperor had made Roman religion at best a quaint or misguided belief to Christian America and at worst a sacrilegious antagonist to Christianity, films after 1945 could add a powerful new political side to this.

The fire of Rome in A.D. 64 also points to twentieth-century history. Studio boss Louis B. Mayer wanted *Quo Vadis* to be a "DeMille-like religious epic," whereas John Huston, who had originally been set to write and direct the film, aimed for "a modern treatment about Nero and his fanatical determination to eliminate the Christians in much the same manner as his historic counterpart and fellow madman, Adolf Hitler, tried to destroy the Jews two thousand years later."[51] Mayer had Huston replaced, and a team of screenwriters was instructed "to eliminate the political parallels and turn the movie into a virtual remake of Cecil B. DeMille's *The Sign of the Cross.*"[52] Remarkably, however, Huston's perspective survives in the finished film. A clear example of the Nero-Hitler

---

50. The following year John Farrow's *The Hitler Gang,* a film about Hitler's rise to power, was to contain a speech with this statement: "We need no God on a distant throne. Adolf Hitler is the Jesus Christ as well as the Holy Ghost of the Fatherland"; quoted from Koppes and Black 1990, 300 (with misspelling "Adolph"). On the insistence of the Production Code Administration these words had to be deleted as blasphemous although they were an exact quotation. On the PCA see Koppes and Black, 13–16. Leiser 1975, 27, comments on Hitler's appearances in *Triumph of the Will:* "He poses as the prophet of a new religion, as the grand master of a mystical order ... an intimidating spectacle for those who were still undecided on the sidelines, a beacon signaling Hitler's power beyond the frontiers of Germany, and a divine service for the faithful."

51. Both quotations are from Huston 1994, 175. German poet Bertolt Brecht may have been the first to make the analogy between Hitler and Nero explicit in two poems written in 1933 that were occasioned by the fire of the Reichstag in Berlin; see *Die Moritat vom Reichstagsbrand* and *Der römische Kaiser Nero* in Brecht 1976, vol. 1, 408–12, and vol. 2, 525. The former poem refers to Göring, not Hitler, but the implication is obvious. For detailed scholarship on the actual relations between Jews and Romans from the first century B.C. on see Smallwood 1981; for a wider-ranging modern study see Feldman 1993.

52. Higham 1993, 389.

analogy occurs immediately after the Fire-of-Rome sequence. Empress Poppaea coaxes Nero to divert the people's suspicion of his own responsibility for the fire onto the Christians. When Nero dictates a proclamation to the Roman people to this effect, Petronius, Nero's arbiter of taste and an independent spirit who is unafraid of his tyrannical master, tries to dissuade him. The dialogue leaves no doubt that Nero is meant to be understood as a precursor of Hitler:

> NERO: I hereby proclaim that the guilt of the burning of our beloved city rests with the foul sect which calls itself Christians. They have spread the lie that it was Nero who burned Rome. I will exterminate these criminals in a manner matching the enormity of their crime. Their punishment will be a warning, a spectacle of terror, to all evil men, everywhere, and forever, who would harm you or harm Rome or harm your emperor, who loves you.
> PETRONIUS: Pause, Nero, before you sign this decree. . . . Condemn these Christians, and you make martyrs of them, ensure their immortality. Condemn *them,* and in the eyes of history you'll condemn yourself.
> NERO: When I have finished with these Christians, Petronius, history will not be sure that they ever existed.

Unlike almost twenty years earlier, when DeMille's Nero had commanded "The extermination of Christians must continue," in 1951 the words "exterminate" and "terror" will have struck many in the audience as an unambiguous reference to Nazi atrocities. Nero's last statement quoted here supports this view, for it is a reminder of the Holocaust. Later in the film, Nero's order after Petronius' suicide ("Burn his books!") echoes Nazi behavior as well. The large model of the new Rome that Nero intends to build on the ruins of the burnt city and that he shows to Petronius and some of his courtiers may remind some viewers of Albert Speer's models for Germania, the new Berlin planned for the Thousand-Year Reich after its projected final victory (*Endsieg*) in World War II.[53]

Nazi-like viciousness finds a dramatic visual expression in the film's depiction of the death of St. Peter. Peter says to the centurion who comes to lead him to crucifixion: "To die as our Lord died is more than I deserve." The centurion snidely answers: "We can change that!" Now there is a cut, and director LeRoy shows us Peter on the cross in a

---

53. So Bertelli 1995, 66. Numerous photographs of Hitler and other Nazi brass looking at Speer's models of Germania exist.

manner intended to shock. The camera slowly tilts up from the ground to reveal Peter crucified upside down, with a musical fortissimo on the soundtrack. This is one of the very few moments in almost three hours of screen time, and the most forceful one as well, that draws the viewers' attention to the film's cinematic technique. According to the principles of classic Hollywood filmmaking, audiences are rarely if ever to become conscious of camera or editing; their attention is not to be diverted from the plot. Here the camera's unusual vertical movement departs from this standard to create a strong emotional reaction in the spectator. According to the Christian tradition St. Peter himself had requested upside-down crucifixion, but in the film this is presented as a particularly choice example of Roman sadism.[54] It is meant to fulfill what Nero, ominously, had said about Peter a little earlier: "Something singular must be done with him."

Altogether, then, the pagan Romans of *Quo Vadis* and any number of such films run a totalitarian military empire and resemble the Nazis of the filmmakers' recent past while ancient Christians take the place of modern Jews. The fact that in such films' plots most of the persecuted Christians are Roman citizens reinforces the obvious point that tyranny turns against its own people. *Quo Vadis* explicitly states this by lifting Suetonius' report that Emperor Caligula wanted the Roman people to have only one neck—the more easily to be killed—and applying it to Nero.[55] "The world is mine, and mine to end," Nero will later say about his empire, a clear reference to Hitler's megalomania and recklessness in bringing war to the world and leading his own country to the brink of annihilation. Such words or those uttered by Marcus Vinicius quoted earlier will have evoked to viewers the Nazi ideology of Aryan superiority and its successful dissemination among the German people. In *Quo Vadis* Petronius comments on Nero's attempt to blame the fire on the Christians: "People will believe any lie if it is fantastic enough." The success of Nazi ideology, not only in Germany and not only in the 1930s and 1940s, fully bears him out.

Besides carrying obvious political connotations, the raised-arm salute also occurs in *Quo Vadis* as a general feature of Roman life. Wrestlers at Nero's banquet, for example, greet him with this gesture, and even

---

54. For Peter's request to be crucified upside down see Eusebius, *History of the Church* 3.1.2. Eusebius claims Origen's *Commentary on Genesis* as his source for the deaths of Saints Peter and Paul under Nero. Cf. Perkins 2000, 138–40, and, for the wider context, Cullmann 1962, 71–157.

55. Suetonius, *Caligula* 30.2. The saying has been given to Nero since at least the early seventeenth century; examples at Gwyn 1991, 439–40.

General Plautius, a good (because Christian) Roman and soon to be a victim of Nero's terror, employs it. We are meant to realize that this mode of saluting was a regular Roman custom but that it became politicized under a tyrant and turned into a sign of blind obedience to the power of the state.

A similar point had been made fourteen years earlier in a new production of Shakespeare presented in New York City. As is still the case, plays by Shakespeare are frequently staged in modern dress to emphasize their timeless qualities or to comment on contemporary situations. The first and most famous instance in which a play by Shakespeare was staged in contemporary dress to make an anti-Fascist point was Orson Welles's Mercury Theatre production *Caesar* (1937). It was highly influential.[56] The American television *Coriolanus,* already mentioned and made the same year as *Quo Vadis,* follows Welles's example; it is set in Mussolini's Italy. The Fascist salute is given once in *Coriolanus* in an unusual variation when a uniformed messenger's right arm is pointing downward in the direction of an officer seated before him.[57] Since then, Fascist

56. Described by Leaming 1986, 170–72, with excerpts from Welles's press release. Details in (the play's producer) Houseman 1972, 296–321. For representative other examples of Fascist overtones or settings in productions of the play see the comments in Shakespeare 1984a, 56 (the play's "Fascist/liberal dichotomy"), 66–67 (on Welles and his influence), and 69–70 (on a 1968 Royal Shakespeare Company production by John Barton and on Trevor Nunn's 1972 Stratford production, with illustration at 70 of Caesar's statue giving a bent-elbow variant of the Fascist salute in the latter). On *Antony and Cleopatra* cf. Shakespeare 1998, 87 (on the architecture in Glen Byam Shaw's 1946 London production); Shakespeare 1994, 36–37 (on Tony Richardson's 1973 production at the Bankside Globe with Octavius Caesar as a Fascist blackshirt). On *Coriolanus* cf. Shakespeare 2000, 80–84 (on German editions and productions of the 1930s with Coriolanus as a Führer figure and on British and American productions of 1935 and 1938), 85–86 (on Peter Hall's 1959 production at the Shakespeare Memorial Theatre, with illustration of the dead body of Coriolanus hung upside down, modeled on Mussolini's fate), and 93 (on a 1980 American production); on *Titus Andronicus* cf. Shakespeare 1984b, 56 (on a 1967 production by Douglas Seale in Baltimore). After World War II the Allies banned *Coriolanus* in West Germany for its alleged Fascist tendencies until 1953.

57. Unusual, that is, in the context of moving images of the salute after 1945. As described above, DeMille's *The Crusades* had already contained a salute in which the right arm was extended downward. In Fascist cinema a comparable posture, with arms stretched out lower than horizontally, appears in two Italian films of the same title and made in the same year, although these are oath scenes, not salutes: *I martiri d'Italia* (1927; "The Martyrs of Italy"), directed by Domenico Gaido and Silvio Laurenti Rosa. Both films are sweeping historical canvases spanning several centuries of Italian history. Rosa's film has the subtitle *Il trionfo di Roma* ("The Triumph of Rome"). Stills from both films showing the oath scenes appear in Gori 1988, figs. 50 and 55; Gori, 48 and 84–85, describes the two versions. He gives filmographical information at 104. Verdone 1970, 207, provides a still of what appears to be a comparable oath scene in a silent film (unidentified, but from Guazzoni's *Messalina*). The body of a young woman, presumably killed, is lying on the ground; several bystanders raise their right arms while one is stretching his down and toward her body.

settings for Shakespearean drama have continued. The most recent cinematic example is Richard Loncraine's *Richard III* (1995), based on the 1994 National Theatre production by Richard Eyre and set during a Fascist coup in 1930s England.

seven

Visual Legacies

Antiquity on the Screen from *Quo Vadis* to *Rome*

A LARGE NUMBER of films and television films made after World War II furnish us with proof that the Roman salute has become a visual stereotype and now appears to be almost ineradicable, and not only in Hollywood. *Quo Vadis* provided other filmmakers with a powerful model.[1] This chapter examines the vagaries and varieties of the raised-arm salute first in the cinema, then, more briefly, on television. I separate these two media, related as they are, to emphasize that the small screen is just as conservative as the silver screen as far as adherence to a tried and supposedly true formula is concerned.

1. Cinema: From *Salome* to *Alexander*

In *Salome* (1953), directed by German expatriate William—originally Wilhelm—Dieterle, Romans and Jews use the expected forms of the raised-arm salute, including Emperor Tiberius, King Herod, and Pontius Pilate. But two members of Herod's palace guard on one occasion display a particularly silly salute when they first rotate their arms. In George Sidney's musical *Jupiter's Darling* (1955), set in the Second Punic War—the title refers to Hannibal, called "the singing conqueror" in the

---

1. By contrast, David Bradley's independent production of *Julius Caesar* (1950) displays only a loose raised-arm salute by Antony and Caesar when Antony offers Caesar the kingly crown at the festival of the Lupercalia. The fist-on-heart salute also occurs.

film's trailer—Fabius Maximus, just made dictator, greets the people with the raised-arm salute in the Roman Forum. Then his mother arrives and greets him the same way. He in return greets her, arm raised, while they are talking to each other. The comedy in these two scenes is unintentional. Apparently, little or no thought or historical consciousness went into their staging. So it is no surprise when we see Sidney's Hannibal giving the raised-arm salute, too.

Philip Saville's *The Silver Chalice* (1954), also set at the time of Nero, has some scenes with the raised-arm salute patterned on *Quo Vadis,* as when Nero's guests at a lavish banquet in his palace or the Roman crowd assembled for a spectacle before Nero's imperial box greet their ruler. Simon Magus, the Samaritan magician and heretic familiar from the *Acts of the Apostles,* returns from Nero's banquet dizzy with hopes of imperial favors and raises his arms in a series of vaguely "Roman" salutes as if he were practicing for his imminent introduction into the emperor's closest circles.[2] In *Demetrius and the Gladiators,* the sequel to *The Robe,* the salute appears perfunctory when the Praetorian Prefect greets Emperor Caligula by raising his *left* hand from the elbow up. In the arena Caligula also greets the crowd by raising his left arm, fingers spread. When he is proclaimed emperor by the Praetorians, Claudius is greeted by acclamation and raised-arm salutes, but not from all.

What about other ancient peoples in post-World War II cinema? In Pietro Francisci's *Attila* (1954; *Attila the Hun*) a high-ranking Roman delegation suing for a peace treaty with the Huns greets Attila's brother with the now standard salute; the latter returns it in the same way, although, being in a position of power, he does so rather condescendingly by barely lifting his right arm. Nevertheless the brief moment reveals that the Huns are familiar with this form of salute and may employ it themselves. In Robert Wise's *Helen of Troy* (1955) King Priam hails an assembly of Trojan warriors with the raised-arm salute before handing over a suspiciously Roman-looking eagle standard to one of his officers. (Figure 27) Earlier, Paris had greeted Priam and Hecuba, his parents, with a raised-left-arm salute and received the "correct" salute from them in return. Some years later, in Giorgio Ferroni's *La guerra di Troia* (1962), Trojan prince Aeneas receives a loose right-arm salute, with elbow bent, from a fellow Trojan—"Hail Aeneas!" is heard on the soundtrack of the English-language version—whereas Agamemnon, supreme commander of the Greeks in the Trojan War, gives permission to continue the funeral games for

---

2. Simon may indeed have worked his magic in Rome, but at the time of Claudius, not Nero. Cf. *Acts* 8.9–24.

Figure 27. *Helen of Troy* (1956). Priam (back to camera) saluting Trojan officer. Warner Bros.

Patroclus with a far more modern-looking raised-arm salute, elbow straight.³ And in Rudolph Maté's *The 300 Spartans* (1962), a film about the Persian invasion of Greece in 480 B.C., the commander of the Ten Thousand Immortals, the Great King's bodyguard, employs the raised-arm salute before the climactic Battle of Thermopylae begins.

Romans may still raise their straight left arms in greeting even after modern history and popular media had made the right arm virtually obligatory. A noncinematic example appears on the cover of a bestselling novel. Rex Warner's *The Young Caesar* (1958) and *Imperial Caesar* (1960) purport to be the autobiography of Julius Caesar. The former was republished as a mass-market paperback by the New American Library of World Literature in 1959 under their imprint Mentor Books—"Good Reading for the Millions."⁴ The color picture on the front cover shows Caesar in a triumphal chariot in Rome, followed by standard bearers. (Figure 28) Caesar has here raised his *left* arm to greet the crowd in attendance; two members of the crowd are shown returning his salute, one raising his right arm, the other his left. Evidently, it does not matter all that much—any arm will do since the gesture is immediately identifiable.

This cover picture would hardly warrant mention if it were not for the fact that the novel's author was an influential classical scholar, whose name was widely popular. Warner (1905–1986) was a well-known poet, historical novelist, and translator.⁵ He had read classics and English at Wadham College, Oxford, where he became friends with W. H. Auden

---

3. The English titles of Ferroni's film are *The Wooden Horse of Troy*, *The Trojan Horse*, and *The Trojan War*.
4. Warner 1959, quoted from back cover.
5. On Warner see Tabachnick 2002.

Figure 28. Rex Warner, *The Young Caesar*. Cover illustration of paperback edition. Author's collection.

Figure 29. *Ben-Hur* (1959). Messala (r.) arriving in Jerusalem. Metro-Goldwyn-Mayer.

and C. Day Lewis. After World War II he was director of the British Institute in Athens. Later, in the United States, he was Tallman Professor of Classics at Bowdoin College (1961–1962) and professor of English at the University of Connecticut (1964–1974). His translations of classical literature were the standard English versions for many years, especially those published in the Penguin Classics series. So the cover image of his most popular novel is remarkable. Would not a scholar of his standing have objected to such a historically inaccurate image? *Should* he not have objected? (Since authors are not always consulted about such matters, it might be fairer to ask whether Warner *could* have objected.) Given the general ignorance of the true origin of the raised-arm salute in the twentieth century even among scholars, it may be best if we assume that Warner probably had no say in the matter.

Now back to the cinema. In the 1959 version of *Ben-Hur,* the most famous and popular Roman-Empire film worldwide, director William Wyler also resorts to the general view of a totalitarian and militaristic Roman Empire that Hollywood had propagated. Wyler, a Jewish émigré from Germany and a committed anti-Fascist, takes care to have his actors display the expected gesture with greater subtlety. Except for Arrius' salute to Tiberius in the scene examined in chapter 6, Romans now raise their right arm no higher than horizontal, as does Messala upon his arrival at the Roman garrison in Jerusalem, of which he is about to take command. (Figure 29) When Arrius arrives on his flagship to take over the Roman fleet, Wyler has his Roman soldiers employ a different salute: right arm raised to chest, fist touching heart, an echo of the American Pledge of Allegiance. When later the cry "Hail Arrius!" is heard, only one arm goes up. Still, Wyler's conception of the Roman Empire continues the cinema's tradition of presenting Rome as a conquering and oppressive military machine. Wyler was familiar with *Quo Vadis.*[6]

---

6. On the Roman Empire in Wyler's *Ben-Hur* see my discussion in Winkler 1998, 184–93.

Figure 30. *The Greatest Story Ever Told.* King Herod (r.) receiving Roman officer. United Artists/Metro-Goldwyn-Mayer.

Richard Fleischer's *Barabbas,* released two years later, features one of the most unusual because most spectacular arena sequences in Roman film epics. Although completely invented, it derives a good measure of excitement from being filmed in an authentic ancient location, the Roman amphitheater of Verona. Accompanied by a military entourage, the undefeated champion of the arena, who is a charioteer and *retiarius* (net fighter) combined, grandly enters the arena on his chariot to salute the emperor in his box. He and his soldiers raise their right arms. Since they all appear in an impressive long shot, they do not utter the verbal greeting (*Morituri te salutant . . .*) that theater audiences might expect at such a moment.

George Stevens's gigantic *The Greatest Story Ever Told* (1965), whose subject is the life of Jesus, shows us King Herod Antipas greeting a Roman officer (Figure 30) and High Priest Caiaphas greeting Pontius Pilate by raising their right arms, if only from the elbow. In Hollywood's ancient Egypt we may observe comparable phenomena. Howard Hawks's *Land of the Pharaohs* (1955) has the people greet their pharaoh with their left or right arms raised, elbows bent and palms held vertically outward; their ruler usually employs a straight-arm salute. Pietro Francisci's *La regina di Saba* (1952; *The Queen of Sheba*) contains a scene in which a tavern keeper salutes his queen, who is visiting incognito, by raising his arm, albeit the left one. In comedy the salute may take an exaggerated form, as when Nero greets his mother Agrippina with his arm raised vertically in Steno's *Mio figlio Nerone* (1956).[7] Early in Mario Bonnard's

---

7. The film's English-language titles are, variously, *O.K. Nero, Nero's Big Weekend, Nero's*

Figure 31. *Solomon and Sheba*. Pharaoh, his court, and Adonijah's henchman (r.) hailing the false king of Israel. Note variety of saluting gestures. United Artists/Metro-Goldwyn-Mayer.

Afrodite, dea dell' amore (1958; *Aphrodite, Goddess of Love*) the Corinthians hail Emperor Nero—off-screen because on board a ship sailing back to Rome—and the on-screen archon of Corinth with raised-arm salutes. The scene, although set in Greece, was filmed in Mussolini's EUR. The film's opening shot shows the gigantic marble sculpture of a nude athlete giving a unique version of the salute: his right arm is raised, elbow bent, but his palm is bent back even further and pointing upward at an angle. In King Vidor's *Solomon and Sheba* (1959) both Jews and Egyptians employ raised-arm salutes. In Jerusalem a priest so greets Solomon in the temple. The pharaoh and some of his courtiers raise their arms to Solomon's treacherous brother Adonijah, adding "Hail!" as they prematurely proclaim him king of Israel. On usurping Solomon's throne, this brother is saluted with the straight-arm salute by his henchman, who may variously raise his left or right arm, also crying "Hail!" Some of the assembled Israelites follow suit. (Figure 31) The indiscriminate use of the gesture on the part of ancient Jews and Egyptians, who are bitter enemies in this biblical epic, appears rather eerie in the light of their descendants' history in the twentieth century.

In *Coriolano, eroe senza patria* (1964; *Coriolanus, Hero without a Country* or *Thunder of Battle*), which is set in the early Roman republic, director Giorgio Ferroni has the Romans even raise their left arms sideways, away from their bodies. That same year, in Ferdinando Baldi's *Il figlio di Cleopatra* (*Son of Cleopatra*), it is Arabs who know and use the raised-arm

---

Mistress, and *Nero's Weekend*. (Take your pick.) Steno is Italian comedy director Stefano Vanzina (or Vanzini).

Figure 32. *Spartacus* (1960). "Hail Crassus!" Julius Caesar (r.) and senators except Gracchus acknowledging the new powers of Crassus. Bryna Productions/Universal.

salute. Earlier, in Mario Bonnard's *Gli ultimi giorni di Pompeii* (1959; *The Last Days of Pompeii*) two rather loose raised-arm salutes occur. The first of these is memorable, in the English-language version, for its charming verbal accompaniment: "Hail friends!" But more important is the loose variant of the raised-arm salute that occurs in Osvaldo Civirani's campy *Ercole contro i figli del sole* (1965; *Hercules against the Sons of the Sun*). These solar sons are none other than Incas. The film is an example of the gleeful mixture of incompatible periods of history, geography, and culture that came to signal the final phase of the Italian muscleman epics.

In the early 1960s the iconography of the raised-arm salute in mainstream or big-budget Roman films began to change further. Stanley Kubrick's *Spartacus* (1960) has little use for the raised-arm salute, for only relatively few examples occur in three and a quarter hours of screen time.[8] Crassus, arriving at the gladiatorial school in which Spartacus is being trained, is greeted with the salute by its servile owner, but only in long shot and at the edge of the huge screen. A little later Crassus greets gladiators with a perfunctory raised-arm reply to their far more formal salute. "Perfunctory" is the best word to describe the forms of the salute nearly every time it occurs in this film. Senators salute Glabrus in the Senate and Crassus in the Forum when he is about to march against Spartacus. (Figure 32) Crassus' staff so welcomes him upon arrival in his army camp. Such relaxed and loose ways of performing the raised-arm salute lack any forceful modern overtones. A revealing example occurs

---

8. On the complicated production history and on various other aspects of this film and its influence see the essays collected in Winkler 2007.

Figure 33. *Cleopatra* (1963). Julius Caesar (r.), unimpressed by Egyptian pomp, salutes King Ptolemy while looking for Cleopatra. Twentieth Century-Fox.

when a legionary greets Crassus in his tent. He throws his right arm up into the air vertically and then down again in a loose-limbed motion. Later a centurion greets Crassus with a comparably loose gesture, his upper arm held horizontally away from his body, his lower arm raised at an angle of about seventy-five degrees to the upper limb. There is nothing as energetic or snappy about the salutes in *Spartacus* as there had been in *Quo Vadis*. To a smaller degree the same is true for Lionello De Felice's *Costantino il grande* (1961; *Constantine the Great* or *Constantine and the Cross*). In the 1963 version of *Cleopatra* Julius Caesar's raised-arm salute to Ptolemy, the boy king of Egypt, is even played for humor. (Figure 33) Neither this Caesar nor his writer-director, Joseph L. Mankiewicz, take the epic proceedings and the stereotypical trappings of Roman-Empire films all that seriously. Amerigo Anton's *Giulio Cesare il conquistadore delle Gallie* (*Caesar the Conqueror*), made the same year, keeps the raised-arm salute for the Roman military, with arms straight or bent at the elbow and usually accompanied by a verbal Latin greeting. ("Ave!" is heard for addresses in both singular and plural.) Nevertheless the film has other forms of salutation just as frequently: manly embraces and right hands closed above the wrist. A variant of the right-fist-over-heart salute may be observed in *David e Golia* (1960; *David and Goliath*), directed by Richard Pottier and Ferdinando Baldi, in which the standard form of greeting is the placement of the open right hand near the left shoulder, accompanied by a slight inclining of the head. Mario Costa's *Il gladiatore di Roma* (1962; *The Gladiator of Rome* or *Battles of the Gladiators*) even shows both the raised-arm salute and the mutual above-the-wrist-grip occurring within a minute of each other in one and the same scene. In the early crowd scenes of *Julius Caesar* (1970), a film version of Shakespeare, director Stuart Burge has the people raise their right arms, but some of his Romans are waving their open hands while the majority, more unusually, are waving their fists. We can imagine how differently directors like Guazzoni or LeRoy could have staged such moments. In these later films the raised arms and the raised-arm salutes are devoid of political connotations and appear because they have so appeared for decades. The same is true for *The Three Stooges Meet Hercules* (1962), a forced comedy directed by Edward Bernds, in which we observe Hercules, riding into the arena, exchange raised-arm salutes with King Odius. Gerald Thomas's *Carry On Cleo* (1965), the only ancient entry in the *Carry On* series of British farces, has several instances of rather loose raised-arm salutes. In later comedies things remain comparable, for instance in the French animated films about the cartoon heroes Asterix and Obelix. For example, in *Astérix et Cléopâtre* (1968; *Asterix and Cleopatra*), directed by René Goscinny, Lee Payant, and Albert Uderzo, a statue of Julius Caesar appears with its right arm raised, and Cleopatra's Egyptian mercenaries give a loose raised-arm salute while getting the gladiators' *Morituri* . . . greeting wrong. Later, in *Astérix et la surprise de César* (1985; *Asterix vs. Caesar*), directed by Gaëtan and Paul Brizzi, and in *Astérix chez les Britons* (1986; *Asterix in Britain*), directed by Pino Van Lamsweerde, similarly loose raised-arm salutes occasionally occur but lack any significance.

In view of the wide use of the raised-arm salute in American and European films set in antiquity, it is important for us to be aware that not all directors believed in the patterns of visual recreations of antiquity that had emerged since the earliest days of cinema. Writer-director Vittorio Cottafavi, who had made both ancient epics and other historical adventure films in the late 1950s and early 1960s, the heyday of these genres in Italy, is an honorable, if also rare, exception to the presentation of history and myth prevalent in popular films. Looking back on his career and on the genre of ancient epics, Cottafavi observed in an interview in 1983:

> La chose que j'ai toujours cherché à faire, c'est d'être cohérent ou respectueux vis-à-vis des manières de vivre des Romains, parce que la plupart des films était faux sur ce point: ils ne connaissaient pas la civilisation romaine, ils n'avaient pas correctement étudié ce qu'étaient la vie et les rapports entre les Romains. . . . Dans les films que j'ai fait sur l'Antiquité, j'ai toujours eu un grand respect pour le sens de la romanité.
>
> What I always sought to do was to be consistent or respectful regarding the Roman way of life, because the majority of films were wrong on

this point: they did not know Roman civilization, they had not studied correctly what life and relationships among the Romans were like. . . . In the films I made about antiquity, I always had great respect for the sense of what it means to be Roman.[9]

The one specific aspect that Cottafavi singled out as the most telling example of falsehood in standard ancient epic films is the raised-arm salute:

> Ainsi on voyait faire le salut avec le bras levé, du genre nazi. Ce n'était pas le salut qu'on faisait à Rome. C'est un geste qu'on peut faire encore aujourd'hui, on peut lever la main et se faire un signe. C'était peut-être une manière de saluer avec respect, ou bien de répondre: l'homme à cheval répond au salut en levant le bras parce qu'il ne peut pas donner une accolade. Pour tous ces gestes—la façon dont mangeaient les Romains, leurs manières de vivre, de bâtir leurs habitations—, j'ai cherché à être véridique, à être assez fidèle aux connaisances dont nous disposons.

> So they [the Romans] were seen giving the salute with their arm raised, the kind the Nazis gave. This was not the salute that one gave in Rome. This is an activity that one can still carry out today; one can raise one's hand and make a sign to one another. This was, perhaps, a way of saluting respectfully or of answering: a man on horseback replies to a salute by raising his arm because he cannot give an embrace. About all such activities—how the Romans ate, their way of life, of building their homes—I've sought to be truthful, to be quite faithful to the knowledge we have at our disposal.[10]

These words and the fact that the interview excerpted here was conducted in French indicate that Cottafavi was as well-educated as he was thoughtful.[11] Even so, at least some of the evidence in his body of work

---

9. Siarri-Plazanet 1999, 98 and 101. Cf. also Cottafavi's words to similar effect about *La rivolta dei gladiatori* as quoted in Rondolino 1980b, 63–64. Cf. below on this film.

10. Siarri-Plazanet 1999, 98.

11. Leprohon 1972, 178–79, calls Cottafavi "cultured" and "a complete professional and probably more besides." Rondolino 1980b makes evident on numerous occasions that this is not an overstatement.—Cottafavi's other Roman films are *Le legioni di Cleopatra* (1959; *Legions of the Nile*, also written), *Messalina Venere imperatrice* (1960; *Messalina*), and *Le vergini di Roma* (1961; *Amazons of Rome* or *Warrior Women*, co-directed). Cottafavi also directed two Hercules films that transcend the standard level of such films: *La vendetta di Ercole* (1960; *The Revenge of Hercules*, *Vengeance of Hercules*, and even *Goliath and the Dragon*) and *Ercole alla conquista di Atlantide* (1961; *Hercules Conquers Atlantis* or *Hercules and the Captive Women*). In later years Cottafavi directed

contradicts him. In his first Roman film, *La rivolta dei gladiatori* (1958; *The Warrior and the Slave Girl* or *Revolt of the Gladiators*), raised-arm greetings both of the standard and of a loose variety occur on the part of Romans and Armenians. (The story is set in the Roman client kingdom of Armenia during the third century A.D.)

Considerable care on the part of a committed filmmaker to show Romans on the basis of his familiarity with their history and culture and at the same time to make antiquity meaningful to his audiences is evinced by Anthony Mann, an exception among American directors of epic. *The Fall of the Roman Empire* (1964), the last silver-screen epic about Rome until the year 2000, is the only film ever made that attempts to do full justice to the greatness of Rome and consciously goes against the stereotypical presentations of Romans in the cinema.[12] The ways in which the raised-arm salute occurs in this film are important because they tell us how persistent the cinematic tradition of raised-arm salutes can be even if a film's emphasis is different from all others and, at the same time, how far the gesture has come by now. Fascist analogies to imperial Rome are not an issue in this film, not even in its first epic set-piece, in which Emperor Marcus Aurelius greets and reviews an assembly of leaders of the Roman Empire and then delivers to them a speech about the greatness of Rome. In this sequence the raised-arm salute occurs several times. Marcus is formally greeted by some but not all of the leaders with the standard salute, for at least as many salutes feature the right hand or fist being placed over the heart. The king of Armenia, soon to play a major part in the film's plot, even stretches out both arms, then crosses them over his chest and bows to the emperor. Marcus returns the raised-arm salute a few times, but usually with his elbow bent. He also holds his raised right arm up in such a way that his palm is turned toward himself, not to those he is greeting. And at the moment that the assembled leaders collectively shout "Hail Caesar!" there is no raised-arm salute anywhere to be seen. It is unlikely that during the preceding decade a film director should have missed such an opportunity of giving his viewers what they would have expected. Evidently, if director Mann had wanted to present Rome as an evil empire of the stereotypical kind, this sequence would have afforded him several good opportunities to do so by reviving the snappy and ubiquitous salutes of *Quo Vadis,* on which Mann had worked under LeRoy. (He had been in charge of the Fire-of-Rome sequence.) But such is not the case in *The Fall of the Roman Empire.* Some time later Marcus and his son Commodus meet on screen for the first time,

---

highly regarded adaptations of Greek tragedies for Italian television.

12. I give an appreciation of this film's qualities in Winkler 1995. See also Winkler 2009.

Figure 34. *The Fall of the Roman Empire.* Commodus saluting the crowd during his triumphal entry into Rome. Samuel Bronston Productions.

and the father welcomes him with a raised-arm salute that carries no Fascist implications at all. Commodus in turn greets his father only by placing his right fist over his heart. This is a common gesture in this film, presented as the standard salute in the Roman army. So the film's first instance of the straight-arm salute takes on a different meaning. When returning General Livius, the film's hero, gives such a salute to his emperor, it is an almost private gesture. Again, when Commodus is proclaimed emperor, the soldiers repeatedly shout "Hail Caesar!" The only salute that occurs at this moment is the placement of the fist over the heart. During his triumphal entry into Rome Emperor Commodus greets the people with a variation on the raised-arm salute from which obvious Fascist overtones are absent because Commodus quite noticeably is holding his fingers spread apart. (Figure 34) The film's second half shows a heated senate debate on the future of the empire in the presence of Commodus. A few senators greet Livius, entering the senate hall, with "Hail Livius!" and raised arms. But Mann also has the emperor's chief henchman raise his right arm, palm stretched out, in the familiar gesture. But this time it is not a salute because this senator is attempting to silence the room before speaking. Mann both follows the established iconography of epic cinema and simultaneously avoids some of its hoary clichés. We may compare Mankiewicz's *Julius Caesar,* already mentioned, in which ostensibly Fascist trimmings of Roman-Empire films are both employed on the screen and subtly counteracted by its writer-director's *mise-en-scène.*[13]

---

13. This is well demonstrated by Wyke 2004. She observes, for instance, that black-and-white photography, costumes, and sets "worked to establish . . . a political association with

Figure 35. *Titus*. An inebriated Emperor Saturninus giving the Roman salute in front of the Fascist *Colosseo quadrato*. Twentieth Century-Fox.

In 1999 Julie Taymor's *Titus* presented to filmgoers an intentionally anachronistic version of Shakespeare's *Titus Andronicus*. Influenced by Federico Fellini, especially *Amarcord*, and Pier Paolo Pasolini, especially *Edipo re* (1967; *Oedipus Rex*) and *Salò, o le 120 giornate di Sodoma* (1975; *Salo, or The 120 Days of Sodom*), Taymor shows us a decadent and Fascist Rome. A number of scenes are set in Rome's EUR in front of the *Palazzo della Civiltà Italiana*. This part of Rome had been built under Mussolini for the *Esposizione Universale di Roma* of 1942. Emperor Saturninus, not entirely sober, gives a snappy raised-arm salute on the steps of the palazzo. (Figure 35) In his army camp Lucius Andronicus, Saturninus' enemy, uses a variation of the hand-over-heart salute and is greeted so as well. We may conclude that Taymor attempts, somewhat uneasily, to appeal to both youthful and older audiences by combining antiquity with the more recent past and by resurrecting explicit Fascist overtones alongside other, more traditional, cinematic conventions.[14]

Not until Ridley Scott's *Gladiator* (2000), in large part an unofficial remake of Mann's film, did the Roman Empire return to the big screen, replete with all the grandeur and decadence that were *de rigueur* in the tradition of Hollywood's Roman films. As had been the case with *The Fall of the Roman Empire*, Commodus in *Gladiator* also triumphantly enters Rome but does not use the right-arm salute on this occasion. When he later greets the crowd in the arena he raises his right arm without holding

---

fascism" while camera and musical score "helped provide . . . an anti-fascist narrative drive" (63); cf. 65 on "fascism, its persuasive attractions, and the need for resistance to it."

14. Anderegg 2004, 180–90 and 203 (notes), gives an overview of the film, with further references.

Figure 36. *Gladiator.* Tigris of Gaul entering the Colosseum on his chariot. Dreamworks/Universal.

it stiff. A little later he raises his left arm, keeping the fingers of his hand apart. *Gladiator* does not make imperial Rome as blatant a precursor of Nazism or Fascism as Hollywood's Roman epics had done in the 1950s. But some visual reminders of Nazi Germany still occur, mainly through the influence of Riefenstahl's *Triumph of the Will.*[15] The raised-arm salute occurs again when a champion gladiator makes a spectacular entrance into the Colosseum. (Figure 36)

By the time of *Titus* and *Gladiator* the explicit analogies to Nazi Germany and Fascist Italy that Roman-Empire films like *Quo Vadis* and others had used were less blatant on the screen because Fascism and Nazism had themselves begun to fade from popular memory. After the age of epic spectacles about the ancients a new evil empire, the Soviet Union, replaced the Roman Empire and furnished equally hissable but more contemporary villains with greater destructive powers.[16] Even Roman films like *Spartacus* and *The Fall of the Roman Empire* had carried some Cold-War overtones. In the early twenty-first century, more than fifty years after the end of World War II and over a decade after the fall of the Soviet Union, Fascists, Nazis, and Communists are no longer all that

---

15. Arthur J. Pomeroy, "The Vision of a Fascist Rome in *Gladiator,*" in Winkler 2004, 111–23, presents a detailed analysis.

16. As an exception I mention, if only to include one example of the bottom-of-the-barrel filmmaking that runs parallel to mainstream cinema, the Italian violence-and-pornography exploitation film *Caligola: La storia mai raccontata* (1981; *Caligula: The Untold Story*), directed, if that is the word, by Joe D'Amato (credited as David Hills in the English-language version). An orgy presided over by Caligula can only begin after raised-arm salutes between emperor and some of the participants have been exchanged. Silliness, even in such a context, knows no bounds.

prominent in the cinema. Historical consciousness today is more diffuse. This is especially true in the case of film audiences whose average age has steadily decreased. Today the majority of mainstream American films are geared to appeal to young viewers, the main providers of box-office returns. So terrorists, serial killers, and assorted psychopaths have supplanted earlier cinematic bad guys. In addition, as *Gladiator* reveals, the rise of computer-generated images has made it tempting and easy for screenwriters and directors to neglect the social and historical backgrounds of their plots, to abandon convincing psychological motivations for good and bad characters alike, and to put most of their creative energies into dazzling action sequences and special effects. In such a cultural climate historical analogies tend to be vague. This is a deplorable tendency in general, but in the case of the raised-arm salute it may actually be for the better since it has to a considerable extent freed the Romans from the stigma of Fascism that had been foisted on them by a potent combination of modern popular culture and totalitarian history. A revealing example for this is a 2002 *New Yorker* cartoon that satirizes the worldwide box-office success of *Gladiator,* which was mainly due to its Colosseum sequences. The cartoon, set in a Roman arena, shows a melée of Christians and lions while a messenger addresses a rather soused and befuddled-looking emperor in his box with the requisite greeting "Hail Caesar!" The messenger's right arm is raised. But his hand is bent back as far as possible, conveying no specific reminiscence of politics or history.[17] Here the raised-arm salute is no more than what it had originally been: a visual cue that denotes something Roman but that is by now without any political or historical significance.

Even when a political comment *is* intended, modern cultural memory of the Romans and "their" salute can be on the vague side. Verbal analogies between the Roman Empire and the United States as a global superpower have been ubiquitous in the news media during the last several years. For instance, an article about President George W. Bush by a newspaper columnist based in Washington, D.C., begins: "He is an unlikely, incomplete and possibly still not wholly willing Caesar"; it ends: "it may not be too early to practice a lusty, 'Hail, Caesar!'"[18] Visual

---

17. Lee Lorenz, "Hail Caesar! This weekend's gross set a new record!" *The New Yorker* (November 11, 2002), 158.

18. Cragg Hines, "Hail W! How Bush Bestrides the World," *Houston Chronicle* (March 23, 2002). With its deliberate echo of Shakespeare the title of this article reinforces the analogy expressed in the passages quoted. Cassius describes Julius Caesar, Rome's most famous—or infamous—strongman, to Brutus in these well-known words: "he doth bestride the narrow world / Like a Colossus" (*Julius Caesar* 1.2.133–34).

analogies appear as well. A clever example is the 2002 drawing by David Levine of President Bush as a Roman warrior in the breast plate and military "skirt" familiar from Hollywood epics. Behind his shield, on which the presidential seal is displayed, the tips of assorted rockets and other weapons are visible.[19] In January 2007 *The New Yorker* featured the president on its cover as an American Nero plucking a lyre behind a lectern, on which the seal is again prominent.[20] Visual comments on the new American empire may even resort to the still prevalent conception of the Roman salute. A photo collage that appeared on the Internet in 2002 is an example. Under the headline "'Hail Bush': a Roman salute for a born again emperor?" a photograph of Bush is merged with an arena scene from *Gladiator*.[21] The president's right arm is raised, slightly bent at the elbow, his palm open and his fingers not touching. His is clearly not a Fascist salute. But the headline and two quotations accompanying the image express the opinion that Bush is an extreme right-wing politician.[22] The point is made without any subtlety. Nor is it completely convincing. But that it is made at all, and in connection with a popular film set in the Roman Empire, shows us that the power of cinema to shape people's pseudohistorical awareness remains undiminished.

Two films depicting antiquity that were released in 2004 have no raised-arm salutes. But this is neither a surprise nor an indication that the salute is a thing of the past. In *The Passion of the Christ* director Mel Gibson and his collaborators are indebted to earlier cinematic representations of ancient Romans and Jews, for example in terms of architecture and costumes and in the manner of this film's crucifixion scene. But Gibson's Romans are far too obsessed with delivering sadistic torture to Jesus to have any time or inclination for social etiquette like acts of greeting. Wolfgang Petersen's *Troy*, loosely based on Homer's *Iliad*, contains only one instance of a traditional cinematic saluting gesture; it is the familiar one in which the right fist is placed over the heart. Although *Troy* is patterned on Robert Wise's *Helen of Troy*, for instance in regard to the

---

19. The drawing was first published in *The New York Review of Books* (February 28, 2002), 44. It is only one representative example of such iconography.

20. Anita Kunz, "While Rome Burns," *The New Yorker* (January 22, 2007), cover. The president's hairstyle is copied from that of the statue of Apollo at Olympia.

21. The collage appeared under the date of March 19, 2002, at http://www.ftlcomm.com/ensign/desantisArticles/2002_600/desantis608/hailbush.html. The site belongs to a Mario de Santis.

22. The quotations are the following: "There ought to be limits to freedom" (Bush) and: "There are reminders to all Americans that they need to watch what they say, watch what they do, and this is not a time for remarks like that; there never is" (White House spokesman Ari Fleischer).

Figure 37. *Alexander.* Alexander on his triumphant entry into Babylon. Warner Bros.

Minoan columns that are prominent features of Trojan architecture in both films (which were produced by the same studio), it seems obvious that director Petersen, a German working in Hollywood, should have no interest in giving straight-arm salutes to any of his characters.[23] Wise, as we have seen, had had no such qualms.

A third film of 2004 set in antiquity was Oliver Stone's *Alexander.* Stone's Alexander repeatedly raises his right arm, fingers apart, when he greets the crowds on his triumphant entry into Babylon. The first instance of his salute is close to the standard form, with arm and hand held straight out. Several following instances are looser, Alexander keeping his fingers from touching each other. (Figure 37) The gesture here looks close to the one Mann had given his Commodus on his triumphal procession through Rome. Stone also includes a scene equivalent to the episode reported by Arrian and discussed in chapter 1, in which Alexander, after receiving a serious wound, shows himself to his army. Now he does so without raising his hand at all, and the soldiers raise their arms only to wave them about. In Stone's film no historical or political comment is intended with these gestures, but the presence of the salute, even if it occurs only briefly, indicates that it is unlikely to vanish from our screens altogether.

That same year, a minor instance of a fake-ancient salute could be observed at the beginning of Joel Schumacher's *The Phantom of the Opera,* the film adaptation of Andrew Lloyd Webber's hugely successful musical. An opera about Hannibal is in rehearsal at the nineteenth-century Paris

---

23. The essays collected in Winkler 2006 examine Petersen's film from various points of view.

Opera. A formation of soldiers is parading on stage and at one time giving the pectoral salute. But these soldiers are a chorus of girls. Mainly because of the women's anatomy as emphasized by their chest armor, the salute here is slightly different. To connoisseurs of the cinematic varieties of Roman salutes this instance may look a trifle bizarre.

2. Television: From *Star Trek* to *Rome*

After the departure of the Roman Empire from the silver screen in the mid-1960s the small screen of television continued to provide viewers with a variant of the raised-arm salute, if sometimes in unexpected contexts. In a 1967 episode of the science-fiction series *Star Trek,* entitled "Mirror, Mirror" and directed by Marc Daniels, Captain Kirk and three of his crew are transported into a parallel universe which appears like a combination of Nazi Germany and the Roman Empire.[24] The United Federation of Planets, a benign political entity modeled on the United States, has here been replaced by an empire whose character traits are patterned on Hitler's Germany: sadistic violence and torture ("Terror must be maintained, or the Empire is doomed"), genocide ("You will die as a race"), and unquestioning obedience to authority, although for the military assassination of one's superior officer is the best way to rise through the ranks. Roman overtones reinforce the message to the viewers that Kirk and his loyal crew are dealing with an evil empire. Vaguely ancient-looking clothing (gold cloth, a sash, an upper-arm bracelet), the mention of someone becoming "a Caesar," and, first and foremost, a new raised-arm salute make the point. This salute, a variation on the pectoral salute already mentioned, begins with the right fist being placed over the heart; then the arm is stretched out (and usually up) before the body, open palm down. At the beginning of the episode the right arm is always extended horizontally, but later at regularly higher angles. (Figures 38–39) The result is simultaneously strange, especially in the futuristic context of the story, and utterly familiar. At one time the henchmen of this empire are characterized as being "like the ancient Gestapo." This paradoxical phrase aptly expresses the standard popular analogy between imperial Rome and Nazi Germany. By contrast, the second *Star Trek* episode dealing with Roman themes—"Bread and Circuses" (1968), directed by Ralph

---

24. Roman-style overtones are a regular feature of this series; most prominent in this regard are the Romulans, an alien race whose society has praetors, senators, and proconsuls and whose origins go back to a small settlement in the marshes which later acquired a Forum and a senate building.

Figures 38–39. *Star Trek:* "Mirror, Mirror." Varieties of the Roman salute in outer space. Paramount.

Senensky—presents viewers with what Captain Kirk calls "a twentieth-century Rome," one that never fell. This surviving Roman Empire still has arena games, slavery, a Proconsul and First Citizen, a Praetorian Guard, and fake neoclassical architecture. The traditional themes of freedom and religious oppression are still the plot's main driving forces, but the usual Fascist trimmings that characterize modern American presentations of Rome are wholly absent. The closest that we come to a raised-arm salute, for instance, is a moment when gladiators raise their right arms but then place their fists over their hearts.

Doubtless the most famous—because most widely watched—Romans of the 1970s are the members of the imperial family in *I, Claudius* (1976),

Herbert Wise's highly successful adaptation of Robert Graves's novels *I, Claudius* (1934) and *Claudius the God* (1935) for the BBC. The series was noteworthy for the adaptation of big-screen themes and visual styles to the small screen. A scholar has summarized these changes:

> Television ... altered the cinematic spectacle of Roman imperial power and corruption. In film, the spectacle is externalized, fully staged in elaborate, often monumental, sets, peopled by vast crowds, and accompanied by special effects. On television in *I, Claudius,* the family becomes the spectacle ... [and] promises to reveal the workings of empire through a domestic drama. ... The limits of budget and of the television screen turn the Hollywood signifiers of imperial Rome (armies on the march, gladiatorial games, fantastical debauches) into what are largely a series of gestures, most of which translate the spectacular into familial scenes or contain it within domestic space. So, for example, scenes at the gladiatorial games focus exclusively on the imperial family in their box relishing the violent struggle of imaginary gladiators to the roar of a Roman mob whose presence is suggested by sound effects. Any fully realized spectacles take place in the enclosed spaces of palace rooms or gardens. ... For the rest, the television audience watches some acts of violent murder and, most often, characters conversing, exchanging confidences, and making speeches.[25]

The effect is repetitive, visually dull, and anti-cinematic. To make the point with only slight hyperbole, in an eleven-hour soap opera about the rich, (in)famous, and dysfunctional we follow endless parades of talking heads in endlessly repeated interiors. But *I, Claudius,* the spiritual precursor of an even longer if more cinematic sex saga co-produced by the BBC thirty years later (on this below), predictably and, given its limitations, almost by necessity adheres to any number of historical and visual stereotypes about the Romans. These include the straight-arm salute. Although it does not occur with the frequency one might have expected a decade or two earlier, it is still prominently on display. "Let the games begin!" proclaims Marcellus after raising his right arm to an off-screen crowd in Episode 1. In Episodes 2 and 3, for instance, messengers in standard-issue Roman uniform bring missives and salute in the accustomed fashion; the first such instance even features a clearly audible heel being clicked (or stamped on the marble floor). With such modern militarism

---

25. Quoted from Sandra R. Joshel, "*I, Claudius:* Projection and Imperial Soap Opera," in Joshel, Malamud, and McGuire 2001, 119–61; quotation at 120.

firmly in place, viewers will feel familiar in this sex-and-violence saga: Roman business as usual.

Boris Sagal's film *Masada* (1981) attempts, with at least some success, a more thoughtful presentation of the Roman Empire but, in view of its subject, the film returns to the standard portrayal of Rome as oppressor, especially at the end. The absence of overtly Fascist iconography is, however, noteworthy. The official Roman army salute is to put the right hand over the heart, open palm down. Nevertheless the legionary commander may still give a version of the familiar raised-arm salute, elbow bent at about a ninety-degree angle. Franc Roddam's three-hour television film *Cleopatra* (1999), strongly indebted to Mankiewicz's version, features the raised-arm salute when Caesar enters Rome, but it does not look particularly militaristic or Fascist. The fist-over-heart greeting, which seems to have been popularized by *The Fall of the Roman Empire*, also occurs here. In Kevin Connor's television film *Mary, Mother of Jesus* (1999) the Romans again appear as precursors of the Nazis, not least in their dramatic function as persecutors of Jews, but they do not exhibit the raised-arm salute. Pontius Pilate raises his right arm at the trial of Jesus, but only to call for silence.

In 2001 distinguished writer-director Jerzy Kawalerowicz made the first Polish version of *Quo Vadis?* (with its titular question mark restored) as a television epic that lasts over four and a half hours. Internationally the film was released in various shortened versions as a theatrical feature. Variations of the familiar salute occur as expected. A Roman officer, for example, greets General Plautius with a raised-arm salute, elbow bent and lower arm and palm held vertically, to deliver a command from Emperor Nero. He then strikes his fist on his heart. It is unlikely that Kawalerowicz, who had been born in 1922, was unaware of the historical and pseudohistorical implications of the gesture. That here he combines a variation of the Fascist salute with a standard cinematic one is telling: he follows filmic tradition but avoids strict analogies between Romans and Nazis.

Further examples appear in the three-hour television film *Imperium: Augustus* (2003), directed by Roger Young and the first of a series of several projected epics about major Roman emperors. These are British-Italian-German co-productions on a large and expensive scale. The one about Augustus has the set pieces and the raised-arm salutes that we expect. The first salute occurs on the part of a Roman centurion, his elbow bent. More examples are seen when Julius Caesar triumphantly enters Rome after his victory at Munda and when, later on, the troops of Mark Antony parade past Octavian through the Roman Forum on the occasion of Antony's return to the East. On one occasion Octavian greets the Roman rabble with the raised-arm salute. Before Cleopatra's dead body in Alexandria Roman legionaries so hail Agrippa, the architect of Octavian's victory at Actium in 31 B.C. Despite its disappointing plot—a soap opera set in Augustus' family and with the historical background to his rule told in extensive flashbacks—the film takes pains to impress viewers with the accuracy of its sets and its cultural savvy. (This Augustus quotes Virgil.) But it cannot shake itself loose from the traditional cinematic iconography of the Roman salute. The same had been the case a year earlier in Uli Edel's television film *Caesar* (or *Julius Caesar*). The senators officially greet Caesar, now made dictator, with the raised-arm salute in the senate house. Earlier, the Roman commoners in the marketplace greet Caesar with arms raised in loose gestures ("Good morning to you, Caesar" and "Hail Caesar") to indicate his popularity. Pompey uses a comparable salute during his triumph. But right arms also go up when the senate votes. In the later installment *Imperium: Nero* (2004), directed by Paul Marcus, the raised-arm salute, with elbow bent, appears as a military form of greeting but does not look particularly Fascist; the standard fist-over-heart salute occurs as well. Emperor Claudius, on his triumphant return to Rome, holds his right arm horizontally in front of his body and then, with fingers slightly apart, to the side when he greets the people lining the sides of the road. When Nero appears at a banquet, one guest gives him the raised-arm salute; Nero himself greets those assembled with his right arm stretched out horizontally, his palm tilted slightly upward and his fingers apart. Similarities to the horizontal salutes in Wyler's *Ben-Hur* are probably unintentional.

Empire (2005), a four-hour television series with multiple directors, purports to tell how Julius Caesar's adopted son Octavius took power to become Augustus, Rome's first emperor. The standard raised-arm salute is on display in the opening sequence, Caesar's return to Rome, and appears with greater emphasis just before Caesar's assassination when Cassius and the senators greet Caesar in the senate hall and again when Mark Antony incites the Roman crowd so to salute Caesar's body in the Forum. The scene last mentioned is a rather unabashedly free reimagining of the most famous part in Shakespeare's *Julius Caesar*. It indicates that the filmmakers were more concerned with telling a new version of a venerable story than with attempting to do justice to the past, either to great works of literature that deal with the same subject or to Roman history itself, to which this film's plotline bears only the most fleeting resemblances. On the other hand, alert viewers will have realized from the beginning that Scott's *Gladiator* and, to a smaller degree, Kubrick's *Spartacus* are the inspiration, if that is the right word, for *Empire*. Less obvious is the visual echo of Gallone's *Scipione l'Africano* in a very brief scene set in the Roman Forum. Kubrick's epic has also cast its long shadow over Robert Dornhelm's television film *Spartacus* (2004), in which raised-arm salutes appear in two scenes in which Romans conduct important business of state. Glabrus, the first Roman commander appointed to fight Spartacus, salutes the senate and is saluted in return with raised right arms, elbows bent. In the same way the senate reacts to the proclamation that Pompey and Crassus have received "the honorable and noble title of Co-Consul of the Roman Empire" after victory over the rebellious slaves. Perhaps the senators' diffidence expressed in their salute is due to this unusually silly formulation, replete with the common American mispronunciation of *consul* as "counsel."

Also in 2005 a kind of Roman salute that attempts strenuously to avoid any similarity to the Nazi or Fascist salute could be observed repeatedly and with even greater impact in the British-American television series *Rome,* directed by divers hands. Continued for a second season that aired in 2007, its plot ranges from Julius Caesar's conquest of Gaul to the deaths of Antony and Cleopatra. Obviously a story of twenty-two hours of screen time that deals largely with conquests, battles, great generals, and empires must demonstrate to its millions of viewers worldwide that the famous Roman war machine was as thoroughly and precisely drilled as that of any modern power (or superpower). So the visual aesthetic (if that is the word) of *I, Claudius* has been abandoned, and *Rome* looks much more like a "real" film, with regular outdoor sequences, action scenes, and other spectacular ingredients. Indoor and outdoor sex and violence are on plentiful display as well. And the military employs a right-arm salute as a regular part of Roman army ritual. As we have seen frequently before, these Romans follow military patterns that are familiar to contemporary audiences and can be heard in commands like "Dismiss!" or addresses of superior officers or Julius Caesar as "sir." But despite all manner of intrigue, corruption, political murder, violence, and explicit sex that are attributed to them, these Romans are not the stereotypical evil conquerors familiar from Hollywood's films of the 1950s. As a result their salute is not the familiar straight-arm salute. Instead, the military salute shown in *Rome* resembles the pectoral salute: first the right hand, palm down, is placed over the heart, then the arm is rapidly extended horizontally or higher to the front of the body. A telling example of how important the gesture is meant to appear to viewers demonstrates how filmmakers can use a fictional but vaguely familiar gesture as a means toward rather subtle characterization even of a major character. (Figures 40–41)

Figures 40–41. *Rome.* Caesar (r.) receiving combination pectoral and straight-arm salute. HBO.

The moment in question occurs shortly before the battle of Pharsalus. Caesar, resting in his army tent, unexpectedly receives bad news about his enemy Pompey Magnus (who ought to be called either Pompeius Magnus or Pompey the Great) from an officer called Fulvio. (He ought to be called Fulvius.) In his excitement Fulvio forgets all military protocol: he omits to salute Caesar before delivering his message. This Caesar, however, closely resembles his historical model, for he keeps his cool even in adversity. He is not about to show concern, much less anguish or panic, at this sudden information before even a single one of his men. To make this point to viewers, the filmmakers have the following brief exchange take place between Caesar and Fulvio in Caesar's tent:

FULVIO: "Sir! Pompey's legions are in the field in battle array."
CAESAR: "Thank you, Fulvio. Have you forgotten how to salute?"
FULVIO: "I haven't, sir! No excuse, *sir!*" [*Salutes.*]
CAESAR: "Gracchus, sound assembly! [*To Fulvio:*] Have Zeno saddle my horse."
FULVIO: "Sir!" [*Salutes again and leaves.*]

This brief scene looks snazzy, and so throughout this long film do many others involving army salutes. They may well have delighted the Christian Falangists of America, whose gesture the actors in *Rome* largely imitate, although presumably neither they nor their writers or directors were aware of the Falangists' salute or realized what ideology they might be thought to express. But there is more. Close analogies to this salute in *Rome* had occurred decades earlier on American television and European cinema screens. The variant encountered in "Mirror, Mirror," the *Star Trek* episode discussed above, is almost if not quite identical, for there the right fist, not the open hand, had been placed over the heart. A salute virtually identical to the one we watch being performed with great smartness in *Rome* had, however, appeared over a period of several years during the 1960s in a series of German Westerns![26] The pectoral salute was the standard greeting of, for instance, the heroic Apache chief, the most romantic reincarnation of the noble savage, and his white bloodbrother, although with the fourth and fifth fingers bent while the right arm goes out from the body. (Figure 42 shows a moment from Harald Reinl's *Winnetou, 1. Teil* of 1963; English title: *Apache Gold*.) These films, immensely popular domestically if less so abroad, are now virtually unknown except among a small number of European aficionados. More familiar is the moment in François Truffaut's *Fahrenheit 451* (1966) in which two members of the fire brigade-cum-police greet each other with the pectoral salute. This film depicts a totalitarian society of the future that is modeled on Nazi Germany, replete with thought control, book burnings, and black helmets and uniforms. (Figure 43) Although the left arm is used for this salute, the implications are obvious.

---

26. On the German Westerns, most of which were loose adaptations of novels or stories by popular author Karl May (1842–1912), a favorite author of Hitler's, see especially Frayling 1998, 103–17 (chapter entitled "Karl May and the Noble Savage").

Figure 42. *Apache Gold*. The salute in the American West as imagined in Western Germany. Rialto Film.

Figure 43. *Fahrenheit 451*. A variant of the salute in a futuristic totalitarian society. Enterprise Vineyard/Universal.

conclusion

It is now time for a comprehensive assessment of the cinematic history of the raised-arm salute. In the preceding chapters we have met a formidable array of ancient peoples from various historical epochs and geographical locations and with separate cultures, customs, symbols, and religions—to name only those aspects that historical films emphasize most.[1] But across any boundaries of space and time, at least in the imagination of filmmakers, all these peoples, nations, and tribes have one thing in common: they are united in their knowledge and ready use of the raised-arm salute. A list of the nationalities we have encountered may be instructive. They are:

Arabs
Armenians
Babylonians
Carthaginians
Egyptians
Etruscans
Gauls
Germans
Greeks

---

1. Bertelli 1995, 39, summarizes the convention of historical film to treat ancient peoples in similar, if not identical, ways and to see all cultures of the past through the lens of our own. Cf. also my comments on film and historical authenticity in "*Gladiator* and the Traditions of Historical Cinema," in Winkler 2004, 16–30, at 16–24.

Huns
Israelites and Jews (from Old and New Testaments)
Lygians
Numidians and other Africans
Persians
Romans
Sabaeans
Thracians
Trojans

This is a veritable league of ancient nations. A complete survey of American and especially Italian spectacles set in any of the ancient cultures or beyond, although impossible to carry out, may well add a few other nations or tribes who are shown to have employed the gesture. As we have seen, New-Testament Jews who employ the raised-arm gesture include Jesus and his disciples. Even Incas, an ancient people from an entirely different part of the world, join these classical ancients. So do nineteenth-century American Indians when presented as yet another exotic people. It does not at all matter if historical enemies share the custom of raised-arm salutes, as do Greeks and their mythical and historical foes, the Trojans and Persians, or Old-Testament Hebrews and Arabs.

Perhaps one more instance of a raised arm is worth mentioning, if mainly for curiosity's sake (or as evidence that someone who has spent years watching historical films is liable to end up suffering from a cinematic raised-arm complex). But my example once more illustrates the importance of gesture for epic films. The creation sequence of *The Bible: In the Beginning . . .* (1966), John Huston's adaptation of the first twenty-two chapters of the Book of Genesis, culminates with the creation of Adam. A series of dramatic dissolves shows us, over clouds of swirling dust, the development of a vaguely human-looking lump of clay into a young man, who slowly rises from the ground and half turns to face the camera in a medium close-up. Huston's set-up of the scene pays indirect homage to the most famous of all images of this moment as painted by Michelangelo on the Sistine Chapel ceiling. Michelangelo's Adam was handsome and athletic; Huston's is as tall and slender as viewers might expect, but he is also quite the Nordic type. (He is played by American actor Michael Parks.) And what is the first thing this Adam does while getting up? As if saluting and thereby acknowledging his creator, he raises—no, not his right but his left arm, fingers slightly apart. (Figure 44) Michelangelo's Adam had also extended his left arm toward God. In Huston's staging Adam's raised arm makes two points, as it were.

180 / *Conclusion*

Figure 44. *The Bible: In the Beginning.* . . . Adam's first gesture at the culmination of the world's creation. Twentieth-Century Fox.

Primarily it reminds viewers of its famous model, but in addition it follows the same strategy that we already witnessed in the silent era: not to obstruct the camera's view, as a raised *right* arm would do. The postures of these two Adams are by no means identical, but the screen Adam equally fits two visual traditions, that of the history of painting and that of epic cinema.

In view of all this, and particularly in view of the ethnic variety we have traced, the conclusion is inescapable that the term "Roman salute" makes no historical sense. But it does make political and ideological sense to all those who see in the Romans a model for power and might and for glorious conquest of others (if not for the less glorious kind of defeat at the hands of these others that we commonly refer to as the fall of Rome). It made sense to D'Annunzio and Mussolini and their followers and to their imitators in Nazi Germany. It still makes sense to the modern epigones of Fascism and Nazism until this day. The history of the gesture from the nineteenth-century stage to the silent screen, on both of which it was free of any ideological messages, and on to its close association with two destructive totalitarian systems tells us much about the vulnerability of a past to the demands of political manipulation, even if that past is so well documented as to provide us with sufficient knowledge to make its use or abuse for political purposes more than suspect. The power of modern media, ubiquitous as they now are, was a precondition for the political turn in the history of the raised-arm salute. The media convey the messages, and in the process they become inextricably identified with these messages. The cinematic history of the *saluto romano* provides us with one of the most illuminating cases in point.

So it seems likely that future feature films or individual television films or whole series set in ancient Rome, such as further installments in the *Imperium* series, or set in other areas and eras of antiquity will continue to feature the raised-arm salute. Various television films dealing with Old and New Testament themes have gained a popularity indicative of the social and religious climate of the late twentieth and early twenty-first century, a phenomenon not likely to abate very soon. An instance is *L'inquiesta* (*The Inquiry*), a three-hour Italian television film directed by Giulio Base and a remake of Damiano Damiani's 1986 film of the same title. The inquiry concerns a Roman investigation into the death of a criminal in Palestine who is, of course, none other than Jesus. In 2006 the investigator still raises his right arm in the familiar way. Ancient times, classical and biblical alike, are experiencing a kind of renaissance in the visual media. In this as in much else, the attractions of myth and fiction prove to be stronger than historical fact. The irresistible urge to mix them is something that filmmakers, chiefly directors and their screenwriters, have long acknowledged. Riccardo Freda, director of several ancient epics including the 1953 *Spartaco,* put it in disarming and indisputable terms: "History is full of possibilities for enthralling scenarios."[2] This is despite often strenuous protestations of scrupulous adherence to history on the part of producers or advertising managers who like to pass off their historical films as being correct in every detail. Such claims are intended to emphasize the extent of the historical research that was conducted for their spectacular productions and also intended discreetly, or not so discreetly, to point out to audiences the enormous costs involved in making such films. This in turn reinforces their box-office appeal.

For enthralling historical scenarios to be marketed successfully and, in the age of the global village, to reach the farthest corners of our world, history need not—indeed, better *had* not—be studied or followed too closely. This is true in practically all ways of life: politics and ideology, spectacles on stage and screen, popular literature, and even the fine arts. Despite the great variability of the raised-arm salute in modern times that we have examined, the gesture is still chiefly identified as Roman. No medium has spread this identification farther than the cinema, which most effectively disseminated the *faux*-Roman iconography and other aspects of Fascism and Nazism that are related to antiquity. As a result the Romans themselves have become stereotypical. They could

---

2. Quoted from Leprohon 1972, 178.

be regarded—and were regarded—as proto-Fascists or proto-Nazis. Many of our contemporaries perceive them as a people hopelessly obsessed by collectivism, militarism, imperialism, and all the evils that ancient and modern history has shown to attend these social and political phenomena.[3]

Even dedicated educators have been seduced by the myth of the Roman salute and the power of cinematic images. Anyone opening the 1987 edition of *Jenney's First Year Latin,* a widely used American high-school textbook, will see, before anything else, not one but two large images with the gesture in full-color display. Both are stills from *I, Claudius.* The former is the book's frontispiece and carries the following text, erroneous even in that the still photo is of Marcellus opening the games (on this cf. chapter 7):

> The pose of a Roman senator addressing the Senate is based on that of the famous life-sized bronze statue called the *Arringatore* ("Haranguer").... it represents a magistrat making a speech. Even in the twentieth century, strongly nationalistic leaders copied this pose when addressing the people.

The second still, spread across the book's two title pages, is explained as showing a "Roman general reporting to the Senate."[4]

So it is time to counteract such distorted beliefs, although no single book can hope to refute all popular prejudices against the Romans. But these pages have attempted such a refutation in one specific regard. If and when cinema goers or television watchers among readers encounter Romans saluting in an all too familiar manner in the future, they will no longer need to wonder why. They will realize that the Romans, who in the course of their long history achieved the most famous empire of all time, did not resemble in nature or spirit certain recent empire builders who, in whole or in part, had modeled themselves on the Romans for the creation of their own, if fortunately much shorter-lived, empires.

Rather than ending my historical and cinematic journey on such a serious note, however, I return to my beginning, specifically Gore Vidal's and Guy Debord's points about history and spectacle, and link them to the year 2008. That year saw the most colossal global spectacle ever, the Olympic Games held in China. A French feature film released before

---

3. Similarly Giardina and Vauchez 2000, 215–16.

4. Quotations from Jenney, Scudder, and Baade 1987. This edition sports a still of the chariot race from Wyler's *Ben-Hur* on its cover. The first edition appeared in 1970; later editions followed.

the Games opened was meant to cash in on the occasion: Frédéric Forestier and Thomas Langmann's *Astérix aux jeux olympiques* (*Asterix at the Olympic Games*). This live-action adventure-comedy derives from the popular French cartoons and films about the intrepid Gauls who give bad headaches (besides other aches and woes) to Julius Caesar and his Romans. This time our Gallic heroes compete in the Olympics, over which Caesar himself presides. The film's farcical plot is simultaneously predictable, witty, and eye-popping, not least through an extensive use of computerized special effects that make the *POW!* and *CRASH!* of traditional cartoons possible among real actors. They also enable the directors to show us the most gigantic Roman army ever put on screen, if only as an apparent reality that is irreal in a double sense since it is neither Roman nor even human. (The massed legionaries are almost all digital figures.) But straight and other raised-arm salutes are still on view. A soldier delivering a message to Caesar first puts his right fist over his heart, then extends his whole arm, holding the upper part horizontally, the lower part and his palm vertically. The villainous Brutus, who here is Caesar's son as he was rumored to have been in antiquity, salutes his father with a military-looking raised-left-arm salute and the words "*Ave César.*" Caesar replies by putting his right fist over his heart, extending it into the standard gesture, and saying "*Ave moi*" ("Hail myself"). This is his standard saluting gesture and favorite saying. The joke, repeated several times, makes clear that Caesar is quite the narcissist. (He likes mirrors.) Since he is played by Alain Delon, to many the best-looking male star in the history of French cinema and quite handsome even in his seventies, all this makes for attractive silliness. But if we consider the real spectacle of the 2008 Olympics, digitally and instantaneously transmitted worldwide, together with the computerized spectacle of this film, we may be forcefully reminded of what Debord said about spectacle that covers the entire globe in the empire of passivity and that has abandoned any sense of history. Spectacle, Olympic and cinematic, exists for its own sake. Forestier and Langmann's Caesar is a good illustration of the permanent presence of spectacle, for this Caesar, obsessed with his own appearance in private and public, knows that he is the best show in town. His raised-arm salutes are not just for the masses but also for and to Caesar. "Hail myself" indeed. We may even go a step beyond this and say: "Hail Spectacle! Hail Cinema! *Spectaturi te salutant*. Those about to watch salute you."

appendices

1. Livy's Account of the Horatii and Curiatii

The Roman historian Livy (59 B.C–17? A.D.) gives the following account of the two sets of brothers and the aftermath of their championship fight. About the middle of the seventh century B.C., hostilities between the cities of Rome and Alba Longa had reached a crisis. At that time Tullus Hostilius was king of Rome; Mettius Fufetius was the last ruler (or king) of Alba. By the third century B.C. the episode of the Horatii and Curiatii had taken a prominent place in the mythic-heroic tradition about early Rome. Livy describes in detail the ceremony accompanying the treaty between the Romans and the Albans, the oldest instance of a formal treaty on record. The oath sworn by both sides as part of this treaty is the only one to appear in the entire story.

My translation of Livy's text (*From the Foundation of the City* 1.24–26) is indebted for some turns of phrase to R. M. Ogilvie, *A Commentary on Livy: Books 1–5* (Oxford: Clarendon Press, 1965; rpt. with addenda, 1970), 109–17, and to *Livy: Book I,* ed. H. E. Gould and J. L. Whiteley (1952; rpt. London: Bristol Classical Press, 1987 and later), 145–53. Ogilvie, 114–15, describes the legal background to Horatius' trial for high treason (*perduellio*), which contained a provision not for acquittal but instead for an appeal to the people (*provocatio*), and his sister's guilt of *proditio* ("treachery," for mourning an enemy). Fetial priests presided over peace ceremonies or declarations of war. The lictors (lit., "binders"), who attended Roman magistrates, carried out their sentences; the *fasces* were their insignia of office and indicated their power to inflict corporal (rods) and capital (axe) punishment. On the etymology of the term *sororium tigillum* ("Sister's Beam") in connection with an archaic rite of passage see Ogilvie, 117.

BY CHANCE THERE were at that time in the two armies two sets of three brothers, quite equal in age and strength. That they were the Horatii and

Curiatii is clear enough, and scarcely any other ancient tradition has been known better. But even in such a famous matter there remains a doubt about the names: to which people the Horatii, to which the Curiatii belonged. Sources tend to either view, although I find more who call the Roman brothers the Horatii, and I am inclined to follow them. To each set of brothers the kings proposed that they should take up the sword on behalf of their country and that supreme rule should go to the victorious side. There was no objection, and a time and place were agreed upon. Before the fight a treaty was struck between the Romans and the Albans on these terms, that whichever country's citizens should win this battle, that people should rule over the other in peace and quiet. Different treaties are concluded on different terms, but in their formalities they are always the same. So we understand it to have been on that occasion, too, with the oldest treaty on record. The Fetial priest asked King Tullus as follows: "Do you command me, king, to enter into a treaty with the representative of the Alban people?" The king so commanded. The priest said: "I ask you, king, for the sacred herbiage." The king replied: "Pluck fresh, untainted grass." The Fetial priest brought a fresh plant from the citadel and then asked the king: "Do you, king, appoint me royal ambassador of the sovereign Roman people, with my sacred implements and companions?" The king answered: "I do, without harm to myself or the sovereign Roman people." Marcus Valerius was the Fetial priest, and he appointed Spurius Fusius as spokesman, touching his head and hair with the sacred grass. Such a spokesman is appointed to pronounce the oath formula by which a treaty is solemnly ratified. He does so in a long incantation, which I need not report here. When finally the terms had been read out, he said: "Hear, Jupiter; hear, representative of the Alban people; hear you, too, Alban people. What has been read out publicly from beginning to end from these wax tablets without any intent of deception, and what has been correctly understood here today, from those terms the Roman people will not be the first to depart. But if it does so depart by public consent and intent of deception, then, Jupiter, on that day strike the Roman people just as I will here strike this pig today, and strike it the more fiercely the greater your power and might." Then he struck the pig with a knife of flintstone. In the same way the Albans carried out their own formal ritual and took their own oath through their supreme leader and priests.

The treaty concluded, the sets of triple brothers took up their arms as agreed. On either side their fellow soldiers encouraged their champions, reminding them that their native gods, their country, their parents, all their fellow citizens at home, everybody in the army would now be watching their weapons and the prowess of their hands. With high-spirited confidence in their abilities, and still hearing the voices of everybody urging them on, they proceeded into the middle between the two armies. On either side the two armies had taken their positions in front of their fortifications; they took no part in the immediate danger but very much in the anxiety over the result, since the sovereignty that was at stake depended on the bravery and good luck of such few. Therefore tense and full of suspense, they gave their whole attention to the spectacle that was by no means pleasant.

On a given signal and with weapons at the ready, the triplets rushed against each other with the courage of a large army, as if they were an entire battle line. Neither side was concerned with their mortal danger but only with their country's fate of sovereignty or slavery as their actions would decide it. On their very first collision, shields clashing and gleaming swords flashing, huge awe struck those watching, and they were left speechless and breathless. Hope of victory did not yet incline to either side. Then they joined in hand-to-hand combat. The swift movements of their bodies, the whirlings of weapons and shields, still indecisive, but also their bloody wounds were on display, for all to see. The three Albans were wounded, but two of the Romans, the one after the other, sank to the ground and breathed their last. At their fall the Alban army raised one shout of joy; the Roman levies, deathly pale, had already lost all hope but not yet their anxiety for the only one left, whom the three Curiatii had now surrounded.

By chance he was unharmed, and although he alone was no match for the three together, he was still boldly confident against each of them individually. So, in order to keep his fights with them separate, he took flight, calculating that they would each pursue him to the extent that their bodies, weakened by wounds, would allow them. When he had fled a bit from the earlier place of battle, he looked back and saw them in pursuit at considerable distance from each other, but one quite close to himself. He turned back and attacked this one with great force, and while the Alban army was still shouting to the other Curiatii to help their brother, Horatius had already killed his enemy and, triumphantly, was rushing toward his next duel. Now the Romans spurred on their warrior with the kind of shouts heard from sports fans who cheer at an unexpected event, and he hastened to end the fighting. So before the third Curiatius, who was not far away, could reach him, he had already killed the second one, too. Now only one was left on either side, and the odds of battle were equal, but the two were not equal in hope or energy. The one went into his third engagement highly confident through his lack of wounds and his double victory; the other, exhausted from his wounds, exhausted from running, dragged himself along, already as good as defeated. The slaughter of his brothers before his eyes, he met his victorious enemy. It was not even a real battle any more. Jubilant, the Roman shouted: "Two men I have already handed over to the shades of my brothers; the third I will dedicate to the cause of this war, so that Roman may rule over Alban." From high above he planted his blade deep in the throat of the other, who could barely hold up his shield, and stripped him of his armor as he was lying on the ground.

Cheering and congratulating him, the Romans received Horatius among them, their joy all the greater as the matter had come very close to the result they had feared. Then both sides turned to burying their dead, but with very different feelings, because the ones were exalted by sovereign rule, the others had become subject to a foreign power. The tombs still are where each man fell, the two Roman ones in one and the same place closer to Alba, the three Alban ones nearer Rome but separated, just as the fights had taken place.

Before everybody left the place, Mettius asked Tullus according to their treaty what he commanded him to do. Tullus ordered him to keep his fighting men in arms: he would use them if there were a war with Veii. So the armies were led back home. Horatius was walking at the head of the Romans, displaying his triple set of spoils. His sister, a young girl, who was engaged to be married to one of the Curiatii, met him before the Capena Gate. She recognized on her brother's shoulders her fiancé's cloak, one she had made herself, tore loose her hair, and weeping called her dead fiancé by his name. The grief of his sister in the midst of his own victory and the great rejoicing of all the people aroused the young man's fury, and he drew his sword and stabbed her to death, berating her at the same time. "Go to your fiancé with your childish love," he shouted, "you who have forgotten your dead brothers and your surviving one, you who have forgotten your country. Thus let every Roman woman go to hell who mourns for an enemy."

Such a deed appeared terrible to all, patricians and commoners, but his recent great service to them stood in the way of any punishment for his crime. Still, he was arrested and brought to trial before the king. So as not to become himself responsible for such a tragic and unpopular sentence and inflicting the death penalty, the king called an assembly of the people and said: "I appoint two prosecutors to judge Horatius for high treason according to our law." This law had the most ominous wording: "Let the committee of two judge cases of high treason; if the defendant appeals from them to the people, let him argue his appeal;

if their judgment stands, let the defendant's head be veiled; let him be hanged by a rope from a barren tree; let him be thrashed either inside or outside the city's walls." According to this law the prosecutors were appointed. They did not believe that they could acquit even someone innocent when they had charged him, so one of them said: "Publius Horatius, I judge you guilty of high treason. Come, lictor, tie his hands." The lictor came forward and was about to tie the rope when Horatius, on the urging of Tullus, who was a more lenient interpreter of the law, said: "I appeal!" So the appeal was brought to the people. During this hearing the father, Publius Horatius, affected everybody most because he declared that, in his judgment, his daughter had deserved to be killed; otherwise he would have punished his son himself, as a father has every right to do. Then he begged the people not to deprive him completely of his children, him whom they had seen only a short time before in the company of such excellent offspring. During this speech the old man embraced his son, pointed to the spoils taken from the Curiatii, which had been set up in the spot that is now called The Spears of Horatius, and exclaimed: "This same man, whom you have just now seen walking in honor and celebrating his victory, can you, people of Rome, really bear to see him bound under the yoke and beaten and tortured? Even the eyes of the Albans could hardly endure such a horrendous sight. Go ahead, lictor, tie his hands which, holding sword and shield, won supremacy for the Roman people. Go ahead, veil the head of this city's liberator; hang him from a barren tree; thrash him either inside the city walls, right among the spears and spoils he took from the enemy, or outside the city walls, right among the tombs of the Curiatii. For where can any of you possibly take this young man where his glorious deeds and honors do not completely absolve him from such an utterly vile punishment?"

The people could not hold out against the father's tears or the son's courage, equally high as it was in any danger, and they acquitted him, more because they admired his bravery than because he had justice on his side. So in order that the evident murder yet be atoned for by some act of expiation, the father was ordered to perform the purification of his son at public expense. When certain expiatory sacrifices had been completed, which from then on became a tradition in the clan of the Horatii, a wooden beam was put up across the street, and the young man, head veiled, was led under it by his father as if under the yoke. It is still in place even today, always repaired at public expense; they call it the Sister's Beam. Horatia's tomb was built of square stones on the spot where she had been struck to the ground.

2. The Roman Salute According to *Il Capo-Squadra Balilla*

The *Opera Nazionale Balilla* was the Fascist party's youth organization. Originally Balilla was the nickname of a boy from Genoa—*balilla* means "urchin"—who had thrown a stone at Austrian soldiers and in this way started the revolution which expelled the Austrians from Genoa in 1746.

The organization's handbook provided young Italians (ages 8–14) with information and instructions necessary to conduct themselves as good Fascists in all areas of public and private life. Section 15 deals with the raised-arm salute. My source of the text quoted below is Carlo Galeotti, *Saluto al Duce! I catechismi del Balilla e della piccola italiana* (Rome: Gremese, 2001), 24–25 and 72–73. This book reprints the fourth edition, dated "Anno XIII" of the Fascist era, i.e. 1934, of *Il Capo-Squadra Balilla* (for boys) and, from the same year, *La Capo-Squadra piccola italiana* (for girls). Both contain illustrations of youngsters giving the raised-arm salute with the requisite dedication and snappiness. Except for some typographical differences and the change from *il Comandante* to *la Comandante* in the girls' edition, the text of Section 15 is identical in both versions. I give the text from pages 17–18 of the boys' handbook, followed by my translation. Section 16, here omitted, lists those to whom such a salute is owed. (The king, the Duce, and the pope head the listing in this order.) Galeotti, 10–11 and 16–17, explains the importance of the salute and the name Balilla and its origin. Heller 2008, 110 (ills. 174–78) and 111, provides instructive illustrations.

The *labaro* mentioned in the text is originally the Christogram, a late Roman and early Christian symbol combining the Greek letters *chi* and *rho* (X and P), which begin the name Chrestos (Christus). The Fascists adopted it as insignia of their militia and combat teams (*assoziazioni combattentistiche*).

Text

15) IL SALUTO

Il saluto è la forma di rispetto comune anche nella vita privata. Il saluto deve essere quello romano che si esegue *portando vivamente il braccio destro in avanti con il gomito all'altezza dell' occhio destro e la mano distesa.*

Se da fermi si saluta nella posizione di attenti; camminando, mentre si esegue il saluto romano, si rivolge lo sguardo a chi saluta, continuando a camminare e muovendo il bracchio sinistro. Il saluto va eseguito col braccio destro anche se il superiore o l'insegna che si saluta rimane sulla sinistra. In occasione di sfilata, rassegna ecc. il solo comandante del reparto saluta alzando il braccio; i Balilla in rango si limitano a prendere la posizione di attenti.

Il saluto romano si fa anche in abito borghese, nella vita civile. La stretta di mano, residuo dei vecchi tempi, è abolita.

Vi è obbligo di saluto anche tra pari grado. Il saluto deve essere fatto circa tre passi prima della persona, bandiera, labaro, gagliardetto che si saluta e tale posizione deve esser mantenuta per circa quattro passi dopo.

Quando si riceve il saluto si deve restituire. Il saluto di un reparto inquadrato è il sequente:

da fermo: saluta il Comandante dando prima l'attenti;

in marcia: saluta il Comandante dando prima l'attenti a destra (o sinistra).

A questo comando i componenti del reparto volgono vivacemente la testa a destra o a sinistra mantenendo questa posizione per circa quattro passi dopo la persona che si saluta. *Nell'attenti a destr'* (o a sinistr') *il naturale movimento delle braccie non deve arrestarsi.*

Translation

15) The Salute

The salute is the common form of respect also in private life. The salute has to be the Roman one, which is executed by *carrying one's right arm lively to the front, with the elbow at the level of the right eye and the hand outstretched.*

When standing still, one greets in the position of standing at attention; when walking while the Roman salute is being given, one's eye is turned toward the person saluted while continuing to walk and moving the left arm. The salute is to be given with the right arm even if the higher-ranking person or the insignia being saluted remain on the left. During a parade, inspection, etc., only the commanding officer of the detachment salutes by raising his arm; the Balilla in the ranks are restricted to standing at attention.

The Roman salute is also given in civilian clothing [when the Balilla is not in uniform] in private life. The handshake, a relic of past times, is abolished.

It is obligatory to salute someone of equal rank as well. The salute must be given about three steps in front of the person, flag, *labaro,* or pennant which is being saluted, and this position must be maintained for about four steps past.

When the salute is being received, it must be returned. The salute of a detachment in block formation is the following:

from standing position: salute the commanding officer by first standing at attention;

on the march: salute the commanding officer by first standing at attention to the right (or left).

At this command the individual members of the detachment turn the head lively to the right or to the left, maintaining this position for about four steps past the person who is being saluted. *When standing at attention to the right* (or to the left), *the natural movement of the arms need not be stopped.*

3. Modern Scholarship on Fascism, Nazism, and Classical Antiquity

The following are among the standard or most readily accessible works on the subject. Except for the documentary film, all contain further references. Paxton, *The Anatomy of Fascism,* and Payne, *A History of Fascism, 1914–1945,* provide a modern introduction to the topic, with updated bibliographies. Works cited in the notes to chapters 1–7 are not again listed here, except to point to any chapters or articles in them that have not been mentioned.

ITALY

Salvatore Pisani, "Faschismus: I. Kunst und Architektur," and Mariella Cagnetta and Claudio Schiano, "Faschismus: II. Politik und Gesellschaft," both in *Der Neue Pauly: Enzyklopädie der Antike,* 13 (1999), cols. 1084–96 and 1096–1105, give detailed overviews with references mainly to Italian and German scholarship, respectively. See further Mariella Cagnetta, *Antichisti e impero fascista* (Bari: Dedalo, 1979); Dino Cofrancesco, "Appunti per un'analisi del mito romano nell'ideologia fascista," *Storia contemporanea* 11 (1980): 383–411; Peter Bondanella, *The Eternal City: Roman Images in the Modern World* (Chapel Hill and London: University of North Carolina Press, 1987), 172–206 (chapter entitled "Mussolini's Fascism and the Imperial Vision of Rome"); Clive Foss, "Augustus and the Poets in Mussolini's Rome," in *Style and Tradition: Studies in Honor of Wendell Clausen,* ed. Peter Knox and Clive Foss (Stuttgart and Leipzig: Teubner, 1998), 306–25; Peter Aicher, "Mussolini's Forum and the Myth of Augustan Rome," *The Classical Bulletin* 7 (2000): 117–39; Nicola Terrenato, "Ancestor Cults: The Perception of Ancient Rome in Modern Italian Culture," in *Images of Rome: Perceptions of Ancient Rome in Europe and the United States in the Modern Age,* ed. Richard Hingley (Portsmouth, RI: Journal of Roman Archaeology, 2001), 71–89; Ann Thomas Wilkins, "Augustus, Mussolini, and the Parallel Imagery of Empire," in *Donatello among the Blackshirts: History and Modernity in the Visual Culture of Fascist Italy,* ed. Claudia Lazzaro and Roger J. Crum (Ithaca and London: Cornell

University Press, 2005), 53–65 and 252–54 (notes); and Jobst Welge, "Fascism *Triumphans:* On the Architectural Translation of Rome," in *Donatello among the Blackshirts,* 83–94 and 257–59 (notes). On the term *romanità,* characteristic of Italian Fascism, see Philip V. Cannistraro, "Romanità," in *Historical Dictionary of Fascist Italy,* ed. Philip V. Cannistraro (Westport and London: Greewood Press, 1982), 461–63; Romke Visser, "Fascist Doctrine and the Cult of the 'Romanità,'" *Journal of Contemporary History* 27 (1992): 5–22; Marla Stone, "A Flexible Rome: Fascism and the Cult of *romanità,*" in *Roman Presences: Receptions of Rome in European Culture, 1789–1945,* ed. Catharine Edwards (Cambridge: Cambridge University Press, 1999), 205–20; and Andrea Giardina and André Vauchez, *Il mito di Roma: Da Carlo Magno a Mussolini* (Rome and Bari: Laterza, 2000), 212–96 (chapter entitled "Ritorno al futuro: la romanità fascista"). Cf. also Luigi Barzini, *The Italians: A Full-Length Portrait Featuring Their Manners and Morals* (1964; rpt. New York: Touchstone, 1996), 117–32 (chapter entitled "Cola di Rienzi or the Obsession of Antiquity," which details analogies between Cola and Mussolini).

GERMANY

Alex Scobie, *Hitler's State Architecture: The Impact of Classical Antiquity* (University Park and London: College Art Association/Pennsylvania State University Press, 1990), especially 9–36 (chapter 1: "Mussolini, Hitler, and Classical Antiquity"); Frederic Spotts, *Hitler and the Power of Aesthetics* (2002; rpt. Woodstock and New York: Overlook Press, 2003), especially 309–98 ("The Master Builder"); Eric Michaud, *The Cult of Art in Nazi Germany,* tr. Janet Lloyd (Stanford: Stanford University Press, 2004), with discussion and illustrations of Nazi art and architecture patterned on classical models; Christian Welzbacher, "'Die geheiligten Bezirke unseres Volkes'–Antikenrezeption in der Architektur des Dritten Reiches als Beispiel für das Nationalsozialistische Historismuskonzept," in *Tradita et Inventa: Beiträge zur Rezeption der Antike,* ed. Manuel Baumbach (Heidelberg: Winter, 2000), 495–513; Volker Losemann, *Nationalsozialismus und Antike: Studien zur Entwicklung des Faches Alte Geschichte 1933–1945* (Hamburg: Hoffmann und Campe, 1977), with special focus on German ancient historians, and "The Nazi Concept of Rome," in *Roman Presences,* 221–35; and Frank-Lothar Kroll, "Geschichte und Politik im Weltbild Hitlers," *Vierteljahresschrift für Zeitgeschichte* 44 (1996): 327–53. See further Volker Losemann, "Nationalsozialismus: I. NS-Ideologie und die Altertumswissenschaften," and Hans-Ernst Mittig, "Nationalsozialismus: II. Kunst und

Architektur," both in *Der Neue Pauly,* 15.1 (2001), cols. 723–54 and 754–67; John T. Quinn, "The Ancient Rome of Adolf Hitler," *The Classical Bulletin* 76 (2000): 141–56; Hans Dietz, "Classics, Ancient History, and Ideological State Institutes in the Third Reich," *Quaderni di storia* 11 (1985): 129–35; Peter Lebrecht Schmidt, "Latin Studies in Germany, 1933–1945: Institutional Conditions, Political Pressures, Scholarly Consequences," in *Texts, Ideas, and the Classics: Scholarship, Theory, and Classical Literature,* ed. S. J. Harrison (Oxford and New York: Oxford University Press, 2001), 285–300; and Karl Christ, "Zum Caesarbild der faschistischen Epoche," in Karl Christ, *Zum Caesarbild der faschistischen Epoche: Reden zur Ehrenpromotion* (Berlin: Freie Universität Berlin, 1993), 15–28. See now especially *Antike und Altertumswissenschaft in der Zeit von Faschismus und Nationalsozialismus,* ed. Beat Näf (Mandelbachtal and Cambridge: Edition Cicero, 2001), and in this the following: Beat Näf, "Zu den Forschungen über Antike und Altertumswissenschaften in der Zeit von Faschismus und Nationalsozialismus" (15–70; an annotated bibliography), Volker Losemann, "Nationalsozialismus und Antike: Bemerkungen zur Forschungsgeschichte" (71–88), and Hans-Ernst Mittig, "Antikebezüge nationalsozialistischer Propagandaarchitektur und -skulptur" (245–65). A source often overlooked is Hermann Giesler, *Ein anderer Hitler: Bericht seines Architekten Hermann Giesler: Erlebnisse, Gespräche, Reflexionen,* 5th ed. (Leoni am Starnberger See: Druffel-Verlag, 1982), with numerous illustrations of models for large-scale pseudo-Roman designs. Giesler's book is in the nature of an *apologia pro vita sua (et pro duce suo).* The documentary film *Architektur des Untergangs* (1989; English-language version: *Architecture of Doom),* directed by Peter Cohen, provides numerous visual illustrations of neoclassical Nazi architecture.

works cited

XI. *Olympiade Berlin 1936: Amtlicher Bericht.* 1937. 2 vols. Berlin: Limpert.
Abel, Richard. 1999. *The Ciné Goes to Town: French Cinema 1896–1914.* 2nd ed. Berkeley, Los Angeles, and London: University of California Press.
Ades, Dawn, ed. 1995. *Art and Power: Europe under the Dictators 1930–45: The XXIII Council of Europe Exhibition.* London: Thames and Hudson.
Aldrete, Gregory S. 1999. *Gestures and Acclamations in Ancient Rome.* Baltimore and London: Johns Hopkins University Press.
———. 2004. *Daily Life in the Roman City: Rome, Pompeii, and Ostia.* Westport and London: Greenwood Press.
Alföldi, Andreas. 1970. *Die monarchische Repräsentation im römischen Kaiserreiche.* Darmstadt: Wissenschaftliche Buchgesellschaft.
Alkemeyer, Thomas. 1996. *Körper, Kult und Politik: Von der "Muskelreligion" Pierre de Coubertins zur Inszenierung von Macht in den Olympischen Spielen von 1936.* Frankfurt am Main and New York: Campus Verlag.
Allert, Tilman. 2008. *The Hitler Salute: On the Meaning of a Gesture.* Tr. Jefferson Chase. New York: Metropolitan Books.
Anderegg, Michael. 2004. *Cinematic Shakespeare.* Lanham: Rowman and Littlefield.
Andreae, Bernard. 1999. *Die römische Kunst.* 2nd ed. Rpt. Darmstadt: Wissenschaftliche Buchgesellschaft, 2000.
Andreoli, Annamaria. 2000. *Il vivere inimitabile: Vita di Gabriele d'Annunzio.* Milan: Mondadori.
———, ed. 2003. *D'Annunzio e Trieste nel centenario del primo volo aereo.* Rome: De Luca.
Antongini, Tom. 1938a. *D'Annunzio.* London: Heinemann/Boston: Little, Brown.
———. 1938b. *Vita segreta di Gabriele D'Annunzio.* Milan: Mondadori.
———. 1957. *Quarant'anni con D'Annunzio.* Milan: Mondadori.
Appelbaum, Stanley. 1980. *The Chicago World's Fair of 1893: A Photographic Record.* New York: Dover.

Argentieri, Mino. 2003. *L'occhio del regime: Informazione e propaganda nel cinema del fascismo*. 2nd ed. Rome: Bulzoni.
Aristarco, Guido. 1996. *Il cinema fascista: Il primo e il dopo*. Bari: Dedalo.
Austin, Gilbert. 1966 (new ed.). *Chironomia, or A Treatise on Rhetorical Delivery*. Ed. Mary Margaret Robb and Lester Thonssen. Carbondale and Edwardsville: Southern Illinois University Press.
Bach, Steven. 2007. *Leni: The Life and Work of Leni Riefenstahl*. New York: Knopf.
Badger, Reid. 1979. *The Great American Fair: The World's Columbian Exposition and American Culture*. Chicago: Nelson Hall.
Baer, John W. 1992. *The Pledge of Allegiance: A Centennial History, 1892–1992*. Annapolis: Baer.
Bagshaw, Mel. 2005. *The Art of Italian Film Posters*. London: Black Dog Publishing.
Ball, Robert Hamilton. 1968. *Shakespeare on Silent Film: A Strange Eventful History*. New York: Theatre Arts Books.
Barnett, Dene. 1987. *The Art of Gesture: The Practices and Principles of 18th Century Acting*. Heidelberg: Winter.
Barsam, Richard M. 1975. *Filmguide to* Triumph of the Will. Bloomington: Indiana University Press.
Barzini, Luigi. 1984. *The Europeans*. Harmondsworth: Penguin. Originally 1983.
———. 1996. *The Italians: A Full-Length Portrait Featuring Their Manners and Morals*. New York: Touchstone. Originally 1964.
Baudrillard, Jean. 1994. *Simulacra and Simulation*. Tr. Sheila Faria Glaser. Ann Arbor: University of Michigan Press.
———. 2002. *Screened Out*. Tr. Chris Turner. London and New York: Verso.
Beard, Mary. 2007. *The Roman Triumph*. Cambridge: Belknap Press/Harvard University Press.
Ben-Ghiat, Ruth. 2001. *Fascist Modernities: Italy, 1922–1945*. Berkeley, Los Angeles, and London: University of California Press.
Ben-Hur (souvenir booklet). 1926. New York: Metro-Goldwyn-Mayer.
Bergemann, Johannes. 1990. *Römische Reiterstatuen: Ehrendenkmäler im öffentlichen Bereich*. Mainz: von Zabern.
Berlin, Isaiah. 1991. *The Crooked Timber of Humanity: Chapters in the History of Ideas*. Ed. Henry Hardy. New York: Knopf.
Bernardini, Aldo, Vittorio Martinelli, and Matilde Tortora. 2005. *Enrico Guazzoni: regista pittore*. Doria (Cosenza): La Mongolfiera.
Berry, Joanne. 2007. *The Complete Pompeii*. New York: Thames and Hudson.
Bertelli, Sergio. 1995. *I corsari del tempo: Gli errori e gli orrori dei film storici*. Florence: Ponte alle grazie. Originally 1989.
———, and Monica Centanni, eds. 1995. *Il Gesto nel rito e nel cerimoniale dal mondo antico ad oggi*. Florence: Ponte alle grazie.
Bertetto, Paolo, and Gianni Rondolino, eds. 1998. *Cabiria e il suo tempo*. Milan: Museo Nazionale del Cinema/Il Castoro.
Bierman, John. 1988. *Napoleon III and His Carnival Empire*. Toronto: McClelland and Stewart.
Binder, Gerhard, ed. 1991. *Saeculum Augustum*. Vol. 3: *Kunst und Bildersprache*. Darmstadt: Wissenschaftliche Buchgesellschaft.
Blasetti, Alessandro. 1939. "Cinematografo storico e documentario." *Film* 2 (January 28).

Bleicken, Jochen. 1963. "Coniuratio: Die Schwurszene auf den Münzen und Gemmen der römischen Republik." *Jahrbuch für Numismatik und Geldgeschichte* 13: 51–70 and plates VII–VIII.
Boegehold, Alan L. 1999. *When a Gesture Was Expected: A Selection of Examples from Archaic and Classical Greek Literature.* Princeton: Princeton University Press.
Bohrer, Karl-Heinz, ed. 1983. *Mythos und Moderne: Begriff und Bild einer Rekonstruktion.* Frankfurt am Main: Suhrkamp.
Boime, Albert. 1987. *Art in the Age of Revolution: 1750–1800.* Chicago and London: University of Chicago Press.
———. 1990. *Art in an Age of Bonapartism: 1800–1815.* Chicago and London: University of Chicago Press.
Boker, George Henry. 1963. Rpt. 1975. Glaucus *and Other Plays by George Henry Boker.* Ed. Scully Bradley. Bloomington: Indiana University Press. Originally 1940.
Booth, Michael R. 1981. *Victorian Spectacular Theatre, 1850–1910.* Boston, London, and Henley: Routledge and Kegan Paul.
———. 1991. *Theatre in the Victorian Age.* Cambridge: Cambridge University Press.
Bordes, Philippe. 1983. *Le Serment du Jeu de Paume de Jacques-Louis David: Le peintre, son milieu et son temps de 1789 à 1792.* Paris: Ministère de la Culture/Editions de la Réunion des musées nationaux.
———. 2005. *Jacques-Louis David: Empire to Exile.* New Haven and London: Yale University Press.
Bordwell, David, Janet Staiger, and Kristin Thompson. 1985. *Classical Hollywood Cinema: Film Style and Mode of Production to 1960.* New York: Columbia University Press.
Borgese, G. A. 1937. *Goliath: The March of Fascism.* New York: Viking. Rpt. 1938.
Boschung, Dietrich. 1993. *Die Bildnisse des Augustus.* Berlin: Mann.
Bosworth, R. J. B. 1998. *The Italian Dictatorship: Problems and Perspectives in the Interpretation of Mussolini and Fascism.* London: Arnold; New York: Oxford University Press.
———. 2002. *Mussolini.* London: Arnold; New York: Oxford University Press.
———. 2006. *Mussolini's Italy: Life under the Dictatorship 1915–1945.* New York: Penguin Press.
Bowser, Eileen. 1990. *The Transformation of Cinema 1907–1915.* New York: Scribner's.
Brecht, Bertolt. 1976. *Gesammelte Gedichte.* Ed. Elisabeth Hauptmann. 4 vols. Frankfurt am Main: Suhrkamp.
Bremmer, Jan, and Herman Roodenburg, eds. 1992. *A Cultural History of Gesture.* Ithaca and London: Cornell University Press.
Brewster, Ben, and Lea Jacobs. 1997. *Theatre to Cinema: Stage Pictorialism and the Early Feature Film.* Oxford: Oxford University Press.
Brilliant, Richard. 1963. *Gesture and Rank in Roman Art: The Use of Gestures to Denote Status in Roman Sculpture and Coinage.* New Haven: Connecticut Academy of Arts and Sciences.
Brodersen, Kai. 2004. *Die Sieben Weltwunder: Legendäre Kunst- und Bauwerke der Antike.* 6th ed. Munich: Beck.
Brookner, Anita. 1987. *Jacques-Louis David.* 2nd ed. New York: Thames and Hudson.
Brunetta, Gian Piero. 1975. *Cinema italiano tra le due guerre: Fascismo e politica cinematografica.* Milan: Mursia.
———. 1993. *Storia del cinema italiano.* 2nd ed. Vol. 1: *Il cinema muto 1895–1929.* Vol. 2: *Il cinema del regime 1929–1945.* Rome: Editori Riuniti.

Bruun, Christer, ed. 2000. *The Roman Middle Republic: Politics, Religion, and Historiography, c. 400–133 B.C.* Rome: Institutum Romanum Finlandiae.
Bulathsinghala, Frances. 2003. "Interview with Black Tigers: Obsession with Death." *Sunday Observer,* July 13. http://www.sundayobserver.lk/2003/07/13/fea27.html.
Bulwer, John. 1974 (new ed.). *Chirologia: Or, The Natural Language of the Hand* and *Chironomia: Or, The Art of Manual Rhetoric.* Ed. James W. Cleary. Carbondale and Edwardsville: Southern Illinois University Press.
Burg, David F. 1976. *Chicago's White City of 1893.* Lexington: University Press of Kentucky.
Buruma, Ian. 2005. "The Indiscreet Charm of Tyranny." *The New York Review of Books,* May 12, 35–37.
Cadalanu, Giampaolo. 1994. *Skinheads: Dalla musica giamaicana al saluto romano.* Lecce: Argo.
Cadars, Pierre, and Francis Courtade. 1972. *Le cinéma nazi.* Toulouse: Losfeld.
Cairns, Douglas, ed. 2005. *Body Language in the Greek and Roman Worlds.* Swansea: Classical Press of Wales.
Callebat, Louis. 1988. *Pierre de Coubertin.* Paris: Fayard.
Calvet, Arlette. 1968. "Unpublished Studies for 'The Oath of the Horatii' by Jacques-Louis David." *Master Drawings* 6: 37–42 and plates 23–31.
Calvino, Italo. 2003. *Hermit in Paris: Autobiographical Writings.* Tr. Martin McLaughlin. New York: Pantheon. Rpt. 2004.
Cammarota, Domenico. 1987. *Il cinema peplum: La prima guida critica ai film di: Conan, Ercole, Goliath, Maciste, Sansone, Spartaco, Thaur, Ursus.* Rome: Fanucci.
Campi, Alessandro. 2007. *L'ombra lunga di Napoleone: Da Mussolini a Berlusconi.* Venice: Marsilio.
Canfora, Luciano. 1980. *Ideologie del classicismo.* Turin: Einaudi.
Cannistraro, Philip V. 1975. *La fabbrica del consenso: Fascismo e mass media.* Rome and Bari: Laterza.
Capra, Frank. 1997. *The Name Above the Title: An Autobiography.* New York: Da Capo. Originally 1971.
Carabba, Claudio. 1974. *Il cinema del ventennio nero.* Florence: Vallecchi.
Carcopino, Jérôme. 1940. *Daily Life in Ancient Rome: The People and the City at the Height of the Empire.* Ed. Henry T. Rowell. Tr. E. O. Lorimer. New Haven and London: Yale University Press.
Cardillo, Massimo. 1983. *Il duce in moviola: Politica e divismo nei cinegiornali e documentari "Luce."* Bari: Dedalo.
Casadio, Gianfranco. 1989. *Il grigio e il nero: Spettacolo e propaganda nel cinema italiano degli anni Trenta (1931–1943).* Ravenna: Longo.
Chimirri, Giovanna Finocchiaro. 1986. *D'Annunzio e il cinema: Cabiria.* Catania: Cooperativa Universitaria Editrice Catanese di Magistero.
Chiurco, G. A. 1929. *Storia della rivoluzione fascista.* Vol. 1: *Anno 1919.* Vol. 2: *Anno 1920.* Florence: Vallecchi.
Christ, Karl. 1996. *Von Caesar zu Konstantin: Beiträge zur römischen Geschichte und ihrer Rezeption.* Munich: Beck.
Ciani, Ivanos. 1999. *Fotogrammi dannunziani: Materiali per la storia del rapporto D'Annunzio-cinema.* 2nd ed. Pescara: Ediars.
Cichorius, Conrad. 1896–1900. *Die Reliefs der Traianssäule.* 4 vols. Berlin: Reimer.
Cincotti, Guido, ed. 1975. *Pastrone e Griffith: L'ipotesi e la storia.* Rome: Edizioni d'Ateneo.

Clark, Barrett H., ed. 1940–1941. *America's Lost Plays.* 20 vols. Rpt. in 10 vols. Bloomington: Indiana University Press, 1963.
Clark, Martin. 1996. *Modern Italy 1871–1995.* London and New York: Longman.
Clayton, Peter A., and Martin J. Price, eds. 1988. *The Seven Wonders of the Ancient World.* London and New York: Routledge.
Coarelli, Filippo, ed. 2000. *The Column of Trajan.* Tr. Cynthia Rockwell. Rome: Editore Colombo.
The Columbian Exposition Album Containing Views of the Grounds, Main and State Buildings, Statuary, Architectural Details, Interiors, Midway Plaisance Scenes, and other Interesting Objects which Had Place at the World's Columbian Exposition, Chicago 1893. 1893. Chicago and New York: Rand, McNally.
Corbeill, Anthony. 2004. *Nature Embodied: Gesture in Ancient Rome.* Princeton and Oxford: Princeton University Press.
Corcoran, Michael. 2002. *For Which It Stands: An Anecdotal Biography of the American Flag.* New York: Simon and Schuster.
Cordova, Ferdinando. 1969. *Arditi e legionarii dannunziani.* Padua: Marsilio.
Corneille, Pierre. N.d. *Théatre complet de Corneille.* Vol. 1. Ed. Maurice Rat. Paris: Garnier.
Cottafavi, Vittorio. 1912. *Nella Libia italiana: Impressioni-studi-recordi.* Bologna: Beltrami.
Crawford, M. H. 1974; corrected rpt., 1995. *Roman Republican Coinage.* 2 vols. Cambridge: Cambridge University Press.
Crow, Thomas. 1995. *Emulation: Making Artists for Revolutionary France.* New Haven and London: Yale University Press.
Cullmann, Oscar. 1962. *Peter: Disciple, Apostle, Martyr: A Historical and Theological Study.* Tr. Floyd V. Filson. Philadelphia: Westminster Press.
D'Alberti, Sarah. 1971. *Giuseppe Antonio Borgese.* Palermo: Flaccovio.
D'Anelli, Aris, ed. 2003. *Giovanni Pastrone (Asti 1882–Torino 1959): Contributo astigiano al cinema muto italiano.* Asti: Provincia di Asti.
D'Annunzio, Gabriele. 1974. *La penultima ventura: Scritti e discorsi fiumani.* Ed. Renzo de Felice. Milan: Mondadori.
Dahl, Curtis. 1956. "Recreators of Pompeii." *Archaeology* 9: 182–91.
———. 1963. *Robert Montgomery Bird.* New York: Twayne.
Dalle Vacche, Angela. 1992. *The Body in the Mirror: Shapes of History in Italian Cinema.* Princeton: Princeton University Press.
David et Rome/ David e Roma. 1981. Rome: Académie de France à Rome/De Luca.
De España, Rafael. 1998. *El Peplum: La antigüedad en el cine.* Barcelona: Glénat.
De Felice, Renzo. 1978. *D'Annunzio politico 1918–1938.* Rome and Bari: Laterza.
———, ed. 2001. *Autobiografia del fascismo: Antologia di testi fascisti 1919–1945.* Turin: Einaudi. Originally 1978.
de Grazia, Victoria, and Sergio Luzzatto, eds. 2003. *Dizionario del fascismo.* 2 vols. Turin: Einaudi.
de Jorio, Andrea. 2000. *Gesture in Naples and Gesture in Classical Antiquity.* Tr. Adam Kendon. Bloomington: Indiana University Press.
de Vincenti, Giorgio. 1988. "Il kolossal storico-romano nell'immaginario del primo Novecento." *Bianco e nero* 49: 6–26.
Debord, Guy. 1994. *The Society of the Spectacle.* Tr. Donald Nicholson-Smith. New York: Zone Books.
Decherney, Peter. 2005. *Hollywood and the Culture Elite: How the Movies Became American.* New York: Columbia University Press.

Demandt, Alexander. 2002. "Klassik als Klischee: Hitler und die Antike." *Historische Zeitschrift* 274: 281–313.
Demisch, Heinz. 1984. *Erhobene Hände: Geschichte einer Gebärde in der bildenden Kunst.* Stuttgart: Urachhaus.
Dowd, David Lloyd. 1948. *Pageant-Master of the Republic: Jacques-Louis David and the French Revolution.* Rpt. Freeport: Books for Libraries Press, n.d. [1969].
Downing, Taylor. 1992. *Olympia.* London: British Film Institute.
Duff, Mark. 2005. "Footballer's 'Fascist Salute' Row." *BBC News,* January 9. http://news.bbc.co.uk/2/hi/europe/4158591.stm.
Eatwell, Roger. 1996. *Fascism: A History.* New York: Viking Penguin. Rpt. 1997.
Edwards, Catharine, ed. 1999. *Roman Presences: Receptions of Rome in European Culture, 1789–1945.* Cambridge: Cambridge University Press.
Eichberg, Henning, Michael Dultz, Glen Gadberry, and Günther Rühle. 1977. *Massenspiele: NS-Thingspiel, Arbeiterweihespiel und olympisches Zeremoniell.* Stuttgart-Bad Cannstatt: Frommann-Holzboog.
Elley, Derek. 1984. *The Epic Film: Myth and History.* London: Routledge and Kegan Paul.
Ellis, Richard J. 2005. *To the Flag: The Unlikely History of the Pledge of Allegiance.* Lawrence: University Press of Kansas.
Elsner, Jas. 1995. *Art and the Roman Viewer: The Transformation of Art from the Pagan World to Christianity.* Cambridge: Cambridge University Press.
Ettlinger, L. D. 1967. "Jacques-Louis David and Roman Virtue." *Journal of the Royal Society of Arts* 115: 105–23.
Eyquem, Marie-Thérèse. 1966. *Pierre de Coubertin: L'épopée olympique.* Paris: Calmann-Lévy. Rpt. 1976.
Falasca-Zamponi, Simonetta. 1997. *Fascist Spectacle: The Aesthetics of Power in Mussolini's Italy.* Berkeley, Los Angeles, and London: University of California Press.
Fantham, Elaine. 1982. "Quintilian on Performance: Traditional and Personal Elements in *Institutio* 11.3." *Phoenix* 36: 243–63.
Farrell, Nicholas. 2003. *Mussolini: A New Life.* London: Weidenfeld and Nicholson.
Fehl, Phillip. 1974. "The Placement of the Equestrian Statue of Marcus Aurelius in the Middle Ages." *Journal of the Warburg and Courtauld Institutes* 37: 362–67 and plates 80–82.
Feldman, Louis H. 1993. *Jew and Gentile in the Ancient World: Attitudes and Interactions from Alexander to Justinian.* Princeton: Princeton University Press. Rpt. 1996.
Fenner, Angelica, and Eric D. Weitz, eds. 2004. *Fascism and Neofascism: Critical Writings on the Radical Right in Europe.* New York and Basingstoke: Palgrave Macmillan.
Fenton, Ben. 2005. "'I'm a Fascist, Not a Racist,' Says Paolo di Canio." *Daily Telegraph,* December 24. http://www.telegraph.co.uk/news/main.jhtml?xml=/news/2005/12/24/wpa01024.xml&sSheet=/news/2005/12/24/ixworld.html.
"Flag Salute Like 'Heil' Ends for School Pupils." 1943. *The New York Times,* June 19, 28.
Flaig, Egon. 2003. *Ritualisierte Politik: Zeichen, Gesten und Herrschaft im Alten Rom.* Göttingen: Vandenhoeck und Ruprecht.
Fogu, Claudio. 2003. *The Historic Imaginary: Politics of History in Fascist Italy.* Toronto, Buffalo, and London: University of Toronto Press.
Franz-Willing, Georg. 1974. *Ursprung der Hitlerbewegung 1919–1922.* 2nd ed. Preußisch Oldendorf: Schütz.

Frayling, Christopher. 1998. *Spaghetti Westerns: Cowboys and Europeans from Karl May to Sergio Leone.* 2nd ed. London and New York: Tauris.
Fritzsche, Peter. 2008. *Life and Death in the Third Reich.* Cambridge: Belknap Press/Harvard University Press.
Fuller, Robert C. 1995. *Naming the Antichrist: The History of an American Obsession.* New York and Oxford: Oxford University Press. Rpt. 1996.
Gabba, E., and K. Christ, eds. 1991. *Römische Geschichte und Zeitgeschichte in der deutschen und italienischen Altertumswissenschaft während des 19. und 20. Jahrhunderts.* Vol. 2: *L'impero romano fra storia generale e storia locale.* Como: Edizioni New Press.
Gabriele D'Annunzio: Grandezza e delirio nell'industria dello spettacolo. 1989. Genoa: Costa and Nolan.
Galeotti, Carlo. 2000. *Mussolini ha sempre ragione: I decaloghi del fascismo.* Milan: Garzanti.
———. 2001. *Saluto al Duce! I catechismi del Balilla e della piccola italiana.* Rome: Gremese.
Galinsky, Karl. 1996. *Augustan Culture: An Interpretive Introduction.* Princeton: Princeton University Press. Rpt. 1998.
Gambacorti, Irene. 2003. *Storie di cinema e letteratura: Verga, Gozzano, D'Annunzio.* Florence: Società Editrice Fiorentina.
Gamboni, Dario, and Georg Germann, eds. 1991. *Zeichen der Freiheit: Das Bild der Republik in der Kunst des 16. bis 20. Jahrhunderts.* Berne: Stämpfli.
Garcia, Gustave. 1888. *The Actor's Art: A Practical Treatise on Stage Declamation, Public Speaking, and Deportment, for the Use of Artists, Students, and Amateurs, including A Sketch on the History of the Theatre, from the Greeks to the Present Time.* 2nd ed. London: Simpkin, Marshall.
Gehl, Walther. 1940. *Geschichte: 6. Klasse: Oberschulen, Gymnasien und Oberschulen in Aufbauform: Von der Urzeit bis zum Ende der Hohenstaufen.* Breslau: Hirt.
Gentile, Emilio. 1990. "Fascism as a Political Religion." *Journal of Contemporary History* 25: 229–51.
———. 1993. *Il culto del littorio: La sacralizzazione della politica nell'Italia Fascista.* Rome and Bari: Laterza.
———. 1996a. *Le origini dell'ideologia fascista (1918–1925).* Rev. ed. Bologna: Il Mulino. Rpt. 2001.
———. 1996b. *The Sacralization of Politics in Fascist Italy.* Tr. Keith Botsford. Cambridge and London: Harvard University Press.
Gentile, Giovanni. 1929. *Origini e dottrina del fascismo.* Rome: Libreria del Littorio.
———. 2002. *Origins and Doctrine of Fascism: With Selections from Other Works.* Ed. and tr. A. James Gregor. New Brunswick: Transaction. Rpt. 2004.
Gerra, Ferdinando. 1974. *L'impresa di Fiume.* Vol. 1: *Fiume d'Italia.* Milan: Longanesi.
Giardina, Andrea, and André Vauchez. 2000. *Il mito di Roma: Da Carlo Magno a Mussolini.* Rome and Bari: Laterza.
Gibbon, Lewis Grassic. 2006. *Spartacus.* New York: Pegasus Books.
Giesen, Rolf. 2003. *Nazi Propaganda Films: A History and Filmography.* Jefferson and London: McFarland.
Gilbert, James. 1991. *Perfect Cities: Chicago's Utopias of 1893.* Chicago and London: University of Chicago Press.
Gili, Jean A. 1985. *L'Italie de Mussolini et son cinéma.* Paris: Veyrier.

Glassberg, David. 1990. *American Historical Pageantry: The Uses of Tradition in the Early Twentieth Century.* Chapel Hill and London: University of North Carolina Press.

Gori, Gianfranco Miro. 1988. *Patria diva: La storia d'Italia nei film del ventennio.* Florence: La casa USHER.

Graham, Cooper C. 2001. *Leni Riefenstahl and* Olympia. Lanham and London: Scarecrow Press. Originally 1986.

Grau, Robert. 1909. *Forty Years Observation of Music and the Drama.* New York: Broadway Publishing Company.

———. 1910. *The Business Man in the Amusement World: A Volume of Progress in the Field of the Theatre.* New York: Broadway Publishing Company.

———. 1912. *The Stage in the Twentieth Century.* New York: Broadway Publishing Company.

———. 1914. *The Theatre of Science: A Volume of Progress and Achievement in the Motion Picture Industry.* New York: Broadway Publishing Company.

Green, Peter. 1991. *Alexander of Macedon 356–323 B.C.: A Historical Biography.* Berkeley, Los Angeles, and London: University of California Press.

Grieveson, Lee, and Peter Krämer, eds. 2004. *The Silent Cinema Reader.* London and New York: Routledge.

Griffin, Gerald. 1970. *Gabriele D'Annunzio: The Warrior Bard.* Port Washington and London: Kennikat Press. Originally 1935.

Groß, Karl. 1985. *Menschenhand und Gotteshand in Antike und Christentum.* Ed. Wolfgang Speyer. Stuttgart: Hiersemann.

Guenter, Scot M. 1990. *The American Flag, 1777–1924: Cultural Shifts from Creation to Codification.* Rutherford, Madison, and Teaneck: Fairleigh Dickinson University Press/London and Toronto: Associated University Presses.

Gumbrecht, Hans Ulrich. 1996. "*I redentori della vittoria:* On Fiume's Place in the Genealogy of Fascism." *Journal of Contemporary History* 31: 253–72.

Gunning, Tom. 1991. *D. W. Griffith and the Origins of American Narrative Film: The Early Years at Biograph.* Urbana and Chicago: University of Illinois Press. Rpt. 1994.

Gutberlet, S. Helena, I.ST.M. 1935. *Die Himmelfahrt Christi in der bildenden Kunst von den Anfängen bis ins Hohe Mittelalter: Versuch zur geistesgeschichtlichen Erfassung einer ikonographischen Frage.* 2nd ed. Leipzig, Strassburg, and Zurich: Heitz.

Gwyn, William B. 1991. "Cruel Nero: The Concept of the Tyrant and the Image of Nero in Western Political Thought." *History of Political Thought* 12: 421–55.

Hall, Jon. 2004. "Cicero and Quintilian on the Oratorical Use of Hand Gestures." *The Classical Quarterly* 54: 143–60.

———, and Robin Bond. 2002. "Performative Elements in Cicero's Orations: An Experimental Approach." *Prudentia* 34: 187–228.

Hamann, Brigitte. 1999. *Hitler's Vienna: A Dictator's Apprenticeship.* Tr. Thomas Thornton. New York and Oxford: Oxford University Press.

Hampton, Benjamin B. *A History of the Movies.* 1970. New York: Arno. Originally 1931.

Hart-Davis, Duff. 1986. *Hitler's Games: The 1936 Olympics.* London: Century.

Hasselbach, Ingo, and Tom Reiss. 1996. *Führer-Ex: Memoirs of a Former Neo-Nazi.* New York: Random House.

Hautecoeur, L. 1912. *Rome et la renaissance de l'antiquité à la fin du XVIIIe siècle.* Paris: Fontemoing.

Hawthorne, Nathaniel. 1983. *Novels.* New York: Viking/The Library of America.

Hay, James. 1987. *Popular Film Culture in Fascist Italy: The Passing of the Rex.* Bloomington and Indianapolis: Indiana University Press.
Hazlehurst, F. Hamilton. 1960. "The Artistic Evolution of David's *Oath.*" *The Art Bulletin* 42: 59–63.
Heller, Steven. 2008. *Iron Fists: Branding the 20th-Century Totalitarian State.* London: Phaidon.
Henig, Martin, ed. 1983. *A Handbook of Roman Art.* Ithaca: Cornell University Press.
Herrmann, Peter. 1968. *Der römische Kaisereid: Untersuchungen zu seiner Herkunft und Entwicklung.* Göttingen: Vandenhoeck und Ruprecht.
Herrmann, Ulrich, and Ulrich Nassen, eds. 1994. *Formative Ästhetik im Nationalsozialismus: Intentionen, Medien und Praxisformen totalitärer ästhetischer Herrschaft und Beherrschung.* Weinheim and Basel: Beltz.
Higham, Charles. 1993. *Merchant of Dreams: Louis B. Mayer, M.G.M., and the Secret Hollywood.* New York: Fine.
Hingley, Richard, ed. 2001. *Images of Rome: Perceptions of Ancient Rome in Europe and the United States in the Modern Age.* Portsmouth, RI: Journal of Roman Archaeology.
Hinton, David B. 2000. *The Films of Leni Riefenstahl.* 3rd ed. Lanham and London: Scarecrow Press.
Hobsbawn, Eric, and Terence Ranger, eds. 1983. *The Invention of Tradition.* Cambridge: Cambridge University Press. Rpt. 2000.
Höfer, Andreas. 1994. *Der Olympische Friede: Anspruch und Wirklichkeit einer Idee.* St. Augustin: Academia Verlag.
Hölscher, Tonio. 1967. *Victoria Romana: Archäologische Untersuchungen zur Geschichte und Wesensart der römischen Siegesgöttin von den Anfängen bis zum Ende des 3. Jhs. n. Chr.* Mainz: von Zabern.
Hoepfner, Wolfram. 2003. *Der Koloß von Rhodos und die Bauten des Helios: Neue Forschungen zu einem der Sieben Weltwunder.* Mainz: von Zabern.
Hofmann, Werner, ed. 1989. *Europa 1789: Aufklärung, Verklärung, Verfall.* Cologne: DuMont.
Holliday, Peter J., ed. 1993. *Narrative and Event in Ancient Art.* Cambridge: Cambridge University Press.
Hopkins, Keith. 1983. *Death and Renewal.* Cambridge: Cambridge University Press.
Horne, Alistair. 2004. *The Age of Napoleon.* New York: Modern Library.
Houseman, John. 1972. *Run-Through: A Memoir.* New York: Curtis Books.
Howard, Seymour. 1975. *Sacrifice of the Hero: The Roman Years: A Classical Frieze by Jacques Louis David.* Sacramento: E. B. Crocker Art Gallery.
Hoyt, Edwin P. 1994. *Mussolini's Empire: The Rise and Fall of the Fascist Vision.* New York: Wiley.
Huston, John. 1994. *An Open Book.* New York: Da Capo. Originally 1980.
Iaccio, Pasquale, ed. 2003. *Non solo Scipione: Il cinema di Carmine Gallone.* Naples: Liguori.
Infield, Glenn B. 1976. *Leni Riefenstahl: The Fallen Film Goddess.* New York: Crowell.
Jacobs, Lewis. 1939. *The Rise of the American Film: A Critical History.* New York: Harcourt, Brace.
Jenney, Charles Jr., Rogers V. Scudder, and Eric C. Baade. 1987. *Jenney's First Year Latin.* Newton: Allyn and Bacon.
Joannis, Claudette. 2000. *Sarah Bernhardt, reine de l'attitude et princesse des gestes.* Paris: Payot.

Johnson, Daniel. 2006. "Hezbollah's Nazi Roots." *The New York Sun*, August 4. http://www.acage.org/articles/?day=03222007&id=0197.
Johnson, Dorothy. 1993. *Jacques-Louis David: Art in Metamorphosis*. Princeton: Princeton University Press.
Joshel, Sandra R., Margaret Malamud, and Donald T. McGuire, Jr., eds. 2001. *Imperial Projections: Ancient Rome in Modern Popular Culture*. Baltimore and London: Johns Hopkins University Press. Rpt. 2005.
Junkelmann, Marcus. 1998. *Die Reiter Roms*. Vol. 1: *Reise, Jagd, Triumph und Circusrennen*. 3rd ed. Mainz: von Zabern.
Kater, Michael H. 2006. *Das "Ahnenerbe" der SS 1935–1945: Ein Beitrag zur Kulturpolitik des Dritten Reiches*. 4th ed. Munich: Oldenbourg.
Kertzer, David I. 1988. *Ritual, Politics, and Power*. New Haven and London: Yale University Press.
Kinkel, Lutz. 2002. *Die Scheinwerferin: Leni Riefenstahl und das "Dritte Reich."* Hamburg and Vienna: Europa Verlag.
Kirkpatrick, Ivone. 1964. *Mussolini: A Study in Power*. New York: Hawthorn.
Kleiner, Diana E. E. 1992. *Roman Sculpture*. New Haven and London: Yale University Press.
Kluge, Volker. 1997. *Olympische Sommerspiele: Die Chronik I: Athen 1896–Berlin 1936*. Berlin: Sportverlag.
Knippschild, Silke. 2002. *"Drum bietet zum Bunde die Hände": Rechtssymbolische Akte in zwischenstaatlichen Beziehungen im orientalischen und griechisch-römischen Altertum*. Stuttgart: Steiner.
Köhler, Ulrico. 1863. "Statua di Cesare Augusto." *Annali dell'Instituto di Correspondenza Archaeologica* 35: 432–49.
Köhne, Eckart, and Cornelia Ewigleben, eds. 2000. *Gladiators and Caesars: The Power of Spectacle in Ancient Rome*. Tr. Anthea Bell. Berkeley and Los Angeles: University of California Press.
Koeppel, Gerhard. 1969. "Profectio und Adventus." *Bonner Jahrbücher* 169: 130–94.
Koon, Tracy H. 1985. *Believe, Obey, Fight: Political Socialization of Youth in Fascist Italy, 1922–1943*. Chapel Hill and London: University of North Carolina Press.
Koppes, Clayton R., and Gregory D. Black. 1990. *Hollywood Goes to War: How Politics, Profits, and Propaganda Shaped World War II Movies*. Berkeley and Los Angeles: University of California Press. Originally 1987.
Kracauer, Siegfried. 1947. *From Caligari to Hitler: A Psychological History of the German Film*. Princeton: Princeton University Press. Rpt. 1974.
———. 1960. *Theory of Film: The Redemption of Physical Reality*. Princeton: Princeton University Press. Rpt. 1997.
Kreimeier, Klaus. 1999. *The Ufa Story: A History of Germany's Greatest Film Company 1918–1945*. Tr. Robert and Rita Kimber. Berkeley: University of California Press. Originally 1996.
Kuron, Victor. 1936. *Die Läufer des Friedens von Olympia nach Berlin*. Berlin: Hobbing.
Landy, Marcia. 1986. *Fascism in Film: The Italian Commercial Cinema, 1931–1943*. Princeton: Princeton University Press.
Langer, Elinor. 2004. *A Hundred Little Hitlers: The Death of a Black Man, the Trial of a White Racist, and the Rise of the Neo-Nazi Movement in America*. New York: Picador. Originally 2003.

Langglotz, Ernst. 1975–1976. "Eine Nachbildung des Helios von Rhodos." *Rendiconti della Pontifica Accademia di Roma di Archeologia* 48: 141–50.
Laqueur, Walter. 1996. *Fascism: Past, Present, Future.* New York: Oxford University Press. Rpt. 1997.
Large, David Clay. 2007. *Nazi Games: The Olympics of 1936.* New York: Norton.
Lazarus, Emma. 2005. *Selected Poems.* Ed. John Hollander. New York: The Library of America.
Leaming, Barbara. 1986. *Orson Welles: A Biography.* New York: Penguin. Originally 1985.
Ledeen, Michael A. 2002. *The First Duce: D'Annunzio at Fiume.* New Brunswick: Transactions. Originally 1977.
Leepson, Marc. 2005. *Flag: An American Biography.* New York: St. Martin's.
Leiser, Erwin. 1975. *Nazi Cinema.* Tr. Gertrud Mander and David Wilson. New York: Macmillan. Originally 1974.
Leon, H. J. 1939. "Morituri Te Salutamus." *Transactions and Proceedings of the American Philological Association* 70: 46–50.
Leprohon, Pierre. 1972. *The Italian Cinema.* Tr. Roger Greaves and Oliver Stallybrass. London: Secker and Warburg/New York and Washington: Praeger.
Levey, Michael. 1966. *Rococo to Revolution: Major Trends in Eighteenth-Century Painting.* London: Thames and Hudson.
Liddy, Gordon. 1997. *Will: The Autobiography of G. Gordon Liddy.* 3rd ed. New York: St. Martin's.
Lindner, Ruth. 1999. "'Sandalenfilme' und der archäologische Blick: Protokoll eines Versuchs." *Thetis* 5–6: 519–36.
Livy. 1987 (and later). *Livy: Book I.* Ed. H. E. Gould and J. L. Whiteley. London: Bristol Classical Press. Originally 1952.
Loiperdinger, Martin. 1987. *Rituale der Mobilmachung: Der Parteitagsfilm "Triumph des Willens" von Leni Riefenstahl.* Opladen: Leske und Budrich.
———. 1988. "Halb Dokument, halb Fälschung: Zur Inszenierung der Eröffnungsfeier in Leni Riefenstahl's Olympia-Film 'Fest der Völker.'" *Medium* 18, no. 3: 42–46.
———, Rudolf Herz, and Ulrich Pohlmann, eds. 1995. *Führerbilder: Hitler, Mussolini, Roosevelt, Stalin in Fotografie und Film.* Munich and Zurich: Piper.
L'Orange, H. P. 1982. *Studies on the Iconography of Cosmic Kingship in the Ancient World.* New Rochelle: Caratzas. Originally 1953.
Lorenz, Stefan. 2000. "Hitler und die Antike." *Archiv für Kulturgeschichte* 82: 407–31.
Lussu, Emilio. 1936. *Enter Mussolini: Observations and Adventures of an Anti-Fascist.* Tr. Marion Rawson. London: Methuen.
———. 1945. *Marcia su Roma e dintorni.* Turin: Einaudi. Rpt. 2002.
Lyttelton, Adrian. 1973. *The Seizure of Power: Fascism in Italy 1919–1929.* New York: Scribner's.
MacAloon, John J. 1981. *This Great Symbol: Pierre de Coubertin and the Origins of the Modern Olympic Games.* Chicago and London: University of Chicago Press. Rpt. 1984.
McBride, Joseph. 2000. *Frank Capra: The Catastrophe of Success.* Rev. ed. New York: St. Martin's.
MacCormack, Sabine G. 1981. *Art and Ceremony in Late Antiquity.* Berkeley, Los Angeles, and London: University of California Press.

McGinn, Bernard. 2000. *Antichrist: Two Thousand Years of the Human Fascination with Evil.* New York: Columbia University Press. Originally 1994.
Mackay, Christopher S. 2005. *Ancient Rome: A Military and Political History.* Cambridge: Cambridge University Press. Rpt. 2007.
McKee, Irving. 1947. *"Ben-Hur" Wallace: The Life of General Lew Wallace.* Berkeley and Los Angeles: University of California Press.
Maier-Eichhorn, Ursula. 1989. *Die Gestikulation in Quintilians Rhetorik.* Frankfurt am Main, Berne, New York, and Paris: Lang.
Malamud, Margaret. 2001a. "The Greatest Show on Earth: Roman Entertainments in Turn-of-the-Century New York City." *Journal of Popular Culture* 35, no. 3: 43–58.
———. 2001b. "Roman Entertainments for the Masses in Turn-of-the-Century New York." *The Classical World* 95: 49–57.
Malvano, Laura. 1988. *Fascismo e politica dell'immagine.* Turin: Bollati Boringhieri.
Mandell, Richard D. 1987. *The Nazi Olympics.* 2nd ed. Urbana and Chicago: University of Illinois Press.
Mangoni, Luisa. 1976. "Cesarismo, bonapartismo, fascismo." *Studi storici* 17, no. 3: 41–61.
Marshall, Anthony J. 1984. "Symbols and Showmanship in Roman Public Life: The Fasces." *Phoenix* 38: 120–41.
Martindale, Andrew. 1979. *The Triumphs of Caesar by Andrea Mantegna in the Collection of Her Majesty the Queen at Hampton Court.* London: Miller.
Martinelli, Vittorio. 2001. *La guerra di D'Annunzio: Da poeta e dandy a eroe di guerra e "comandante."* Udine: Gaspari.
Marx, Karl. 1963. *The Eighteenth Brumaire of Louis Bonaparte.* New York: International Publishers. Rpt. 1998.
Mayer, David, ed. 1994 *Playing Out the Empire: Ben-Hur and Other Toga Plays and Films, 1883–1908: A Critical Anthology.* Oxford: Clarendon Press.
Medina, L. H. N.d.. *The Last Days of Pompeii.* New York: French.
Meisel, Martin. 1983. *Realizations: Narrative, Pictorial, and Theatrical Arts in Nineteenth-Century England.* Princeton: Princeton University Press.
Mezzetti, Fernando. 1978. *Borgese e il fascismo.* Palermo: Sellerio.
M-G-M Presents Quo Vadis. 1951. No publishing data provided.
Mielsch, Harald. 2001. *Römische Wandmalerei.* Darmstadt: Wissenschaftliche Buchgesellschaft.
Miller, Margarette S. 1976. *Twenty-Three Words.* Portsmouth: Printcraft Press.
Minkova, Milena, and Terence Tunberg. 2005. *Reading Livy's Rome: Selections from Books I–VI of Livy's* Ab Urbe Condita. Wauconda, IL: Bolchazy-Carducci.
Moeller van den Bruck, Arthur. 1923. *Das dritte Reich.* Berlin: Der Ring.
———. 1932. *Das Recht der jungen Völker: Sammlung politischer Aufsätze.* Ed. Hans Schwarz. Berlin: Verlag Der Nahe Osten.
———. 1934. *Germany's Third Empire.* Tr. E. O. Lorimer. London: Allen and Unwin.
Mommsen, Hans, ed. 2001. *The Third Reich Between Vision and Reality: New Perspectives on German History, 1918–1945.* Oxford: Berg. Rpt. 2002.
Morsberger, Robert E. and Katharine M. 1980. *Lew Wallace: Militant Romantic.* New York, St. Louis, and San Francisco: McGraw-Hill.
Morstein-Marx, Robert. 2004. *Mass Oratory and Political Power in the Late Roman Republic.* Cambridge: Cambridge University Press.

Moses, Montrose J., ed. 1964. *Representative Plays by American Dramatists from 1765 to the Present Day.* Vol. 1: *1765–1819;* vol. 2: *1815–1858.* New York: Blom. Originally 1918.
Mosse, George L. 1989. "Fascism and the French Revolution." *Journal of Contemporary History* 24: 5–26.
Musser, Charles. 1990. *The Emergence of Cinema: The American Screen to 1907.* New York: Scribner's.
Mussolini, Benito. 1951–1981. *Opera Omnia di Benito Mussolini.* Ed. Edoardo and Duilio Susmel. 36 vols. Florence: La Feniche.
———. 1998. *My Rise and Fall.* New York: Da Capo.
"National School Celebration of Columbus Day: The Official Program." 1892. *The Youth's Companion* 65 (September 8): 446–47.
Neumann, Gerhard. 1965. *Gesten und Gebärden in der griechischen Kunst.* Berlin: de Gruyter.
Neville, Peter. 2004. *Mussolini.* London and New York: Routledge.
"New Flag Salute Ruled." 1940. *The New York Times,* October 16, 10.
Niver, Kemp R. 1976. *Klaw and Erlanger Present Famous Plays in Pictures.* Ed. Bebe Bergsten. Los Angeles: Locare Research Group.
———. 1985. *Early Motion Pictures: The Paper Print Collection in the Library of Congress.* Ed. Bebe Bergsten. Washington: Library of Congress.
Nouvel-Kammerer, Odile, ed. 2007. *Symbols of Power: Napoleon and the Art of the Empire Style 1800–1815.* New York: Abrams.
Ogilvie, R. M. 1965. *A Commentary on Livy: Books 1–5.* Oxford: Clarendon Press. Rpt., with addenda, 1970.
Oliva, Gianni, ed. 2002. *Interviste a D'Annunzio (1895–1938).* Lanciano: Rocco Carabba.
Orvieto, Paolo. 1988. *D'Annunzio o Croce: La critica in Italia dal 1900 al 1915.* Rome: Salerno.
Panofsky, Erwin. 1969. *Problems in Titian, Mostly Iconographic.* New York: New York University Press.
Parisi, Luciano. 2000. *Borgese.* Turin: Tirrenia Stampatori.
———. 2002. "Giuseppe Antonio Borgese." *Dictionary of Literary Biography.* Vol. 264: *Italian Prose Writers, 1900–1945.* Detroit: Gale. 58–74.
Parks, Tim. 2005. "The Illusionist." *The New York Review of Books,* April 7, 54–58.
Pasinetti, P. M. 1953. "*Julius Caesar:* The Role of the Technical Adviser." *Film Quarterly* 8: 131–38.
Pasini, Annamaria Cavalli. 1994. *L'unità della letteratura: Borgese critico scrittore.* Bologna: Patron.
Passerini, Luisa. 1991. *Mussolini immaginario: Storia di una biographia 1915–1939.* Rome: Laterza.
Pastrone, Giovanni. 1977. *Cabiria: Visione storica del III secolo a. C.: Didascalie di Gabriele D'Annunzio.* Turin: Museo Nazionale del Cinema.
Paul, Marilyn H. 1992. "I Pledge Allegiance...." *Prologue* 24: 390–93.
Paxton, Robert O. 2005. *The Anatomy of Fascism.* New York: Vintage. Originally 2004.
Payne, John Howard. 1963. The Last Duel in Spain *and Other Plays by John Howard Payne.* Ed. Codman Hislop and W. R. Richardson. Bloomington: Indiana University Press. Originally 1940.

Payne, Stanley G. 1995. *A History of Fascism, 1919–1945.* Madison: University of Wisconsin Press.
Pearson, Hesketh. 1956. *Beerbohm Tree: His Life and Laughter.* London: Methuen.
Pearson, Roberta E. 1992. *Eloquent Gestures: The Transformation of Performance Style in the Griffith Biograph Films.* Berkeley, Los Angeles, and Oxford: University of California Press.
———, and William Uricchio. 1990. "How Many Times Shall Caesar Bleed in Sport: Shakespeare and the Cultural Debate About Moving Pictures." *Screen* 31: 243–62.
Perfetti, Francesco. 1988. *Fiumanesimo, sindacalismo e fascismo.* Rome: Bonacci.
———, ed. 1993. *D'Annunzio e il suo tempo.* 2 vols. Genoa: Sagep.
Perkins, Pheme. 2000. *Peter: Apostle of the Whole Church.* Minneapolis: Fortress Press. Originally 1994.
Pfaff, William. 2004. *The Bullet's Song: Romantic Violence and Utopia.* New York: Simon and Schuster.
Pick, Daniel. 2005. *Rome or Death: The Obsessions of General Garibaldi.* London: Cape.
Porterfield, Todd, and Susan L. Siegfried. 2006. *Staging Empire: Napoleon, Ingres, and David.* University Park: Pennsylvania State University Press.
Prause, Karl. 1930. *Deutsche Grußformeln in neuhochdeutscher Zeit.* Breslau: Marcus.
Presicce, Claudio Parisi. 1990. *The Equestrian Statue of Marcus Aurelius in Campidoglio.* Ed. Anna Mura Sommella. Tr. Andrew Ellis and Carol Rathman. Milan: Silvana.
Prolo, Maria Adriana. 1951. *Storia del cinema muto italiano.* Vol. 1. Milan: Poligono.
Quaranta, Guido. 1998. "Il saluto romano è molto Popolare." *L'Espresso* 44, no. 9 (March 5): 59.
Quennell, Peter. 1971. *The Colosseum.* New York: Newsweek.
Rainsford, William S. 1970. *The Story of a Varied Life: An Autobiography.* Freeport: Books for Libraries. Originally 1922.
Ramsaye, Terry. 1986. *A Million and One Nights: A History of the Motion Picture Through 1925.* New York: Simon and Schuster. Originally 1926.
Rankov, Boris. 1994. *The Praetorian Guard.* London: Osprey. Rpt. 1996.
Ratcliff, Carter. 1990. "Painting's Constitution." *Art in America* 78: 208–15 and 263.
Redi, Riccardo. 1999. *Cinema muto italiano (1896–1930).* Venice: Marsilio.
———, ed. 1994. *Gli ultimi giorni de Pompei.* Naples: Electa Napoli.
Reece, R. [Robert]. 1850. *The Very Last Days of Pompeii: A New Classical Burlesque.* London: Hailes Lacy.
Regardie, Israel. 1997. *The Golden Dawn: A Complete Course in Practical Ceremonial Magic.* Ed. Carl Llewellyn Weschcke. 6th ed. St. Paul: Llewellyn Publications. Rpt. 2002.
Reich, Jacqueline, and Piero Garofalo, eds. 2002. *Re-Viewing Fascism: Italian Cinema, 1922–1943.* Bloomington and Indianapolis: Indiana University Press.
Reichardt, Sven. 2002. *Faschistische Kampfbünde: Gewalt und Gemeinschaft im italienischen Squadrismus und in der deutschen SA.* Cologne, Weimar, and Vienna: Böhlau.
Renzi, Renzo, ed. 1992. *Il cinema dei dittatori: Mussolini, Stalin, Hitler.* Bologna: Grafis Edizioni.
Rhodes, Anthony. 1960. *D'Annunzio: The Poet as Superman.* 1959. Rpt. New York: McDowell, Obolensky.
Riall, Lucy. 2007. *Garibaldi: Invention of a Hero.* New Haven and London: Yale University Press.

Richards, Jeffrey H., ed. 1997. *Early American Drama.* New York and London: Penguin.
Ridgeway, James. 1995. *Blood in the Face: The Ku Klux Klan, Aryan Nations, Nazi Skinheads, and the Rise of a New White Culture.* 2nd ed. New York: Thunder's Mouth Press.
Riefenstahl, Leni. 1995. *A Memoir.* New York: Picador. Originally 1993.
Roberts, Warren. 2000. *Revolutionary Artists: Jacques-Louis David and Jean-Louis Prieur: The Public, the Populace, and Images of the French Revolution.* Albany: State University of New York Press.
Rochat, Giorgio. 1997. *Gli arditi della Grande Guerra: Origini, battaglie e miti.* 2nd ed. Gorizia: Libreria Editrice Goriziana. Rpt. 1999.
Romer, John and Elizabeth. 2000. *The Seven Wonders of the World: A History of the Modern Imagination.* London: Seven Dials. Originally 1995.
Rondolino, Gianni. 1980a. *Torino come Hollywood (capitale del cinema italiano: 1896–1915).* Bologna: Cappelli.
———. 1980b. *Vittorio Cottafavi: Cinema e televisione.* Bologna: Cappelli.
Rosenblum, Robert. 1969. *Transformations in Late Eighteenth Century Art.* 2nd ed. Princeton: Princeton University Press.
———. 1970. "A Source for David's 'Horatii.'" *The Burlington Magazine* 112, no. 806: 269–71 and 273.
Rossi, Cesare. 1958. *Trentatre vicende mussoliniane.* Milan: Casa Editrice Ceschina.
Rossi, Marco. 1997. *Arditi, non gendarmi! Dall'arditismo di guerra agli arditi del popolo 1917–1922.* Pisa: BFS [Biblioteca Franco Serantini].
Rother, Rainer. 2002. *Leni Riefenstahl: The Seduction of Genius.* Tr. Martin H. Bott. London and New York: Continuum.
Russak, J. B., ed. 1965. *Monte Cristo by Charles Fletcher as Played by James O'Neill and Other Plays by Julia Ward Howe, George C. Hazelton, Langdon Mitchell, William C. De Mille.* Bloomington: Indiana University Press. Originally 1940.
Ryan, Nick. 2004. *Into a World of Hate: A Journey Among the Extreme Right.* New York: Routledge.
Rydell, Robert W. 1984. *All the World's a Fair: Visions of Empire at American International Expositions, 1876–1916.* Chicago and London: University of Chicago Press.
———. 1996. "The Pledge of Allegiance and the Construction of the Modern American Nation." *Rendevous* 30, no. 2: 13–26.
Sadoul, Georges. 1951. *Histoire générale du cinéma.* Vol. 3: *Le cinéma devient un art: 1909–1920.* Pt. 1: *L'avant-guerre.* 2nd ed. Paris: Denoël. Rpt. 1973.
Salierno, Vito. 1988. *D'Annunzio e Mussolini: Storia di una cordiale inimicizia.* Milan: Mursia.
Salvemini, Gaetano. 1973. *The Origins of Fascism in Italy.* Ed. Roberto Vivarelli. New York: Harper.
Saxon, A. H. 1989. *P. T. Barnum: The Legend and the Man.* New York: Columbia University Press.
Scheid, John, and Valérie Huet, eds. 2000. *La Colonne Aurélienne: Autour de la colonne Aurélienne: Geste et image sur la colonne de Marc Aurèle à Rome.* Turnhout: Brepols.
Scheide, Frank, and Hooman Mehran, eds. 2004. *Chaplin: The Dictator and the Tramp.* London: British Film Institute.
Schieder, Wolfgang, ed. 1983. *Faschismus als soziale Bewegung: Deutschland und Italien im Vergleich.* 2nd ed. Göttingen: Vandenhoeck und Ruprecht.

———. 1994. *Italia docet: Der italienische Faschismus als Vorbild in der Krise der Weimarer Republik.* Århus: Center for Kulturforskning.
Schiller, Gertrud. 1971. *Ikonographie der christlichen Kunst.* Vol. 3: *Die Auferstehung und Erhöhung Christi.* Gütersloh: Mohn.
Schnapper, Antoine, and Arlette Sérullaz, eds. 1989. *Jacques-Louis David 1748–1825.* Paris: Editions de la Réunion des musées nationaux.
Schneider, Herbert W., and Shepard B. Clough. 1929. *Making Fascists.* Chicago: University of Chicago Press.
Schöning, Jörg, ed. 1989. *Reinhold Schünzel: Schauspieler und Regisseur.* Munich: Edition Text + Kritik.
Seidensticker, Bernd, and Martin Vöhler, eds. 2001. *Urgeschichte der Moderne: Die Antike im 20. Jahrhundert.* Stuttgart and Weimar: Metzler.
Seldes, George. 1935. *Sawdust Caesar: The Untold History of Mussolini and Fascism.* New York and London: Harper.
Seton-Watson, Christopher. 1967. *Italy from Liberalism to Fascism: 1870–1925.* London: Methuen/New York: Barnes and Noble. Rpt. 1981.
Shakespeare, William. 1984a. *Julius Caesar.* Ed. Arthur Humphreys. Oxford: Clarendon Press.
———. 1984b. *Titus Andronicus.* Ed. Eugene M. Waith. Oxford: Clarendon Press.
———. 1988. *Julius Caesar.* Ed. Marvin Spevack. Cambridge: Cambridge University Press.
———. 1994. *The Tragedy of Anthony and Cleopatra.* Ed. Michael Neill. Oxford: Clarendon Press.
———. 1995. *Antony and Cleopatra.* Ed. John Wilders. London and New York: Routledge.
———. 1998. *Antony and Cleopatra.* Ed. Richard Madelaine. Cambridge: Cambridge University Press.
———. 2000. *Coriolanus.* Ed. Lee Bliss. Cambridge: Cambridge University Press.
Short, K. R. M., ed. 1983. *Film and Radio Propaganda in World War II.* Knoxville: University of Tennessee Press.
Siarri-Plazanet, Nadine. 1999. "Entretien Vittorio Cottafavi: Des films contre le pouvoir." *Positif* 456 (February): 97–102.
Siddons, Henry. 1807. *Practical Illustrations of Rhetorical Gestures and Action, Adapted to the English Drama.* London: Phillips.
Silone, Ignazio. 1934. *Der Fascismus [sic]: Seine Entstehung und seine Entwicklung.* Zurich: Europa-Verlag.
———. 2002. *Il fascismo: Origini e sviluppo.* Ed. Mimmo Franzinelli. Tr. Marina Buttarelli. Milan: Mondadori.
Simon, Erika. 1986. *Augustus: Kunst und Leben in Rom um die Zeitenwende.* Munich: Hirmer.
Singer, Ben. 2001. *Melodrama and Modernity: Early Sensational Cinema and Its Contexts.* New York: Columbia University Press.
Sittl, Carl. 1890. *Die Gebärden der Griechen und Römer.* Leipzig: Teubner.
Smallwood, E. Mary. 1981. *The Jews under Roman Rule: From Pompey to Diocletian: A Study in Political Relations.* Leiden: Brill.
Smith, Woodruff D. 1986. *The Ideological Origins of Nazi Imperialism.* New York and Oxford: Oxford University Press. Rpt. 1989.
Solomon, Jon. 2001. *The Ancient World in the Cinema.* 2nd ed. New Haven: Yale University Press.

Sontag, Susan. 2002. *Under the Sign of Saturn.* New York: Picador. Originally 1980.
Souvenir Album: Scenes of the Play Ben-Hur. 1900. New York.
Spotts, Frederic. 2003. *Hitler and the Power of Aesthetics.* Woodstock and New York: Overlook Press. Originally 2002.
Starobinski, Jean. 1982. *1789: The Emblems of Reason.* Tr. Barbara Bray. Charlottesville: University Press of Virginia.
Stephanus of Byzantium. 1849. *Stephani Byzantini Ethnicorum quae supersunt.* Ed. August Meineke. Berlin: Reimer.
Stilp, Florian. 2001. *Mariage et suovetaurilia: Essay sur le soi-disant "Autel de Domitius Ahenobarbus."* Rome: Bretschneider.
Sullivan, Francis A. 1967. "*Tendere manus*: Gestures in the *Aeneid.*" *The Classical Journal* 63: 358–62.
Sydenham, Edward A. 1952. *The Coinage of the Roman Republic.* Rev. G. C. Haines. Ed. L. Forrer and C. A. Hersh. London: Spink.
Tabachnick, Stephen E. 2002. *Fiercer Than Tigers: The Life and Works of Rex Warner.* East Lansing: Michigan State University Press.
Taylor, Richard. 1998. *Film Propaganda: Soviet Russia and Nazi Germany.* 2nd ed. London and New York: Tauris.
Terhune, Albert Payson. 1915. *The Story of Damon and Pythias.* New York: Grosset and Dunlap.
Toland, John. 1976. *Adolf Hitler.* Vol. 1. Garden City: Doubleday.
Trevor-Roper, H. R., ed. 2000. *Hitler's Table Talk, 1941–1944: His Private Conversations.* 3rd ed. Tr. Norman Cameron and R. H. Stevens. New York: Enigma Books.
Trimborn, Jürgen. 2007. *Leni Riefenstahl: A Life.* Tr. Edna McCown. New York: Faber and Faber.
Tyler, Royall. 1965. *Four Plays by Royall Tyler.* Ed. Arthur Wallace Peach and George Floyd Newbrough. Bloomington: Indiana University Press. Originally 1940.
Uricchio, William, and Roberta E. Pearson. 1993. *Reframing Culture: The Case of the Vitagraph Quality Films.* Princeton: Princeton University Press.
Usai, Paolo Cherchi. 1985. *Giovanni Pastrone.* Florence: La Nuova Italia/Il Castoro.
———, ed. 1999. *The Griffith Project.* Vol. 1: *Films Produced in 1907–1908.* London: British Film Institute.
Vachtová, Ludmila. 1968. *Frank Kupka: Pioneer of Abstract Art.* Tr. Zdenek Lederer. New York and Toronto: McGraw-Hill.
Valentini, Valentina. 1995. *Un fanciullo delicato e forte: Il cinema di Gabriele D'Annunzio.* Rome: Biblioteca del Vascello.
Vardac, A. Nicholas. 1949. *Stage to Screen: Theatrical Method from Garrick to Griffith.* Cambridge: Harvard University Press.
Vedder, Ursula. 1999–2000. "Der Koloß von Rhodos: Mythos und Wirklichkeit eines Weltwunders." *Nürnberger Blätter zur Archäologie* 16: 23–40.
———. 2003. "Weltwunder." *Der Neue Pauly,* 15.3, 1110–17.
Verdone, Mario. 1970. *Spettacolo romano.* Rome: Golem.
Vidal, Gore. 1992. *Screening History.* Cambridge: Harvard University Press.
———. 1996. *Palimpsest: A Memoir.* New York: Penguin. Originally 1995.
Wagner, Richard. 1983. *Dichtungen und Schriften: Jubiläumsausgabe in zehn Bänden.* Ed. Dieter Borchmeyer. Frankfurt am Main: Insel.
Wallace, Lew. 1893. "How I Came to Write Ben-Hur." *The Youth's Companion* 66 (February): 57.

---. 1898 (published 1897). *The Wooing of Malkatoon* and *Commodus*. New York and London: Harper.

---. 1906. *Lew Wallace: An Autobiography.* 2 vols. New York and London: Harper.

Warner, Rex. 1959. *The Young Caesar.* New York: Mentor Books. Originally 1958.

"West Virginia Banishes 'Nazi' Salute in Schools." 1942. *The New York Times,* February 2, 17.

Wilgoren, Jodi. 2003. "White Supremacist Is Held in Ordering Judge's Death." *The New York Times,* January 9, A 16.

Wind, Edgar. 1941–1942. "The Sources of David's *Horaces.*" *Journal of the Warburg and Courtauld Institutes* 4: 124–38 and plates 30–33.

Winkler, Martin M. 1995. "Cinema and the Fall of Rome." *Transactions of the American Philological Association* 125: 135–54.

---. 1998. "The Roman Empire in American Cinema After 1945." *The Classical Journal* 93: 167–96.

---, ed. 2001. *Classical Myth and Culture in the Cinema.* New York: Oxford University Press.

---, ed. 2004. *Gladiator: Film and History.* Oxford: Blackwell.

---, ed. 2006. *Troy: From Homer's Iliad to Hollywood Epic.* Oxford: Blackwell.

---, ed. 2007. *Spartacus: Film and History.* Oxford: Blackwell.

---, ed. 2009. *The Fall of the Roman Empire: Film and History.* Oxford: Wiley-Blackwell.

Witt, Mary Ann Frese. 2001. *The Search for Modern Tragedy: Aesthetic Fascism in Italy and France.* Ithaca and London: Cornell University Press.

Witte, Karsten. 1995. *Lachende Erben, toller Tag: Filmkomödie im Dritten Reich.* Berlin: Vorwerk 8.

Woodhouse, John. 1998. *Gabriele D'Annunzio: Defiant Archangel.* Oxford: Clarendon Press.

Wright, Rosemary Muir. 1995. *Art and Antichrist in Medieval Europe.* Manchester and New York: Manchester University Press.

Wyke, Maria. 1997. *Projecting the Past: Ancient Rome, Cinema and History.* New York and London: Routledge.

---. 2004. "Film Style and Fascism: *Julius Caesar.*" *Film Studies* 4 (Summer): 58–74.

---, ed. 2006. *Julius Caesar in Western Culture.* Oxford: Blackwell.

Zilliacus, Henrik. 1983. "Grußformen." *Reallexikon für Antike und Christentum,* 12, cols. 1204–32.

Zorn, John W., ed. 1968. *The Essential Delsarte.* Metuchen, NJ: Scarecrow Press.

index of film titles

A

Affairs of Messalina, The, 117n54
Afrodite, dea dell' amore, 157
Agrippina, 86n21
Alexander, 168
Amarcord, 164
Amazons of Rome, 161n11
American History X, 2n2
Amphitryon (Aus den Wolken kommt das Glück), 133
Androcles and the Lion, 75–76
Antony and Cleopatra, 87
Apache Gold, 176
Aphrodite, Goddess of Love, 157
Assassinat du Duc de Guise, L'. 78n6
Asterix and Cleopatra, 160
Astérix aux jeux olympiques; Asterix at the Olympic Games, 183
Astérix chez les Britons, 160
Astérix et Cléopâtre, 160
Astérix et la surprise de César, 160
Asterix in Britain, 160
Asterix vs. Caesar, 160
Attila; Attila the Hun, 152

B

Balconi e cannoni: I discorsi di Mussolini, 103n18
Barabbas, 156
Barbarian, The; Barbarian Ingomar, The, 84–85
Battaglia del grano, La, 116n49
Battles of the Gladiators, 159
Behold the Man, 136
"Beim nächsten Kuß knall ich ihn nieder!," 133n35
Ben-Hur: A Tale of the Christ (1907), 73n39, 83–85
Ben-Hur: A Tale of the Christ (1925), 66, 70n34, 71, 73n39, 79–80, 135–36
Ben-Hur: A Tale of the Christ (1959), 66, 73n39, 139, 155, 173, 182n4
Bible: In the Beginning, The, 179–80
Bruto; Brutus, 86

C

Cabiria, 81n10, 87, 94–121, 134, 141
Caduta di Troia, La, 99
Caesar. See Julius Caesar (2002)
Caesar and Cleopatra, 75–76
Caesar the Conqueror, 159
Caio Giulio Cesare, 88–89
Caligola: La storia mai raccontata; Caligula: The Untold Story, 165n16
Campo di Maggio, 110n35
Carry On Cleo, 160

Cartagine in fiamme; Carthage in Flames, 117n51
Cento giorni, 110n35
Chariots of Fire, 129n20
Christus, 91
Cleopatra (1917), 41
Cleopatra (1934), 82, 135, 137–38
Cleopatra (1963), 159
Cleopatra (1999), 172
Cleopatra: The Romance of a Woman and a Queen, 91
Colosso di Roma, Il, 62
Constantine and the Cross; Constantine the Great, 159
Coriolano, eroe senza patria, 157
Coriolanus (TV), 62, 149
Coriolanus, Hero without a Country, 157
Costantino il grande, 159
Crusades, The, 138, 149n57

D

Damon and Pythias, 92–93
David and Bathsheba, 76
David and Goliath; David e Golia, 159
Day of Vengeance, 40
Defeat of Hannibal, The. See *Scipione l'Africano*
Demetrius and the Gladiators, 40, 152
Divide and Conquer, 140
Duel of Champions, 46n16

E

Ecce Homo, 136
El Cid, 62
Elektra, 80n9
Empire, 173–74
Enchanted Forest, 133–34
Ercole alla conquista di Atlantide, 161n11
Ercole contro i figli del sole, 158
Ewiger Wald, 133–34

F

Fabiola, 86n21, 125
Fahrenheit 451, 176
Fall of an Empress, The, 86–87n21
Fall of the Roman Empire, The, 62, 162–65, 172
Fall of Troy, The, 99
Figlio di Cleopatra, Il, 157
Flash Gordon, 140
French Cancan, 53n38
From the Manger to the Cross, 85

G

Giulio Cesare il conquistadore delle Gallie, 159
Gladiator of Rome, The, 159
Gladiator, 40, 164–67, 173
Gladiatore della Tracia, Il, 90n30
Gladiatore di Roma, Il, 159
Golgotha, 136
Goliath and the Dragon, 161n11
Good Morning, Eve!, 135
Great Dictator, The, 7–8
Greatest Story Ever Told, The, 156
Guerra di Troia, La, 152

H

Helen of Troy, 152, 167
Hercules against the Sons of the Sun, 158
Hercules and the Captive Women; Hercules Conquers Atlantis, 161n11
Hermannsschlacht, Die, 127
Hero of Rome, 62
Hitler Gang, The, 146n50
Hitler: A Film from Germany; Hitler—Ein Film aus Deutschland, 123

I

I, Claudius, 170–71, 174, 182
Imperium: Augustus, 172
Imperium: Nero, 173
Indian Fighter, The, 64
Ingomar the Barbarian. See *Barbarian, The*
Inquiesta, L'; Inquiry, The (1986, 2006), 181
Intolerance, 91, 95n3

J

Jeremiah Johnson, 64

Judex, 55
Judith of Bethulia, 70n34
Julius Caesar (1914), 88–89
Julius Caesar (1950), 151n1
Julius Caesar (1953), 67, 163
Julius Caesar (1970), 160
Julius Caesar (2002), 173
Julius Caesar: An Historical Tragedy, 80, 84, 85n16
Jupiter's Darling, 151

K

King of Kings, The, 135

L

Land der Liebe, 133
Land of the Pharaohs, 156
Last Days of Pompeii, The (1913), 89
Last Days of Pompeii, The (1926), 40
Last Days of Pompeii, The (1935), 136
Last Days of Pompeii, The (1959), 158
Legioni di Cleopatra, Le, 161n11
Legions of the Nile, 161n11
Leni Riefenstahl: Die Macht der Bilder, 128n18
Life and Passion of Jesus Christ, The, 81–83

M

Maciste, 115n46
Maciste alpino, 115n46
Maciste of Turin, 115n46
Manslaughter, 136
Maratona, 129
Marcantonio e Cleopatra, 87
Marseillaise, La, 55
Martiri d'Italia, I, 149n57
Marvelous Maciste, 115n46
Mary, Mother of Jesus, 172
Masada, 172
Merry Widow, The, 135n38
Messalina (1923), 86n21, 149n57
Messalina (1951), 117n54
Messalina (1960), 161n11
Messalina Venere imperatrice, 161n11
Mio figlio Nerone, 156

Mort de Jules César, La, 84

N

Nazis Strike, The, 146
Nero and the Burning of Rome; Nero, or The Fall of Rome, 85–86n19
Nero's Big Weekend; Nero's Mistress; Nero's Weekend, 156n7
Nerone, 85

O

O.K. Nero, 156n7
Olympia; Olympische Spiele, 127–28, 131
100 Days of Napoleon, 110n35
Orazi e Curiazi, 46n16
Our Hitler, 123

P

Passion of the Christ, The, 167
Passion Play, The, 70n34, 77
Passion Play of Oberammergau, The, 77, 81
Perplexities of Maciste, The, 115n46
Phantom of the Opera, The, 168
Prelude to War, 140, 145
Profession: Neo-Nazi, 2n2

Q

Queen of Sheba, The, 156
Quo Vadis? (1913), 80n9, 81n10, 87, 125
Quo Vadis? (1924), 70n34, 95n2, 125
Quo Vadis (1951), 5, 10–11, 66, 141–49, 152, 155, 159, 162, 165
Quo Vadis? (2001), 172

R

Rameses, King of Egypt, 88
Regina di Saba, La, 156
Rêve de Shakespeare, Le, 84
Revenge of Hercules, The, 161n11
Revolt of the Gladiators (1958), 162
Revolt of the Gladiators, The (1913/1914), 90–91
Richard III, 150

Rivolta dei gladiatori, La, 161n9, 162
Robe, The, 40, 152
Roma, 114
Rome, 174–76
Rosa di Tebe, La, 88

S

Salò, o le 120 giornate di Sodoma; Salo, or The 120 Days of Sodom, 164
Salome, 151
Scipione l'Africano; Scipio Africanus, 8, 117–20, 174
Serpent of the Nile: The Loves of Cleopatra, 139
Shakespeare Writing Julius Caesar, 84
Sieg des Glaubens, 128n18
Sign of the Cross, The, 135, 137, 146
Sign of the Pagan, 40
Silver Chalice, The, 152
Sins of Rome: Story of Spartacus, 91n32
Solomon and Sheba, 157
Son of Cleopatra, 157
Spartaco (1913/1914), 90–91
Spartaco (1953), 91n32, 181
Spartacus (1913/1914), 90–91
Spartacus (1960), 158–59, 165, 173
Spartacus (2004), 174
Spartacus e i dieci gladiatori; Spartacus and the Ten Gladiators, 40
Spartacus the Gladiator, 91n32
Star Trek, 169–70, 176

T

Tag der Freiheit: Unsere Wehrmacht, 128n18
Ten Commandments, The (1923), 136
Ten Commandments, The (1956), 136, 138

They Died with Their Boots On, 64
300 Spartans, The, 153
Three Stooges Meet Hercules, The, 160
Thunder of Battle, 157
Titus, 164–65
Trionfo di Roma, Il, 149n57
Triumph des Willens; Triumph of the Will, 61, 118, 127, 133, 140n43, 141, 143, 146n50, 165
Trojan Horse, The, 153n3
Trojan War, The, 153n3
Troy, 167

U

Ultimi giorni di Pompei, Gli (1913), 81n10, 89
Ultimi giorni di Pompei, Gli (1926), 40
Ultimi giorni di Pompei, Gli (1959), 158

V

Vanishing American, The, 62
Vendetta di Ercole, La; Vengeance of Hercules, 161n11
Vergini di Roma, Le, 161n11
Vie et la passion de Jésus-Christ, n. s., La, 81–83

W

Warrior and the Slave Girl, The, 162
Warrior Women, 161n11
Why We Fight, 140, 145
Winnetou, 1. Teil, 176
Wonderful Horrible Life of Leni Riefenstahl, The, 128n18
Wooden Horse of Troy, The, 153n3

general index

A

acclamatio, 20, 62
adlocutio, 20, 33, 37
adventus, 20, 22, 30
Aeneid, The (Virgil), 25–26, 89
Aeschylus, 112n38
Alexander the Great, 28–29, 168
Alma-Tadema, Sir Lawrence, 84n13, 90
Altar of Domitius Ahenobarbus, 31
American Falangist Party, 5–6, 10, 143
Ammianus Marcellinus, 20
Amphitryo (Plautus), 133
Anabasis of Alexander, The (Arrian), 28–29
André, Georges, 128
Angelico, Fra. *See* Fra Angelico
Anton, Amerigo, 159
Antongini, Tommaso, 102
Antoninus Pius. *See* Column of Antoninus Pius
Antony and Cleopatra (Shakespeare), 62, 87, 138
Antony, Mark. *See* Mark Antony
Arch of Constantine, 17
Arch of Titus, 17
Archelaus of Priene, 29–30
arditi, 3–4n6, 105, 112
Aristophanes, 112n38
Arminius, 127
Arrian, 28, 168
Arringatore (statue), 33, 182
Auden, W. H., 153
Augustus, 20n7, 34n53, 52, 91, 138, 149n56, 172–73. *See also* Prima Porta statue
Aule Metelle, Aulus Metellus. *See Arringatore*
Ave Caesar! Morituri te salutant (Gérôme), 40

B

Balch, George T., 60n11
Balch's salute, 60n11
Baldi, Ferdinando, 46n16, 157, 159
Balilla, 190–92
Banim, John, 92
Bara, Theda, 41
Bargnetto, Luigi Romano, 115n46
Barnum, P. T., 58n6, 59
Barrett, Wilson, 65
Barzini, Luigi, 125–26
Base, Giulio, 181
Baths of Caracalla, 58

217

Beaufort, Jacques-Antoine, 46n15
Beerbohm Tree, Herbert, 84n13
Belasco, David, 69n29
Bellamy, Francis J., 60
Ben-Hur (stage play), 65, 70–75, 77
Ben-Hur: A Tale of the Christ (Wallace), 64, 79
Berlin, Isaiah, 52
Bernds, Edward, 160
Bernhardt, Sarah, 101
Bird, Robert Montgomery, 67, 70, 75
Bismarck, Otto von, 122
Blasetti, Alessandro, 119
Blumenberg, Hans-Christoph, 133n35
Boime, Albert, 50–51, 54
Bologna, Giovanni, 130
Bonnard, Mario, 156, 158
Borgese, Giuseppe Antonio, 106–9
Bradley, David, 151n1
Brecht, Bertolt, 146n51
Brizzi, Gaëtan, 160
Brizzi, Paul, 160
Brookner, Anita, 47, 51
Brutus, Marcus, 47, 139, 183
Buffon, Comte de, 49
Bulwer-Lytton, Edward, 64, 89
Burge, Stuart, 160
Burne-Jones, Edward, 87
Bush, George W., 166–67

C

Caesar. *See* Julius Caesar
Caesar (Welles, after Shakespeare), 149
Caligula, 33, 145, 148, 152, 165n16
Calnan, George Charles, 130
Calvino, Italo, 113–14
Camillus, 119
Campo di Maggio (Forzano), 110n35
Canzone di Garibaldi, La (D'Annunzio), 118n55
Capo-Squadra Balilla, Il, 190–92
Capra, Frank, 140
Caraffe, Armand Charles, 48n21
Carcopino, Jérôme, 37–38, 40
Carducci, Giosue, 106–7
Carnaro, Republic of, 111. *See also* Fiume

Carra, Lawrence, 62
Cartagine in fiamme (Salgari), 98
Caserini, Mario, 89–90
Castle, William, 139
Chaplin, Charles, 7–8
Charlemagne, 53, 110n35, 122
Christian Falangist Party, 6n8, 176
Christianity, Christians, 64–65, 87, 142, 146–48, 166. *See also* Jesus Christ
Cichorius, Conrad, 18
Civirani, Osvaldo, 158
Claudius (emperor), 39–40, 152, 173
Claudius the God (Graves), 171
Cleopatra, 41, 91, 137, 139, 160, 173–74
Coarelli, Filippo, 18
coins, Roman, 45–46
Cole, Thomas, 59
Colosseum, 39, 59n8, 91n32, 165–66
Colossus of Rhodes, 29
Colossus of Rhodes (City) (Kupka), 129n24
Column of Antoninus Pius, 31
Column of Marcus Aurelius, 17–18
Column of Trajan. *See* Trajan's Column
columna rostrata, 58
Commodus, 162–64, 168
Commodus: An Historical Play (Wallace), 65, 73
Connor, Kevin, 172
Constantine the Great, 35n55
Constantius II, 20
Coriolanus (Shakespeare), 62, 149
Corneille, Pierre, 43
Costa, Mario, 159
Cottafavi, Vittorio, 160–61
Coubertin, Pierre de, 129n21
Course of Empire, The (Cole), 59
Couture, Thomas, 33n50
Craig, Gordon, 95n2
Crassus, M. Licinius, 91, 158–59, 174
Cup: A Tragedy, The (Tennyson), 69
Curiatii, Curiatius, 12, 44–45, 56, 185–89

D

D'Amato, Joe, 165n16

D'Annunzio, Gabriele, 3–4, 12, 94–115, 118, 120–21, 125, 180
D'Annunzio, Gabriellino, 95n2
Daily Life in Ancient Rome (Carcopino), 37–38
Damiani, Damiano, 181
Damon and Pythias (Banim), 92
Daniels, Marc, 169
Daves, Delmer, 40
David, Jacques-Louis, 12, 42–55, 130
De Felice, Lionello, 159
Death of Caesar, The (Gérôme), 47, 80–81
Debord, Guy, 6–8, 11, 182–83
Delon, Alain, 183
Delsarte, François, 69
DeMille, Cecil B., 82, 135–38, 146–47
Dieterle, William, 151
Dionysius I of Syracuse, 92–93
Dionysius of Halicarnassus, 43, 45
Dionysus and Ariadne sarcophagus, 31
Distribution of the Eagle Standards, The (David), 51–53
Domitian, 21–22, 30, 145
Domitius Ahenobarbus. *See* Altar of Domitius Ahenobarbus
Doré, Gustave, 82, 85
Dornhelm, Robert, 174
Drei Schweizer, Die (Füssli), 43
Duvivier, Julien, 136

E

Edel, Uli, 173
Edison, Thomas Alva, 59n7
Edwards, J. Gordon, 41
Elektra (Strauss), 80n9
Enobarbus, Domitius, 138–39
Erlanger, Abraham Lincoln, 77–79
Erskine, Chester, 75
Euripides, 112n38
Eyre, Richard, 150

F

Fabius Maximus, 152
Farrow, John, 146n50

fasces, 2, 8, 48, 113, 145
fascio di combattimento, 111
Faustina, 31
Fellini, Federico, 114, 164
Ferree, Barr, 57
Ferroni, Giorgio, 62, 152, 157
Feuillade, Louis, 55
fides, Fides, 24–25, 26n28, 28
Fiume, 3–4, 101–9, 111–13, 118, 121
Fleischer, Richard, 156
foedus, 25–26
Forestier, Frédéric, 183
Forrest, Edwin, 75n45
Forzano, Giovacchino, 110n35
Fra Angelico, 91
Francisci, Pietro, 152, 156
Franco, Francisco, 52
Freda, Riccardo, 91n32, 181
Frederick the Great, 124
Freeman, Walter W., 77
French, Daniel Chester, 58
Führergruß, 125, 143
Füssli, Johann Heinrich, 43

G

Gaido, Domenico, 149n57
Gallone, Carmine, 8, 40, 117–20, 127, 174
Gardner, Helen, 91
Garibaldi, Giuseppe, 108, 118–19n55
Garrick, David, 69n29
Gaskill, Charles S., 91
Gérôme, Jean-Léon, 40, 47, 80–81, 87
Giambologna. *See* Bologna, Giovanni
Gibson, Mel, 167
Gilder, Richard Watson, 58
Giolitti, Giovanni, 111
Giorda, Marcello, 119
Giovagnoli, Raffaello, 90n31
Gladiator, The (Bird), 67, 75
Goebbels, Josef, 133n36, 134, 146
Goliath: The March of Fascism (Borgese), 106
goose step, 126, 131
Göring, Hermann, 133, 146n51
Goscinny, René, 160
Grand Camée de France, 31

Graves, Robert, 171
Graziosi, Giuseppe, 34
Griffith, D. W., 84–85, 91, 95n3
Guazzoni, Enrico, 86–89, 117, 149n57, 160

H

Hadrian, 20n7, 40n67
Halm, Friedrich, 84
Hannibal, 23, 94, 96, 98–99, 118–20, 127, 151–52, 168
Harrison, Benjamin, 59
Hawks, Howard, 156
Hawthorne, Nathaniel, 34–35
Hercules, 114–15, 158, 160, 161n11
Hills, David. *See* D'Amato, Joe
Hitler, Adolf, 5, 7, 51–52, 55, 104, 107, 109, 122–28, 132–34, 143, 145–48, 169, 176n26
Hobsbawm, Eric, 109
Hollaman, Rich G., 77
Homer, 108, 167
Horace (Corneille), 43
Horace (poet), 25, 96
Horatii, Horatius, 12, 42, 44–45, 54–56, 130, 185–89
Hudson, Hugh, 129n20
Huston, John, 146, 179

I

I, Claudius (Graves), 171
Iliad, The (Homer), 167
Imperial Caesar (Warner), 153
Ingomar, the Barbarian (Lovell), 84
Ingres, Jean Auguste Dominique, 53
Irving, Henry, 69

J

Jacoby, Georg, 95n2
Jenny's First Year Latin (textbook), 182
Jesus Christ, 36n58, 77, 81–83, 85, 91, 106, 135–36, 146n50, 167, 179, 181
Johnson, Dorothy, 48, 51
Julius Caesar, 27, 43, 47, 54, 61, 76, 80, 82, 86, 88–89, 98, 107, 109–10, 126, 137–39, 153, 159–60, 166n18, 172–76, 183
Julius Caesar (Shakespeare), 67, 79, 151n1, 160, 166n18, 173
Julius Civilis, 46–47
Justinian, 34n55

K

Kawalerowicz, Jerzy, 172
King, Henry, 76
Kiralfy, Imre, 59
Klaw, Marc, 77–78
König, Leo, 127
Koster, Henry, 40
Kubrick, Stanley, 158, 173–74
Kühnengruß, 2n2
Kupka, Frantisek (Franz), 129n24

L

L'Orange, Hans Peter, 36
Langmann, Thomas, 183
Last Days of Pompeii, The (Bulwer-Lytton), 64
Last Days of Pompeii, The (stage play), 65, 75
Lazarus, Emma, 29n36
Le Bargy, Charles, 78n6
Leclerc, Georges-Louis. *See* Buffon, Comte de
Leigh, Vivien, 75
Leonardo da Vinci, 91
LeRoy, Mervyn, 141, 143, 147, 160, 162
Levey, Michael, 54
Levine, David, 167
Lewis, C. Day, 155
Liddy, G. Gordon, 61
Liguoro, Giuseppe di, 91
Livy, 12, 23, 43, 45, 185–89
Loncraine, Richard, 150
Lovell, Maria, 84
Lucan, 27–28
Lucretia, 46n15
Lussu, Emilio, 103n18
Luther, Martin, 124

M

Maciste, 99, 114–15, 116n48
Macistus, Makistos, 115n45
Mack, Roy, 135
MacKaye, Steele, 69–70
Maggi, Luigi, 85, 115n46
Maistre, Joseph de, 52
Malaparte, Curzio, 116n49
Mankiewicz, Joseph L., 67, 159, 163, 172
Mann, Anthony, 62, 162–64, 168
Mantegna, Andrea, 21n8
Mao Zedong, 52n37
Marble Faun, The (Hawthorne), 34
Marcus Aurelius, 33–37, 162. *See also* Column of Marcus Aurelius
Marcus, Paul, 173
Mark Antony, 88, 138–39, 172–74
Martial, 22
Marx, Karl, 53
Maté, Rudolph, 153
May, Karl, 176n26
Mayer, Louis B., 146
Mazzini, Itala Almirante, 101
Medina, Louisa H., 75
Méliès, Georges, 84
Metamorphoses (Ovid), 97n6
Michelangelo Buonarroti, 179
Miner, Worthington, 62n16
Mort de César, La (Gérôme), 47, 80–81
Mucius Scaevola, 62
Mussolini, Benito, 4–5, 7–8, 34, 51–53, 102, 103n18, 104, 106–7, 109–18, 119n57, 122, 124, 126–27, 141, 149, 157, 164, 180
Mussolini, Vittorio, 117
Muybridge, Eadweard, 59n7

N

Napoleon Bonaparte, 51–53, 110n35
Napoléon sur le trône impériale; Napoleon I on His Imperial Throne (Ingres), 53
Nero (emperor), 5, 10, 33, 59, 85, 87, 135, 137, 142–43, 145–49, 152, 156–57, 167, 172–73

Nero (son of Germanicus), 37
Neroni, Nicola Fausto, 129
New Yorker, The (magazine), 166–67
Niblo, Fred, 79, 135–36
Nickell, Paul, 62n16
Nietzsche, Friedrich, 102
Ninchi, Annibale, 119
Nonguet, Lucien, 81–82
Nostro, Nick, 40

O

Oath of the Horatii, The (David), 12, 42–55, 93
Octavian, Octavius. *See* Augustus
Olcott, Sidney, 83–85
Olympic Games, 56, 127–33, 140, 182–83
Olympic salute, 13, 128–32
Orator (statue). *See Arringatore*
Origen, 148n54
Ovid, 24, 26–27, 97n6

P

Pagano, Bartolomeo, 115
Palermi, Amleto, 40
Parks, Michael, 179
Pascal, Gabriel, 75
Pasinetti, P. M., 67, 70
passo romano, 126
Pastrone, Giovanni, 94, 96–99, 101, 115–16
Paul, Saint, 148n54
Paxton, Robert, 111
Payant, Lee, 160
Pericles, 107
Peter, Saint, 87, 147–48
Petersen, Wolfgang, 167–68
Petronius, 26n27, 147–48
Pharsalia, The (Lucan), 27
Pilate, Pontius. *See* Pontius Pilate
Pilotto, Camillo, 119
Pindar, 112n38
Piranesi, Giovanni Battista, 91n32
Pizzetti, Ildebrando, 97n4, 117
Plato, 10, 112n38
Plautus, 133

Pledge of Allegiance, 12, 57, 59–62, 70, 155
Plutarch, 25
Pollack, Sydney, 64
Pollice Verso (Gérôme), 87
Pompey the Great, 27, 88, 173–76
Pontius Pilate, 83, 135–36, 151, 156, 172
Poppaea, 85, 147
Pottier, Richard, 159
Prima Porta statue (Augustus), 33–34
profectio, 20
Punica (Silius Italicus), 28

Q

Quintilian, 23
Quo Vadis? (Sienkiewicz), 64

R

Rains, Claude, 75
Ranous, William V., 84n14
Reidersche Tafel, 36n58
Reinl, Harald, 176
Rembrandt van Rijn, 46–47
Renoir, Jean, 53n38, 55–56
Richard III (Shakespeare), 150
Riefenstahl, Leni, 61, 118, 127–28, 130–31, 132n32, 140n43, 143, 165
Robespierre, Maximilien, 50
Roddam, Franc, 172
Rodin, Auguste, 8
Rodolfi, Eleuterio, 90n29
Roma (goddess), 31
Roosevelt, Franklin D., 5, 6n8
Rosa di Cipro, La (D'Annunzio), 97n6
Rosa, Silvio Laurenti, 149n57
Rose, Frank Oaks, 83–84
Rossi, Cesare, 105n23
Rostand, Edmond, 101n11

S

Sadoul, Georges, 98–99
Sagal, Boris, 172
Saint-Gaudens, Augustus, 66
Salgari, Emilio, 98

Saturninus (emperor), 164
Saville, Philip, 152
Sawdust Caesar (Seldes), 111
Schoedsack, Ernest B., 136
Schumacher, Joel, 168
Schünzel, Reinhold, 133
Scipio Africanus, P. Cornelius (the Elder), 8, 98–99, 117–19, 127
Scipio Africanus, P. Cornelius (the Younger), 117n51
Scott, Ridley, 40, 164, 173
Seitz, George B., 62
Seldes, George, 110
Senensky, Ralph, 169–70
Serment de Brutus sur le corps de Lucrèce, Le (Beaufort), 46n15
Serment de l'armée fait à l'Empereur . . . , Le (David), 51–53
Serment des Horaces, Le (Caraffe), 48n21
Serment des Horaces entre les mains de leur père, Le (David). See *Oath of the Horatii, The*
Serment du jeu de paume, Le (David), 49–51
Shakespeare, William, 62, 65, 79, 84, 87, 138, 149–50, 151n1, 160, 164, 166n18, 173
Shaw, George Bernard, 75
Sherman, William Tecumseh, statue of, 66
Sidney, George, 151–52
Siehm, Wilhelm Georg, 133n37
Sienkiewicz, Henryk, 64, 141–42
Sign of the Cross, The (Barrett), 65
Silius Italicus, 28
Sirk, Douglas, 40
Sittl, Carl, 37
Skinheads, 2, 14
Sohn der Wildnis, Der (Halm), 84
Sonjewski-Jamrowski, Rolf von, 133n37
Spartaco (Giovagnoli), 90n31
Spartacus, 67, 75n45, 91, 158, 174
Spectatorium, 70
Speer, Albert, 133, 147
Springer, Hans, 133
Stalin, Joseph, 52n37
Starobinski, Jean, 48, 50–51

Statius, 22
Statue of Liberty, 29
Steno, 156, 157n7
Stephani, Frederick, 140
Stephanus of Byzantium, 115n45
Stevens, George, 156
Stone, Oliver, 168
Strabo, 115n45
Strauss, Richard, 80n9
Streicher, Julius, 146
Stroheim, Erich von, 135n38
Suetonius, 39–40, 47, 148
Sulla, L. Cornelius, 88–89
Syberberg, Hans-Jürgen, 123

T

Tacitus, 24, 46–47
Taylor, Ray, 140
Taylor, Robert, 6
Taymor, Julie, 164
Tennis Court Oath, The (David), 49–51
Tennyson, Alfred Lord, 69
Terry, Ellen, 69
Thomas, Gerald, 160
Three Swiss, The (Füssli), 43
Tiberius, 139–40, 151, 155
Titus (emperor), 142
Titus Andronicus (Shakespeare), 164
Toland, John, 126
Toth, Andre de, 64
Trajan, 18, 36n60. *See also* Trajan's Column
Trajan's Column, 17–18, 36n60, 50n28
triumph, *triumphus,* 21n8, 142–45
Truffaut, François, 176
Turner, Otis, 92–93

U

Uderzo, Albert, 160

Upham, James B., 60

V

Valerius Maximus, 24
Van Lamsweerde, Pino, 160
Vanzina (Vanzini), Stefano. *See* Steno
Vardac, Nicholas, 68–69
Varus, Quinctilius, 127
Vespasian, 30, 142
Vidal, Gore, 9–10, 66, 182
Vidali, Giovanni Enrico, 90, 91n32
Vidor, King, 157
Virgil, 24–26, 89, 96, 173

W

Wagner, Richard, 123
Wallace, Lew, 64, 71, 73, 79
Walsh, Raoul, 64
Warner, Rex, 153–55
Webber, Andrew Lloyd, 168
Welles, Orson, 149
Wise, Herbert, 171
Wise, Robert, 152, 167–68
World's Columbian Exposition (1893), 57, 129n21
Wyler, William, 66, 139–40, 155, 173, 182n4

Y

Young Caesar, The (Warner), 153
Young, Roger, 172
Youth's Companion, The (magazine), 59–60

Z

Zecca, Ferdinand, 81–82

www.ingramcontent.com/pod-product-compliance
Lightning Source LLC
Chambersburg PA
CBHW020651230426
43665CB00008B/398